The CALL
of the
LAST FRONTIER

The CALL
of the
LAST FRONTIER

The True Story of a Woman's Twenty-Year Alaska Adventure

MELISSA L. COOK

Hoodoo Books, LLC
Burlington, Wyoming

Hoodoo Books, LLC
P.O. Box 172
Burlington, Wyoming 82411
hoodoobooks.com

ISBN: 978-1-956413-04-5 (hard cover)
ISBN: 978-1-956413-03-8 (paperback)
ISBN: 978-1-956413-05-2 (large print)
ISBN: 978-1-956413-01-4 (ebook)

Library of Congress Control Number: 2021917719
10 9 8 7 6 5 4 3 2 1

Cover design, front cover image, maps, author photograph, interior and eBook design, and content editing by Elgin Cook, copy editing and proofreading by Rachel Robson of 100% Proof, final proofread by Kimberly Steinke of Parker Mayne Editorial, first paragraph back cover book description written by Larry Kaniut

To see the photo section in color and catch up with Melissa, visit her author website at: www.melissacook.us.

The Call of the Last Frontier is a true story—my story, from my perspective. I have written it to the best of my memory. Any discrepancies are unintentional.

To Elgin

For our parents—gone too soon.

Robert Ray Tyler, 1939–2015

Patricia Anne O'Flaherty, 1940–2017

Robert Michael Simmons, 1936–2011

Kenneth Cook, 1935–2011

Connie Ruth Christopherson Cook, 1942–2018

Alaska comes from the Aleut word *Alyeska*,
meaning mainland or great land.

Table of Contents

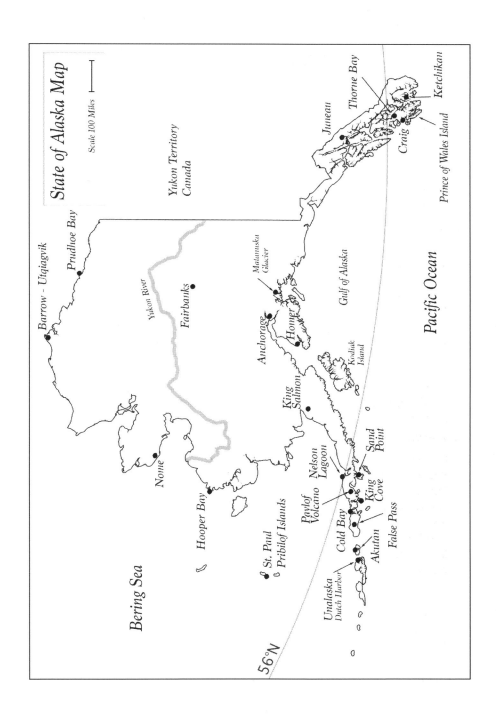

State of Alaska Map

Scale 100 Miles

Bering Sea

Pacific Ocean

Barrow - Utqiagvik
Prudhoe Bay
Yukon Territory
Canada
Yukon River
Fairbanks
Nome
Hooper Bay
Matanuska Glacier
Anchorage
Homer
Gulf of Alaska
Kodiak Island
Juneau
Thorne Bay
Ketchikan
Craig
Prince of Wales Island
King Salmon
Sand Point
Nelson Lagoon
King Cove
Pavlof Volcano
Cold Bay
False Pass
Akutan
St. Paul
Pribilof Islands
Unalaska
Dutch Harbor
56°N

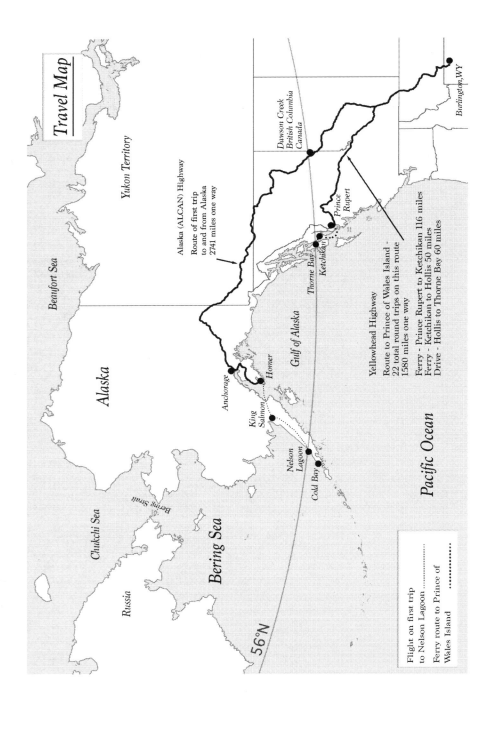

Travel Map

Beaufort Sea

Yukon Territory

Alaska

Chukchi Sea

Bering Strait

Russia

Bering Sea

Anchorage

Homer

King Salmon

Nelson Lagoon

Cold Bay

Gulf of Alaska

Pacific Ocean

56°N

Alaska (ALCAN) Highway
Route of first trip
to and from Alaska
2741 miles one way

Dawson Creek
British Columbia
Canada

Burlington, WY

Prince Rupert

Thorne Bay
Ketchikan

Yellowhead Highway

Route to Prince of Wales Island -
22 total round trips on this route
1580 miles one way

Ferry - Prince Rupert to Ketchikan 116 miles
Ferry - Ketchikan to Hollis 50 miles
Drive - Hollis to Thorne Bay 60 miles

Flight on first trip
to Nelson Lagoon ....

Ferry route to Prince of
Wales Island ....

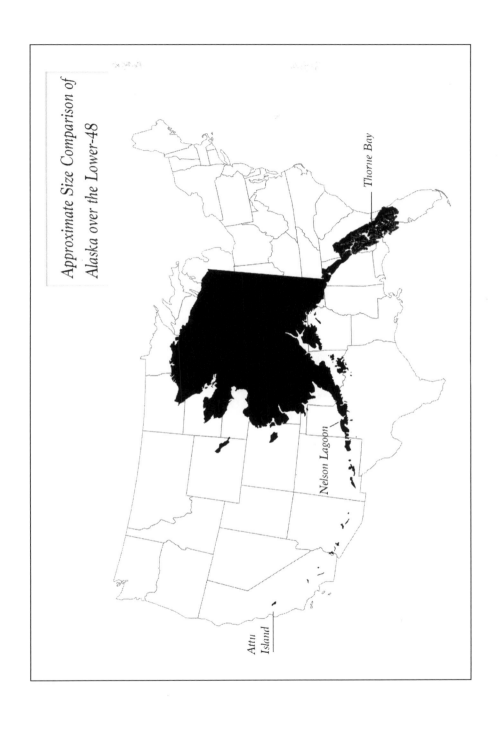

Approximate Size Comparison of
Alaska over the Lower-48

PROLOGUE: Alone on a Beach

I am alone on a beach in Alaska. I have been isolated here for eighteen months and might as well be on another planet. It is wintertime, and a storm is blowing mist off the Bering Sea waves as they crash onto the black sand at my feet. I cradle my frozen self and stare out across the endless white caps of the angry sea. My coat is soaked, but I don't care. *I know people are out there,* I remind myself, *for all the good they will do me here.*

Memories from my childhood in Detroit surface, and I leave this sandy spit for the busy city streets, if only in my imagination. I remember the hustle of people along the city sidewalks and the conversations heard as people pass by, hurrying to their destinations. I picture myself standing on a busy street corner with the smell of fresh wet pavement and the sound of water splashing under the tires. A sprinkle of spring rain touches my face and then I am pulled back to my reality. Thick Alaskan raindrops painfully pelt my tender skin as the wind picks up. Cold rain runs down my bright red cheeks, and the sting shifts to a freezing numbness. My tongue licks the ocean's salty mist from my lips.

A rusty blue Suburban sits on a dune in the distance, overlooking the beach from a primitive road. My family awaits my return, watching the storm's action from the warmth of the old school vehicle. No one else ventured out today.

"Come out of the storm!" The raging waves and wind drown out my husband's voice. He is becoming impatient and worried as I stand in the furious wind. He hollers to me. "You're soaked. Let's go!"

I steal another moment of solitude. Efforts to transplant myself back to Detroit fail. I face the turbulent sea before me. Not a soul is in sight; I feel so alone on this spit. *How did I end up here of all places?* I feel stuck, helpless to change my circumstances. The tiny Aleut village of thirty winter residents is a mile down the black sand road. I seldom see any of them. Only nine school-aged children cross my path daily, and even then, they have little to say.

The creak of the rusty Suburban door is lost in the ferocious wind. My husband's voice radiates across the beach as he steps out into the storm. "Come on!" He is worried about me. Am I losing my grip as he did last winter? He recognizes the signs of cabin fever.

As I turn my back to the sea, the wind presses my red coat against my body. Rain peppers my backside, drenching my remaining dry spots as I work my way back down the beach and climb the hill to my waiting family. They are all I have out here. We spend every waking hour together, and yet my loneliness reaches to the depths of my soul at times.

When you live in a city like Detroit, it's hard to believe there is a place like this. When you live in a place like this, it's hard to believe there is a city like Detroit.

– Melissa L. Cook, 1996

OUR ARRIVAL

ALASKA—THE LAST FRONTIER

1995

ONE

Meat Market

"I have never seen anything like this!" Our jaws dropped at the stunning view of the glacier and snow-capped mountains from the Alaska Airlines jet window. It was, simply put, breathtaking.

"Teachers attending the job fair can rent a cab for ten dollars to take them from the airport to the hotel," I informed Elgin. We hailed a cab headed into the city of Anchorage for our four-day visit. The white mountains in the distance added to our excitement. It was a gorgeous April afternoon at fifty degrees.

"The Captain Cook Hotel," I instructed the driver. Fifteen minutes later, we stood at the entrance of three bronze buildings towering over the streets below. The luxury hotel felt extravagant for our tight budget. It was luxurious inside with bellhops at each door—not exactly what we had expected for Alaska.

"I can get them," Elgin told the porter reaching for our bags. He had never been to a hotel with luggage service.

Our elegant room overlooked the Cook Inlet. "Let's get something to eat, then organize our paperwork for tomorrow and go to bed early," Elgin recommended. We had not come here to fool around. We needed two jobs, and the hotel was brimming with teachers.

"I saw a pizza place in the lobby," I suggested.

The crowded elevator stopped on each floor, and I wondered if using the stairs may have been quicker. We found ourselves seated in a fancy restaurant eating a tiny European-style pizza. We should have ordered a large. Still hungry, we squeezed through hordes of talkative people to return to the room.

Beep. Beep. Beep. The alarm clock sounded. *Ring. Ring.* The front desk rang with our backup wake-up call. We planned to be first in line and refused to take any chances on a missed alarm. I rolled over in the magnificent bedding and looked for Elgin whose feet had already hit the floor.

"What time did you get to sleep?" I murmured, half-awake, as I stretched across the pile of extra pillows scattered on the king-size bed. I had never seen so many pillows on one bed.

"Who knows? The sun set at nine thirty, but it was light until midnight. The noise from the street below and people talking in the halls didn't help either. Hurry! We don't want to be late." He stepped into the bathroom for his morning shower. A true Wyoming cowboy, he always struggled to sleep in the city. I grew up in Detroit and Tucson, so I barely noticed the noise.

We rushed around, preparing for our day. Before leaving the room, we stood in front of the mirror. Elgin was slender and clean-cut in his smart, dark suit. At five feet, I wore a complementing dress and had long auburn hair. Though in our late twenties, our youthful appearance often caused others to mistake us for teenagers.

We exited the room carrying one briefcase. It strategically held only five envelopes for school districts at the top of our list. We planned to return to the room to reload repeatedly throughout the day. We presented ourselves as neat and organized, not overwhelmed with piles of papers in our arms. Before the trip, we put together an individualized packet for each of Alaska's fifty-two school districts. The envelopes contained a letter of application, completed job form, college transcripts, letters of references, a business card, and a clipped photograph. We came prepared.

The crowded elevator failed to clue us in on what was up ahead. Nervousness radiated through the packed, silent enclosure. When the doors opened, the group proceeded in unison down the hall. Teachers and administrators gathered in the grand conference room. With name tags in hand, we stepped through the doors and into an enormous human meat market. One thousand teachers and an untold number of administrators were in attendance. And let me tell you, not all of them were on their best behavior.

Posters filled the walls with school district logos, photos, and maps. Anchorage, Fairbanks, and Juneau representatives were handing out flyers but not accepting applications. Several unattended tables overflowed with piles of résumés while long lines had formed in front of most districts. We had a *holy smokes* moment staring at the mass of candidates.

"Where should we go first?" I asked, glancing around the vast room.

"The Aleutians. Cliff said Sand Point is a good place to live," Elgin responded. His cousin, Cliff Alexander, had lived in Alaska for twelve years and advised us on preferable areas of the state. We spotted the Aleutians East Borough School District and waited in line, eager to submit our paperwork.

"We are accepting applications right now. Look for your name on the board tomorrow morning to see if we have selected you for an interview." The line advanced with considerable speed to our relief. "Thank you," the short, bushy-longer-haired, bearded man nodded as he took our folders. Yikes! The district at the top of our *hope for* list barely made eye contact with us.

"Let's apply with the North Slope next. They pay the most," I suggested. The North Slope Borough School District line stretched across the room and moved at a snail's pace.

"No. I think we better focus on handing out more applications. That line could take forever," Elgin said with a hint of controlled panic. Calculatingly, we removed one packet at a time from the briefcase. We smiled even when shoved here and there by frustrated teachers carrying armloads of résumés squeezing through the crowd. Teachers scattered paperwork across the floor when bumped by the masses. We helped those closest to us while keeping one foot in line. There was no time for lunch.

By afternoon, we found ourselves in the ever-constant crowd of teachers in the North Slope line. Three rows formed in front of several men in suits performing one-to-two-minute screening interviews. We remained calm, staring ahead, formulating our thoughts for our turn. Chuck Coons, a middle-aged administrator in jeans and a dress shirt, casually stood off to the side, watching the crowd. The line rapidly filled in behind us.

Mr. Coons strolled along our row, stopped in front of us, and held out his hand. "Chuck Coons, North Slope Borough School District." Shocked, we shook his hand. He took our folders without opening them and escorted us out of line. "Why do you want to teach for the North Slope?" the disgruntled teachers ahead of us complained under their breath. They had been in line first.

"How many years of teaching experience do you have?" Mr. Coons questioned me.

"This will be my first year teaching," I smiled with confidence.

"It's our policy not to hire first-year teachers; we require at least three years of classroom teaching experience. A classroom aide position may be available though," he informed me with a smile.

"Sorry. I'm not in the market for an aide position. We will only accept full-time teaching positions in the same town," I attempted to hide my disappointment and slight loss of confidence. Chuck appeared amused but went on to explain they hired teachers who could handle the classroom because the district was difficult.

"As a new teacher, I'm completely moldable to your teaching practices. And I can handle a classroom," I added, with more conviction than I felt. Openings were slim pickings, and we were in competition with hordes of teachers.

"You're tenacious, but in a good way," he smiled while handing me a slip. "This was the first of three interviews. You are moving on to the second. The next interview is in one hour. Good luck."

"Let's take a break," Elgin suggested. Hungry but not caring to wait in the restaurant's jam-packed line, we rested in our room with over half our packets handed out already.

"Why are they hosting a job fair with only fifty openings? A thousand teachers are out there!" Elgin sounded panicked. "We spent a small fortune coming here and need two of those jobs." He landed hard on the bed. We stared at each other in disbelief and defeat. He was right; we were broke. The stress was excruciating. "This was a lousy idea." We gazed at the breathtaking view from our window.

"Kodiak refused to take our applications, and it wasn't even ten thirty in the morning," I added.

"Kenai hires Alaska Natives first. We don't have a chance with them either," Elgin muttered under his breath.

TWO

Adventurers Go Home

Two hours had passed. I sat in the coveted second interview with the North Slope. The interviewer jumped right in with his only question, "What will you do when a student assaults you? Before you answer, note I said *when* and not *if*." I am clueless on how I replied. "I will not waste your time. The North Slope plans to offer you a teaching contract somewhere in our district. I urge you to consider other places. The North Slope is a harsh place, especially for young white children." With that, he ushered me back into the hallway where I waited for Elgin in shock. Shock because we were receiving contract offers, and we hadn't even reached the third interview. Shocked because my second interview had lasted less than five minutes. Shocked because the interviewer caught me totally off guard with his assault question. His words echoed in my mind, "*when*, and not *if*."

We entered the main conference room and strolled by the tables, stopping at Chugach School District. The booth posters depicted schools in remote logging communities.

"Welcome!" Roger Sampson held out his hand while Rich DeLorenzo stood next to him with a friendly smile. We agreed to a couple's interview in one hour. Most bush districts interviewed teaching couples together.

The hour-long interview took place in their hotel room. Roger and Rich presented an excellent team spirit filled with enthusiasm for their school district, consisting of several small logging camps with kindergarten through twelfth-grade student bodies. The school was in session six days per week. The administrators boasted of the six-month school year calendar with an extended winter break for the seasonal logging shutdown.

"We have one and a half teaching positions to offer you." Roger held out a sheet of paper. "Here is a copy of our pay scale and benefits."

"We have a family and both need full-time contracts," I stated, ignoring the documents before me. The disappointment was apparent in my tone.

The pay was significant, but so was the twenty-year retirement, our primary motivator for being here. If one of us accepted less than full-time, our stay in the state would extend beyond twenty years.

"Classroom aide hours may be available to fill in the rest of the day at a lower pay," Rich offered sympathetically.

"We will have to decline. Thank you for the opportunity," Elgin replied, our enthusiasm dampened by the turn of events. We had no clue the interviews were for one and a half positions.

"We understand and wish you luck. If you have questions about other districts, ask. We know this state and the administrators here; you cannot be too careful." Our paths would continue to cross with Roger and Rich in the future, though we never worked together.

Elgin and I headed back to our hotel room, emotionally and physically exhausted, not to mention starving.

We found a convenience store down the street and ate cheap, soggy sandwiches for dinner. The tension was still high despite the promised teaching contracts coming from the North Slope. The administrator's words haunted me, and eerily, he nailed it. A student did physically assault me in my first year of teaching.

"Ready for the social?" I asked. Reserved, Elgin avoided such events like the plague. However, this one was different, he would have to attend.

Entering the crowded conference room, we made a beeline for the Aleutians East table. Sand Point was our top choice, so it made sense to sit and speak informally with their administrators. The same short, bushy-haired man sat and grasped his auburn beard, looked us over, and then extended his hand to Elgin. "Chick Beckley." A low rumble of conversation hung over the room. Teachers and administrators made small talk, some desperate to find a job, while others welcomed a chance to catch up with old friends, acquaintances, or former coworkers.

Chick appeared interested as we introduced ourselves. A speaker on stage interrupted, "Welcome to the Alaska Teacher Placement Job Fair. If you are here in search of an adventure, go home! Alaska is looking for teachers, not adventure seekers!"

Funny. I was the teacher seeking a job, not an adventurer, yet adventure arrived on my doorstep almost daily for the next twenty years. She should have begged adventurous teachers to apply for bush jobs, it may have increased the teacher retention rate. Teachers left year-after-year during our tenure in Alaska. The primary reason—they were not adventurous enough. The speaker *should have* said, "Adventurers with teaching certificates apply here! It's the adventurer's mentality and stick-to-it mindset that will shepherd you through the long, dark winters and endless rain and mud. It is the hardiness of the adventurer that will combat the loneliness and cold. You require inner strength when you need a friend and discover yourself in a fishbowl with few lifelines outside your own resourcefulness. It takes imagination to self-entertain night-after-long-night to survive the school years here."

"Outdoorsmen welcome!" the speaker *should* have announced with enthusiasm. Many in the audience would chop wood in the bitter cold, catch dinner from the frosty streams, and dig out several feet of snow to exit their homes and open the schools. Some would carry rank honey bucket bags of feces and urine from their bathrooms through wind, rain, and snow to a village communal disposal. Or they might have no-flush toilets connected to a suction grid that automatically sucked out toilet deposits with an antifreeze chemical.

"Rain gear, parkas, long johns, Xtratuf boots, waterproof shoes, chain saws, powerful handguns, 10-ply tires, fleece clothing, and plenty of grit should be on your shopping list if you land a job in Alaska's bush," she should have continued. "You will need it all and then some. Once you arrive, supplies will be limited unless there is a local store, and beware, prices are usually exorbitant. You'd better be hardy too because it's cold *every single day* of the school year here." Now *that* speech would have caused us to sit up and think twice about what we were getting ourselves into by moving to rural Alaska. At least she would have prepared us for the treacherous road ahead. *This* speech was not given that evening.

We discovered the reality of bush life soon enough. New Alaskans learned quickly to live without or leave. Most teachers quit within a year or two. Some resigned in the middle of the school year. Others packed up and hightailed it home in the middle of the night because the Alaskan lifestyle was too much for them.

Then and now, Alaskans made do with what they had, wore things completely out, repurposed, reused, created new out of scrap, and essentially became creative in solving their own problems. It was expensive to ship items to remote communities, and money was tight for the average Joe. Don't let those fortune stories and rumors of high salaries fool you. Many bush Alaskans were downright poor. And if this lifestyle wasn't adventure, I surely don't know what is.

The speaker drew door prizes following her welcoming. "Melissa Cook," I won the grand prize, an attractive wooden clock in the shape of Alaska with ivory numbers.

"Hey! Lucky you!" Chick Beckley said in surprise.

I hope my good fortune continues, I thought. I would require all the luck of my Irish bloodline to make this trip worth the expense.

THREE

Room 203

On the second day, we awoke jobless and unsure of how job fairs worked. Panic boiled under the surface as we rolled our tired bodies out of bed.

"May as well hand these out today," Elgin said. We had a handful of applications to submit to our lowest priority districts, then we had to wait for our names to be posted on the bulletin board. We decided not to accept the North Slope teaching positions if the district did indeed offer them.

Chuck Coons from the North Slope had pulled us aside to chat during the previous night's social event. He explained that he had watched us as we roamed the conference room in the morning and hoped we would stop at his table. That shed light on why he pulled us out of line for the interview yesterday. "Administrators study everyone in the room. We watch to see how people behave during stressful situations like this." He encouraged us to look elsewhere for work. "If it means you go home without a job, do it. Don't bring your boys to the Slope. If you had your choice of any place in the state, where would you go?" We told him our top choice was Sand Point. He smiled and nodded as though he understood.

Chuck had been a bright spot in our evening, but it was morning now. More keenly aware of being observed from afar by prospective employers, we carried ourselves with confidence. Standing silently in the cramped elevator, Elgin stared at his cowboy boots. I noticed one lady's apparent interest in our name tags.

"Elgin and Melissa Cook," she read our names out loud with excitement. "Please tell us your secret." The other teachers stared as our confusion prompted her to explain. "You don't know? Most of the districts have requested to interview you." Astonishment swept over us.

The elevator doors opened, and we made our way into the conference room, scanning for the bulletin board. "Cooks! Elgin and Melissa Cook." A short, middle-aged man dressed in tan khaki pants and a dress shirt with somewhat disheveled hair hurried toward us, waving his papers to catch our attention. The packets with our photographs must have worked because I had never seen this person before in my life.

"I represent the Lower Yukon School District. We have teaching contracts for both of you at Hooper Bay School. Please come with me to discuss the details."

"We haven't even interviewed with your school district," I replied without thinking as we swiftly made our way to the other end of the conference room.

"We have already called your references and checked you out. You will be a perfect fit for our district." He promised us the moon: fantastic new teacher housing, excellent teaching atmosphere, plenty of district support with an outstanding principal. "Sign here," he held out the last page of the contract.

"We need to talk this over and review the contract before we sign it," Elgin replied, not wanting to be too hasty. The offer dumbfounded us, making it a little suspicious. "May we speak with the principal?"

The man squirmed. "I'm sorry. Our principal is not available right now, but I can assure you the Lower Yukon is an excellent district."

"My wife and I should discuss it first. May we take these?" Elgin held the contracts in his hand. The disappointed administrator agreed but said we only had until noon. No later. They preferred to fill positions early.

When we turned away from the table, Chuck Coons rushed toward us. "What did he say?" He seemed concerned. Still in disbelief, I told him of the job offers and the noon deadline.

Chuck was already writing on a sticky pad. He tore off the note and handed it to Elgin. "Here. Take this note to room 203. Knock on the door. Tell them I sent you and that you have contract offers expiring at noon with the Lower Yukon," he spoke with earnestness and speed.

"Who's in room 203?" His urgency puzzled me.

"The Aleutians East," he replied.

"Don't you work for the North Slope? Why . . ."

"I'll be the principal in Sand Point next year. Go quickly," he urged. You can only imagine our complete and utter delight. Sand Point was in the Aleutians East Borough School District and at the top of our wish list. A smile spread across my face as we turned to go.

We followed orders well. To the elevators, down the hall, room 203 up

ahead. A young man seated in a chair beside the door held his résumé in hand while eyeing us as we approached. His wife sat erect with a pile of papers on her lap and a stuffed bag at her feet. Elgin knocked gently three times and took a step back while my mind raced. *Chuck Coons is the new Sand Point principal!*

"They are interviewing in there," the waiting man curtly informed us.

"And we're next," the woman snapped.

The door opened, and a tall man with dark hair responded, "Yes." Inside, a nervous young couple seated on the couch looked our way.

"Sorry to interrupt. Mr. Coons told us to knock on the door and give you this," Elgin handed him the note. "He instructed us to tell you we have contract offers until noon with the Lower Yukon."

"Okay, thank you." The door closed. We stood there wondering what to do with ourselves.

"If you already have contracts, what are you doing here?" The young man seemed irritated. We stepped back against the wall, unsure of how to respond. In less than a minute, the door opened.

"Thank you for your time," Bob Robertson showed the candidates from the couch to the door. The waiting couple rose from their seats, but Mr. Robertson motioned them to sit. "We will be with you in a few minutes. Elgin and Melissa, come on in." The door closed behind us. I don't know about Elgin, but I felt a little guilty.

FOUR

The Interview

"So, you have an offer from the Lower Yukon School District valid until noon," Mr. Robertson stated. "We better get this interview rolling then. Meet Tom Ryan, our superintendent," the stout, older man nodded. "And this is Chick Beckley. He is our assistant superintendent and technology director."

"I met you at the table last night. The lucky one, right?" Chick remembered.

"Yes." I smiled. We took a seat on the couch while the administrators sat across from us in elegant, tall chairs.

"My name is Bob Robertson, and I'm the principal of King Cove School. You impressed Mr. Coons. He pointed out your applications last night, and we reviewed your information. Elgin, can you tell us more about yourself?"

"Sure. I'm from a farming community of two hundred people in Wyoming. My degree is in elementary and middle school education. I also have a master's degree in curriculum and instruction. For two years, I taught in a one-teacher school in rural Montana about two hours from any services. Then we moved to my hometown, where I've taught third grade for the past three years."

"Please tell us more about your teaching experience in Montana," Tom Ryan leaned forward, interested.

"As the only teacher, I took care of everything related to the school, from teaching three students in multiple grade levels to keeping the building clean and maintained. I was also responsible for completing the school's administrative paperwork. We lived twenty-five miles down a gumbo road. When it was wet, it became slick mud that packed under the vehicle and hardened like cement if we let it dry. We had to clean the mud out from around all of the tires and wheel wells every time we drove on the road if it was wet."

"Melissa, please tell us about yourself," Bob asked.

"I grew up in Detroit, Michigan, and Tucson, Arizona. When I was nineteen, I married Elgin and moved to Burlington, Wyoming. After he finished college, we moved to Montana, and I took the last classes for my degree as independent study while staying home with our three boys. I had planned to be a lawyer, but once we moved back to Burlington the closest law school was seven hours away. I enjoyed substitute teaching, so I chose to get a second bachelor's degree to become a high school teacher instead. I am certified in grades 5–12 social science, K–12 health, and 5–9 math."

"Please describe your rural experience," Tom said.

"When we lived in Montana, our home was next door to the school. The housing was an old rundown trailer in the middle of nowhere on an isolated road two hours from any services. We hauled all of our water from a neighbor's home ten miles away. Because we were so far from town, I stocked up on groceries and froze milk by the gallon. We shared a party line with three other families but the service wasn't good. Ice and wind knocked out the phone lines for days and weeks at a time. When the phones worked, we had to call the operator to make a phone call. There was only one TV channel, and the reception wasn't great. Half the time it was just static on the screen. For fun, we target shot a 22-rifle off the back porch."

"Why do you want to move to Alaska?" Ah, now that was a tricky question because I remembered the speaker telling adventurers to go home. Having recently finished college, I needed to work to afford our student loan payments. Elgin and I had decided if we were going to move, we wanted to make the move worthwhile. Alaska's salary and retirement benefits made the state attractive, and we figured if we could live in rural Montana for two years, we could live anywhere. I would like to point out that there was a road to our home in Montana. Okay, so it was a gumbo mud road, but it was still a road.

"Do you have a strong marriage?" Chick's question surprised us both. "Moving to a remote site is tough, but if your marriage is not solid, the isolation will tear you apart. Last year, the teaching couple in Nelson Lagoon divorced in the middle of the school year. That two-teacher site went through four teachers in nine months. It would be best for those students to have you stay for two years. Can you verbally commit to that if we offer you contracts before noon today?"

We confirmed our strong relationship and verbally agreed to the two-year commitment. But the truth was, after nine years of marriage, we had recently discovered we had nothing in common. Not one shared interest. Desperate for jobs in the same location, we ignored Chick's warning. In debt from college and just starting out in life, we felt we had to take the risk.

Toward the end of the interview, Bob informed us, "We have two full-time teaching positions opening in Nelson Lagoon and plan to offer them to you. We expect a resignation to come in any minute. Can you wait until then to sign with the Lower Yukon? We'll leave a message on your hotel phone or meet you at the conference room door at noon."

"Yes. That will be fine," Elgin nodded.

How could I not be excited? I knew nothing about Nelson Lagoon. However, this was our target district.

"Do you have a 44-magnum or at least a gun powerful enough to take down an Alaska brown bear?" That was not a typical question asked of teachers during the hiring process. Bob was serious. "You shouldn't take students outside without a gun. Two years ago, in King Cove, an Alaska brown bear killed and ate part of a six-year-old boy walking home at night with his mother and sister. We don't fool around with these bears here. They will kill you!" I suspect my mouth was hanging open at this point in the interview. The Aleutians East Borough School District had one dead child; they did not want another one—that was crystal clear.

Yeah, I will not be taking the kids outside! I made a mental note to myself. We would seldom spend recess outdoors in Nelson Lagoon in the years that followed.

Elgin didn't blink an eye at the question and confirmed he did own an appropriate firearm and would be bringing it. Darn straight he was bringing it!

"Melissa, please leave your dresses at home. Last year, the teacher always wore a dress to school. In Nelson Lagoon, the strong, gusty winds blew the dress over her head several times in front of the students. We prefer you not wear a dress." This request provided insight into conditions we would face, but it went right over our heads.

Elgin and I stepped out of the room to a disgruntled couple giving us the stink eye before smiling at the administrators when we cleared the doorway. Bob welcomed them into the room.

Though we were thrilled at the prospect of being offered two full-time positions in Nelson Lagoon, the fact was the district did not have the ability to offer us contracts until a resignation was turned in. Until then, we needed to keep looking. We decided to follow up on the Lower Yukon contract offers and returned to our hotel room to call the principal at the school to see what he had to say about his school and district.

I will admit, I may have had a little skip in my step leaving room 203 that day. Chuck Coons was going to be the principal of Sand Point, which meant we had a chance of someday getting into our top choice school.

From Hooper Bay to Nelson Lagoon

An administrator from Kodiak School District stepped into the hallway when the door closed to room 203. Kodiak was also at the top of our *hope for* list. I wasted no time. "Hello. We're Elgin and Melissa Cook. We would really like to work for your district, but when we tried to turn in our paperwork yesterday morning, they weren't accepting applications." I attempted to make eye contact, hoping for a connection.

"The interview schedule is full. Excuse me," the administrator sidestepped us and escaped toward the elevator. Kodiak was surely a no-go for us this year. He probably wouldn't have been fun to work for anyway or maybe he was too busy. A decade later, our paths crossed again, but by then the shoe was on the other foot.

We rushed to our hotel room. "I'm calling the Hooper Bay principal," Elgin said, picking up the phone to make the call.

"Ugly. Darn right ugly out here! The snow piles up so deep you can't go anywhere. When it isn't snowing, you're knee-deep in mud. You will walk to the grocery store in the blowing, freezing snow to buy high-priced food. Teacher housing is a tiny mobile trailer half-buried in the mud. The second bedroom only has room for two beds, which will mean two of your boys will have to share a bed. The district doesn't allow your children in the classroom before or after school, so you'll need daycare for forty-five minutes in the morning and afternoon. There aren't too many people I would trust my kids with here in this village. Also, be sure to look at the contract closely. They will charge *both of you* rent and utilities, which amounts to a huge chunk of your paycheck." The picture was grim.

Oh, Lord. What could we be getting ourselves into moving here? We thanked the principal for his candid responses, hung up the phone, and stared at one another. Fear. That's what I felt, pure fear.

"That guy at the table lied to us," Elgin broke the silence. "We should not accept those jobs."

"What if we don't receive contracts from the Aleutians East? Let's check to see who else posted our names for an interview." Our busy schedule up to this point had provided no time to visit with the districts requesting interviews.

We loaded a few more packets into our briefcase and headed to the elevator. The administrator from Lower Yukon spotted us when we entered the room and hustled over. "So, are you ready to sign?"

"Not yet. We're still considering it," Elgin replied.

"Okay. Noon. You have until noon." He returned to his table but continued to monitor our whereabouts.

Chuck Coons from the North Slope showed up a moment later. "Did you speak with Tom Ryan?" He seemed excited.

"Yes. They hope to offer us contracts but are waiting for a resignation." Concern was evident in my voice.

"That resignation is coming in. Please don't sign the Lower Yukon contracts without talking to me first. I will be right over there," he pointed to his table.

"We won't," we assured him in unison.

We worked our way across the room, stopping to chat about Lower Yukon with the logging camp district administrator Roger Sampson. We wanted to take him up on his offer of advice during our recent interview.

"Hello, Cooks." Roger stood with a smile, spreading his arms wide in a welcome. "We still have those jobs available if you've changed your minds?"

"We are signing them!" The Lower Yukon administrator appeared out of nowhere and butted into our conversation, leaning on the table between Roger and us.

"Not yet. You said we have until noon," Elgin reminded him in a friendly but matter-of-fact manner.

The administrator continued his intrusions at other school district tables. We ditched the guy by taking a break back in our room to wait for a phone call from Bob Robertson. The phone failed to ring, so we returned to the conference entryway to meet up with the Aleutians East administrators. It was almost noon. Our afternoon schedule filled up with interviews. However, the thought of letting the Lower Yukon deadline pass without signing flat-out rattled me.

The Lower Yukon administrator nagged, "It's close to noon. Let's get this over with and sign you up for next school year." He certainly received points for tenacity, but not the good kind.

"We will wait until noon," Elgin said with a touch of anger. The man bowed, took a step back, and returned to the conference room.

"I'll meet you at the table then," I heard him say as he retreated. It was 11:57 a.m.

"Elgin, I cannot believe you talked to him like that! You realize this entire state only has *fifty* jobs available?"

"He won't leave us alone. I've had it!" Elgin fumed. "We couldn't speak seriously with any other districts."

"Elgin and Melissa," shouted Tom Ryan from the Aleutians East as he rushed down the hall with Chick Beckley. "We have contracts for you to sign."

Believing the pesky administrator was back, Elgin growled, "It's *not* noon, and I don't want to hear another word about it! Is that clear?" His response astonished us all.

I tugged at his shirt and pointed to the men. "That is Tom Ryan with the Aleutians East Borough." Elgin quickly apologized.

"We have an appointment but secured the resignation and can officially offer you both full-time teaching contracts. We'll fill you in on the details later," Tom dashed across the lobby with a briefcase and stack of papers while Chick hustled alongside him.

Stunned, we stood there in silence for a few moments. The reality of our achievement set in. We had jobs with the number one district on our wish list and with a day and a half to spare. Overwhelming relief replaced our anxiety. Entering the conference room grinning ear-to-ear, we celebrated with Chuck Coons.

The Lower Yukon administrator took the news better than expected, "Next time. Best of luck to you."

After canceling our afternoon interviews, we escaped to the teacher's lounge to relax and celebrate. A teacher we met the day before welcomed us into the room. He had decided to move to Hawaii instead of pursuing a job in Alaska and offered to take us to dinner to celebrate. The next day we all went sightseeing and checked out Cook Inlet, Portage Glacier, and the gorgeous scenery of Turnagain Arm.

Welcome to Alaska!

North to Alaska

"Are you ready to go?" Elgin loaded the back end of the Bronco with a tent, sleeping bags, and a cooler full of food. Unsure of what to expect on the Alaska Highway, also known as the Alcan, we picked up the *Mile Post 1995*. This legendary travel guide identified accommodations, recreational sites, and services such as gas stations on the highway.

Standing in the doorway, I took in the old ranch house one last time. It had seen its better days, but it was home and still full of our belongings. Recovering from severe pneumonia and unable to pack, I had no idea what special items remained. "The house doesn't even look like we're leaving," I sighed and closed the door. Aside from what we packed in the Bronco and the year's supply of groceries and a few personal items we dropped off at the barge in Seattle in May, everything we owned was still in that house. Elgin's sister TaMara planned to sell everything at a yard sale the following week.

We drove the short distance to say goodbye to Elgin's parents, Kenny and Connie. Choking back tears, we piled the boys into the Bronco and traveled through Montana into Alberta, Canada. We imagined our destination to be the Great Yellowstone National Park of the North. It was the beginning of a thrilling adventure. On that day, we moved a world away from our family and farming community of 186 people in Burlington, Wyoming. We were excited—and to be honest—a little afraid.

On the outskirts of Calgary, Alberta, we pulled into a campground for the night. "Beware of the bears, they have been in the area searching for a free meal. Put your food away," the clerk warned.

The highway continued to deteriorate the further we drove through British Columbia. We passed up a primitive cabin near Dawson Creek in favor of our tent, despite my fear of hungry bears. The next day, the rough road led us through secluded areas of the Yukon Territory.

Country stores surfaced sporadically along the way, though we decided we'd rather starve than pay the exorbitant prices. Even a cup of fresh water costs money. No free bathrooms either. The previous travelers must have invented the term *highway robbery*! Motels popped up along the highway but a tent was more appealing than most of the lodging options we could afford. Those in our price range offered outhouses for bathrooms and a couple had no electricity or heat. No, thank you!

Miles upon endless miles of wilderness crossed our front window. And the view—let me tell you about the views! Glacier-carved lakes with brilliant hues of green and blue fed the creeks and rivers below. Steep layers of rugged, snow-capped mountains with luscious, thick, green trees blanketed the land at the lower elevations. The rocky banks along the roadside broke out into a scattering of names spelled out in stone by previous travelers. We stopped and added "COOK" to the collection.

Somewhere in the Yukon, I noticed the time. "Gees! It's already nine forty-five. We need to find a place to camp," I urged Elgin as he drove the snaky road. The extended daylight fooled us. We squeaked into the nearest campground right before closing time, giving the boys renewed energy. Thrilled to be out in the open to stretch their legs, they played tag while Elgin and I set up the tent. I prepared dinner over a Coleman cookstove. Giggles and screams of delight rang out through the woods surrounding the campsite. Time escaped us again.

"Quiet out there!" a man yelled, horrifying me as I realized it was now 11:00 p.m.

"Sorry!" Embarrassed, I apologized and served my family a half-cooked dinner. Feeling like total idiots, we gulped our food and dog-piled into the two-room tent. Not another peep came from our direction.

"Mom?" Everett squirmed in his sleeping bag.

"What?" I whispered.

"It's not dark outside yet." In a few minutes, they fell asleep, exhausted from the long day of travel—everyone except me. Wide-eyed and restless, I listened for bears and stared at my sleeping babies. Ethan was a mere five years old. Everett was turning seven in two weeks and Sutton had recently celebrated his eighth birthday. All blonds. All boys. All thin. But not all excited about this significant change.

In the chill of the frosty morning, I stretched my short body in the warm sleeping bag, dreading the inevitable moment of climbing out. I had been on supplemental oxygen as treatment for pneumonia for a month before our departure. Without the extra oxygen, fatigue caused me to drag.

"Time to go," Elgin announced, packing his sleeping bag into its cover. "Wake up, boys. You can sleep in the Bronco."

We bumped along the road's incessant frost heaves making the Alcan Highway feel like a roller coaster ride, twisting, turning, narrow, and rough enough to jar one's teeth loose. We endured in silence for a while. At one point, Elgin announced, "Dang, this road looks like the guy driving the Caterpillar ran down a snake!" The Bronco filled with giggles.

"Look, boys! It's the Alaska sign." Canada had been a long haul, and we were ready to return to the United States. As we crossed the border, we all cheered except for poor Sutton, who put his head into the blanket his Grandma Connie had given to him and cried. He did not want to leave Grandma and Grandpa Cook or Wyoming. My heart went out to him. Sutton kept his watch and bedroom clock set to Wyoming time for the next eleven years. He returned to Wyoming for college in 2006, never coming back to Alaska.

We drove far into the night. The boys had fallen asleep on the backseat by the time Elgin pulled over in exhaustion. "Let's sleep here tonight." The Bronco faced the distant Matanuska Glacier on the Glenn Highway with Palmer and Anchorage up ahead.

Elgin slept on the backseat with Ethan on his chest, while Sutton snuggled in his blanket on the backseat floor. Everett slept in the front with me while I stayed awake, watching for bears from the safety of the vehicle. I was grateful not to be outside camping in a tent, though a hotel would have been preferable.

The sun dipped to the horizon, skimmed below it, and then rose again. Darkness never fully arrived. The midnight sun illuminated the glacier and surrounding mountains. Reverence and wonderment filled my soul as I realized we would soon call Alaska home.

SEVEN

Never Mail Yourself a Gun

Arriving in Anchorage by noon, we rushed to finish last-minute errands before heading south the next morning to Homer. The Alaska Marine Highway transported residents along the coast of Alaska, and we planned to catch the ferry sailing to Cold Bay. First up, the post office for the gun I had mailed to myself. Yep, you read that correctly. I mailed myself a gun. It wasn't easy getting a handgun to Nelson Lagoon since they were illegal to bring through Canada.

"How do you mail a gun to rural Alaska?" I had asked the local postmaster in Cody, Wyoming, a few weeks earlier. The smartphone and wealth of information found on the internet today did not exist then.

"You take it to a gun dealer and have them mail it to another gun dealer there," he said.

"What if no gun dealer exists where we are moving?" I explained the isolated location of our new home.

"You can mail it to yourself general delivery and pick it up at the Anchorage post office," he informed me. I followed the postmaster's instructions. What could go wrong? Of course, shipping it to Anchorage meant I could have sent it between gun dealers or directly to Nelson Lagoon, but that would be hindsight now, wouldn't it?

"My name is Melissa Cook, and I have a general delivery package to pick up," I announced, stepping up to a window of the busy Anchorage post office.

"Just a minute," the man returned with my box. "I'm curious. Why did you mail yourself a package general delivery?"

I did not have to answer that, but being my talkative self, I did. "Because handguns are illegal in Canada."

"There's a gun in this box?" Alarmed, he scrutinized the package with heightened interest. "Wait here." He left, taking my package with him.

Minutes passed before he returned. The serious look on his face intimidated me. Another man stood beside him, holding my now opened package in his hands. "You know it's against the law to mail a gun, don't you?" His sternness frightened me.

"I didn't know how to send it. Nelson Lagoon doesn't have a gun dealer. The postmaster in Wyoming told me to mail it general delivery to myself, so I did." I tried not to become too defensive.

"You are facing six months in prison. It's a federal crime to mail a firearm. Follow me." The second guy did the talking now, and he was not fooling around.

"What do you mean jail time?" The panic in my voice caused people to stare as I defended myself tooth and nail now. "I called the postmaster and followed his instructions. You cannot arrest me for his mistake! That's not right!" Holding back tears, my alarm betrayed me in my raised voice.

"Please step over here ma'am." His unfriendliness and inability to comprehend my circumstances were irritating. We stood at the end of the counter, away from the gawkers. "Who told you to mail this gun?" he questioned me.

"I don't remember his name! I didn't expect to need it. He was the postmaster of the Cody Post Office in Wyoming. That's all I know." That was the truth of it; there was not much more to say. "It seems to me if the post office tells you to do something, and it's wrong, then blame them, not me!" Nervousness revealed itself in my cracking speech.

"I'll be back in a minute," the Anchorage postmaster stepped into his office. The worker kept a close eye on me. The wait was excruciating.

My mind raced with thoughts as I waited. *I don't have the money to pay for a lawyer. What if I go to jail? Oh, gees!* The bystanders, aware of my circumstances, had left the building.

Stuck waiting in the Bronco with the boys, Elgin could not easily come into the building. With no cell phone, I had no way to text message or call him. While I worried about going to jail, unaware, Elgin watched the clock and sweated, wondering if we would have enough time to take the driver's license test and finish shopping.

At last, the man returned, "I spoke to the postmaster in Cody. He claims he did not tell you to mail a gun to yourself. Mailing a firearm is a serious offense."

My jaw dropped, tears filled my eyes, but I was mad too. "I don't know why the postmaster is denying it. I know what he said because I called to be sure. How can you send me to jail for listening to him?"

"Because he denies saying it!"

"He told me to mail it!" We hit an impasse, a showdown of stories. He paused and stared at me.

"Our new school district requires us to bring a gun to Nelson Lagoon for the bears. They will not permit us to take the students outside without the gun because a bear killed a child in King Cove two years ago." We all paused.

"I assume you're telling me the truth. I doubt you would admit to mailing a gun if you knew it was illegal. Never mail yourself a gun again!" With that, he handed over the package.

"I won't. Never again!" I promised in disbelief, half expecting the police to arrive any minute to haul me away.

EIGHT

Pipe Dreams

The next morning, we headed south in the packed Bronco along the dramatic Turnagain Arm toward Homer. The windshield wipers ran frantically in the pouring rain while water splashed on the highway with each passing car. I wish I could say the surrounding beauty of this scenic highway impressed the boys, but a week of travel had numbed them.

Five hours later, we arrived in a blustery Homer. We passed a slew of flopping tents set up along the rocky roadside on our way to the ferry terminal. The occupants endured the treacherous storm as the savage wind beat their tents. A few drenched and freezing campers battled the wind to secure their belongings outside.

"Yikes! Those poor people." I surveyed the scene as we drove by.

We parked near the harbor, and I hopped out of the Bronco. "I'll check in. Be right back." Leaning my shoulder into the wind, I held my hood tightly under my chin and ran for the ferry terminal. Rain-soaked passengers filled the building, some with suitcases, others without. I didn't have to wait long; I heard the dreadful news from where I stood.

"The ferry broke down and won't be leaving tonight. The maintenance crew is waiting on a part which should arrive in three days, weather permitting."

We rented the last room available in the little seaside town. Cousin Cliff's friend, Frank Milliman, waited until we settled into the hotel and then drove our Bronco back to his home in Anchorage, where it would stay in his yard for the winter. Without a vehicle, our food options became severely limited, but at least we were not outside in a tent.

We had expected to board the Alaska Marine Highway ferry for a four-day boat ride to Cold Bay. Then a PenAir bush flight would take us into Nelson Lagoon, eighty miles away. Not sure how to travel to Nelson Lagoon other than our current plan, I called the Homer airport. "We'd like to charter a flight to Nelson Lagoon," I requested. Traveling by the seat of our pants now, it hadn't occurred to us to call the school district for help.

My request for a flight shocked the pilot, George Nathan. "Lady, have you looked outside? There is a nasty storm out there! The forecast is ugly for days. And where is Nelson Lagoon anyway?" He thought I was a nut, for sure.

"It's over by Cold Bay on the Bering Sea side of the peninsula," my weak description probably caused the pilot to shake his head. The village was a three-hour flight in a single-engine plane along the Alaska Peninsula, 450 miles as the crow flies. Each morning and afternoon, we phoned the charter service to check on the possibility of flying. On the third day, the storm broke.

"Come quickly. We'll make a run for it before the storm closes in," ordered the pilot.

"Time to go!" We rushed to the tiny airport and paid the unplanned expense of $2,200 using my mother-in-law's credit card. We climbed into the six-seater plane and flew down the coast to our new home.

The Great Yellowstone National Park of the North we called it, and that about sums up our original expectation—a pipe dream. Life has its harsh realities and rude awakenings. Nothing could have prepared us for the immense changes about to befall us. The previous teacher, Cole Lehmann, had tried to show us by sending a videotape of the village when he transferred from Nelson Lagoon to King Cove. You'd think watching it might have given us some insight. It didn't.

George, the pilot, handed each of us our first set of earplugs to block out the aircraft noise. My last set of plugs sits right here beside my keyboard today. I still find spare earplugs in my coat pockets, purse, and cubbyholes in our truck, evidence of our many bush flights in Alaska.

"Here we go!" George exclaimed as the Cessna 206 back taxied on runway twenty-two. Gorgeous mountains filled the windows as we turned around at the end of the runway. The plane sped down the tarmac until it lifted into the partially sunny skies. My heart sang with delight as we soared above the gorgeous land and sea.

We flew over Cook Inlet with the Pacific Ocean out to our left. The scenic flight was stunning beyond imagination. The roar of the engine echoed through the plane, forcing us into silence. We each became lost in the thrill of the view as we peered through the windows at the surrounding mountains. For once, the boys set their Game Boys aside to watch.

Kodiak Island emerged in the distance through the left windows. We flew across the Alaska Peninsula making a quick pit stop for fuel in King Salmon, 193 miles from Homer. Continuing our journey, we passed by Aniakchak National Monument which included a dramatic snow-capped volcano.

We watched the impressive mountainous area gradually transform into something far less spectacular. The change alarmed me. Vivid colors grew dull. Extensive mudflats emerged with countless static ponds dotting the horizon. The scenery grew dreary. Thick, gray cloud cover overtook the blue skies. Beauty depleted with each mile, like a tub of water going down the drain. Swear words escaped in whispers under my breath, and I didn't usually swear.

As we flew on, the coastal land was barely above sea level. The mountains in the distance to the south lost their flair. The ride seemed endless. Then a stunning volcano came into view—Mount Veniaminof. A massive eruption in 1750 had left an impressive caldera in its center. We would watch the sun rise over this volcano for the next couple of years.

A few minutes later, George announced, "Nelson Lagoon up ahead!" It was nowhere in sight.

"Where?" I hollered over the sound of the engine from the backseat.

George tipped the plane's wings for us to see an itty-bitty sand spit stretching from the mainland, like an extended thumb from a hand. A scattering of buildings, black sand roads, and a landing strip loomed as we approached the village. Waves rolled onto the beach on the Bering Sea side of the spit while calm waters along the seven-mile-wide lagoon caressed the sands of the other. We were landing on a sand mound protruding above the sea in the middle of nowhere and planned to live on it! The shock silenced me as my heart thumped inside my chest. The plane made its final approach and dropped onto the gravel strip.

"Nelson Lagoon," George declared.

When the pilot opened the door, none of us made a move. Not even the boys. No way. *Were we crazy? This wasn't funny! We eagerly signed up for this? What happened to the Great Yellowstone National Park of the North?*

Elgin and I stared at one another, both contemplating the same thing. *Do we get off this plane?* It came down to finances. We had shipped all the possessions we had left in the world, along with a nine-month supply of food. Penniless, we had no choice but to deplane.

A villager pulled up in his pickup truck right next to the aircraft to meet the unscheduled flight out of curiosity. There was no way to send word of our arrival. "I have your new schoolteachers," George informed him.

"Way cool, man." The resident offered us a ride in his two-door pickup truck.

We piled our suitcases and children into the back end of the rusty blue truck. Elgin and I climbed in with the kids and watched George take off, the sound of the engine fading in the distance. Surrounded by water, we rode the one mile to the village, wide-eyed and in shock.

We were in for the adventure the speaker at the job fair had warned us not to come to Alaska expecting.

NELSON LAGOON, YEAR 1

ON THE BERING SEA

1995–96

Stay Clear of the Windows

The truck turned off the main village road, circling the teacher housing unit (or teacherage), ending our ninth day of travel. To our right was the school district's metal cargo container. The slightly ajar door revealed a fifty-five-gallon barrel with a hand pump attached—the school's gas station. Beside the shipping container was a deteriorating one-room structure—an emergency jail. It butted up against another tiny building—the village generator. To the left was the remodeled school district duplex. The school's old, rusty, blue Suburban was parked in the driveway. Our two Polaris four-wheelers sat in the front yard. The ATVs indicated our shipment had arrived which was a good thing since there was no grocery store here.

Lana Gundersen picked up our arrival over the radio and greeted us at the doorstep. She turned out to be our lifeline to sanity in Nelson Lagoon. Lana, one of two non-Native residents in the village, was married to a local. Delighted to have new teachers in town, she showed us the school district's two apartments. The boys ran between rooms investigating.

Each apartment had seven hundred square feet, two-bedrooms, and adequate furniture. White linoleum ran from the front entry, down the hall, and into the bathroom and kitchen, while gray outdoor carpeting covered the tiny living room and bedroom floors. A shared, narrow laundry and storage room ran between the two units. The teacher housing put the promised Hooper Bay mobile trailer half-buried in the mud to shame, but it was, by no means, luxurious.

Someone had stacked our moving boxes in the kitchen and dining room; many of them were left wide open. "What's this?" Elgin asked, staring at the half-empty boxes. "Someone robbed us!"

"At least they left us some food." I peered into a box with a few remaining items. Digging through the boxes, I discovered our new school clothes were missing too, and they still had the tags on them. I was deeply disappointed. Finding clothes that fit me was no easy task and would not happen out of a catalog. It would be months before I could purchase decent clothing. The superintendent guessed the thief mailed the stolen items back to the store for a refund.

Lana gave us the lowdown on the village. "Stay clear of the windows at night," she warned. "The guy across the street shoots his gun haphazardly when he's drunk. If you hear shooting, duck." I was grateful none of our windows faced that neighbor's house.

Hours after Lana left us to unpack, our first visitor knocked at the door. There stood a heavyset Aleut man in his forties with a guitar in hand and alcohol on his breath. "You're my only friends," he declared after finding his way into a chair in our tiny kitchen.

"We just met you," Elgin uttered with a hint of irritation and suspicion.

"You are. I'm telling you, I have no friends but you. Let me play you a song." The lyrics enlightened us on a supposed murder in the village two months prior. "He was my brother," he sang with sadness.

"What do you think of Nelson Lagoon?" Cole Lehmann called from King Cove the first evening. Elgin shared the details of our arrival, the theft of our food and clothing, and the visitor's story with his guitar. "I loaned that guy fifty dollars and asked for it whenever I saw him. One or two requests for the money, and he avoided me like the plague. Best money I ever spent!" He laughed. We lent the man twenty dollars and seldom saw him again.

Our friendship with Cole Lehmann developed into a lasting one. Over the years, we compared notes on school districts and teaching assignments. With a common interest in technology, we met at conferences and the job fair. He even joined us in Wyoming on vacation.

The first night in Nelson Lagoon, I lay awake adjusting to the smaller bed and listening for gunshots coming from the neighbor's house. Two years! That is how long we had agreed to stay, but I didn't know if we could do it. Some promises were more difficult to keep than others. It took four teachers to complete one school year at this two-teacher site and none of them had agreed to stay. I admitted to myself, Alaska wasn't all I had expected it to be, at least not yet.

No Airport Coffee Shop

Two days flew by as we emptied moving boxes at home and organized the classrooms. We resisted our children's pleas to see the village—there would be plenty of time for that. Late on the second afternoon, we rushed to the airstrip to await our next bush flight.

Before spotting the plane, we heard the hum of the engine in the distance. All eyes turned to the breezy sky, watching for wings through the thick cloud cover lingering overhead. Once in sight, the plane roared one hundred feet above us. Excitement filled the old school Suburban. It delighted our boys to see another bush plane, let alone to fly in it.

"It's a Cherokee Six, Dad." Sutton could hardly sit still.

"I'm shocked they made it in with this wind," Elgin replied.

We climbed aboard the PenAir flight headed southwest leaving the Bering Sea side of the peninsula to cross over to the Pacific Ocean and on to King Cove for a teacher in-service. *Bump, bump.* The plane jarred with each air pocket as we cruised four hundred feet above a scattering of large, static ponds surrounded by beach grass. Blowing ocean spray and an occasional high tide reached the ponds closest to the shoreline. Nelson Lagoon drew its water from one such pond, which explained the disgusting taste. The water was unbearable to swallow unless I refrigerated it, and in the weeks ahead, we all adjusted to chronic, partial dehydration.

The vastly unfamiliar terrain of treeless mountains and the Bering Sea had our eyes glued to the windows. We soon discovered our flight plan included a dicey remote airstrip.

Flying into King Cove challenged even the best pilots. On the better days, swift, swirling wind with unpredictable changes combined with the close mountain peaks and Belkofski Bay kept pilots on guard. On ugly days, the famous hurricane-like conditions made flying into King Cove terrifying. Not to mention that, for a newbie like me, the approach resembled a box canyon.

The plane jolted in the gusty wind, while the mountains seemed too close. Sudden squalls blew through the valley and across the runway, forcing the pilot into a severe crosswind landing. The plane jerked and bumped its way through the maneuver, scaring the hell out of me. Landing while battling a punishing crosswind was unnerving, given I wasn't expecting it.

Bob Robertson greeted us on the airstrip and chauffeured our family four miles down the gravel road to the fishing village of eight hundred people. The restaurant closed before our arrival, leaving us hungry. I had failed to feed my family before we left Nelson Lagoon. Bob contacted the store owner to open the market for us to grab a snack. I learned to *always* tote plenty of food in my luggage if I didn't want to go hungry or eat something I didn't recognize.

"How did y'all get to Nelson Lagoon? It has puzzled us." Bob spoke with a slight Arkansas accent. "I worried when we didn't see you at the ferry terminal." We told him about our flight across the peninsula in George's single-engine plane.

"Oh boy! I bet it was a long flight. I've never heard of anyone chartering a single-engine plane out this far. We got caught up in the ferry mess too. My family and I camped out in the storm for days. The school district chartered a plane to Sand Point for employees stranded at the terminal. The weather was terrible!"

"We saw the tents in the blowing rain. That looked awful," I agreed.

"And cold. Let me tell you, it was cold out there!" We chatted as we strolled the damp village street.

We realized we had joined a select group—a new Alaskan family where people watched out for one another. The sparse population in bush communities meant everyone mattered in a time of crisis, regardless of whether you liked one another. At times, one's own survival was at stake.

Our hotel room was directly above the bar. Bob left us to return to his young family. "See y'all in the morning," he pointed out the direction to the school.

"Open the window. It's hot in here," Elgin complained as he hauled the suitcases into the room. The boys pulled out a few toys to play with while I scanned the village from the second-floor window. A putrid smell filled the room as a cool breeze blew past the fish cannery. The temperature dropped, but the smell, oh the *smell*! It was intolerable.

"Close it, quick!" The odor was repulsive and nauseating. Ugh.

Our night was oppressive and insufferable. When suffocating from the heat was worse than the vile smell, the window opened. Gagging, it promptly closed. We lay half-naked on the beds, sweating. Wasn't this Alaska, the land of snow and ice? Though temperatures were in the low fifties outside, the hotel room was sizzling, noisy, and rank.

Cigarette smoke rose from the bar through the bathroom vent and music blared half the night, vibrating the walls and floor. Even the toilet water bounced to the beat. Between songs, the chattering of the drinking crowd below replaced the rhythm of the unwelcome tunes.

The next morning, our exhausted family hurried through the chilly morning mist on foot along the quiet road to the school. King Cove teenagers greeted us at the doorway and took charge of the boys, escorting them to a classroom for playtime. The Aleutians East Borough School District provided childcare at no cost to the teachers. How's that for family friendly?

The staff chatted in the lunchroom, reuniting after a summer apart. A handful of fresh faces observed the scene, including us. We took a seat, bagel and juice in hand.

Two teachers visited next to us. "My dad came to see me last spring. I let him know I would meet him at the airstrip when I heard his plane approaching the village. He couldn't grasp that the flight schedule isn't to the minute out here."

"I told my parents they could get stuck in Cold Bay overnight if a storm kicked up," the other teacher added.

"I gave up and told my dad I would be there waiting for him. Then he worried about inconveniencing me and said he'd be waiting at the airport coffee shop." With that, both teachers burst out laughing. King Cove's airstrip had no services—not even a shelter for waiting passengers. I smiled to myself. It definitely was a different world out here.

Teachers from Sand Point and King Cove stuck together, having little to do with the small school staff. The group functioned as two entities. Teachers from the remote villages of Nelson Lagoon, Akutan, Cold Bay, and False Pass bonded quickly. With upcoming volleyball and basketball seasons, we would visit regularly.

The district provided meals in the school cafeteria for outer site staff and their children during our stay in King Cove. Nothing fancy, but we didn't starve.

Bob Robertson arranged for a tour by school bus to a nearby creek filled with spawning salmon one rainy evening. What an adrenaline rush! Detroit born and raised, I had seen nothing comparable to it. Abundant salmon launched their slimy, mammoth bodies out of the creek, soared through the air, and plunged back into the water one on top of another. Dead bodies floated in and along the water's edge. The stench of rotting flesh was something else. Oh, my. I held in my urge to gag.

During the exhausting five-day marathon in-service, we were introduced to electronic mail and received our first email account from this cutting-edge school district. Though we enjoyed the social aspect and meeting Cole Lehmann in person, it was time for us to head home to Nelson Lagoon.

Let me tell you a secret. The King Cove airstrip was in one freaking crazy landing location, and our arrival meant we were now obligated to leave. Flying in a bush aircraft through swirling and shifting winds was not at the top of my bucket list. No wonder two fatal plane crashes happened in the nearby mountains.

Once in the air and past the mountains, cruising over the tundra, I felt relief until the pilot pointed out his window. "See that wreckage? A plane crashed on its way into Nelson Lagoon ten years ago. No one died in that one."

Great!

Years later, Guy Morgan, a pilot from Cold Bay, described flying into King Cove for the E&E News, "Sometimes it's like we're trying to be aerobatic pilots when we're not aerobatic pilots. It's not for the faint of heart. Pilots described flights between the King Cove and Cold Bay airports as 'very tricky,' 'a risk,' 'pretty violent,' and 'the scariest plane ride of your life.' . . . infamous for some of the world's most sudden and extreme weather" (Scott Streater and Phil Taylor, February 27, 2013).

ELEVEN

Smoke Rises from the Bering Sea

Taking a break from the mad dash to prepare for classes, we gathered the boys on four-wheelers and took our first ride on the beach. It was late August, though it felt similar to fall in Wyoming with overcast skies and cool temperatures. Unbeknown to us, we would be cold for the next twenty years.

The black sand beach revealed an even darker color barely beneath the surface when we drove, stepped, or played on it. *Volcanoes must be the source,* I thought as I held out my hand, allowing the peculiar grains to slip through my fingers into the chilly, constant wind.

Further down the beach, an unbearable stench led to the discovery of a dead sea creature half-buried in the sand. *Eew,* did it stink! Elgin and the boys plugged their noses while I held my jacket over my face. We did not stop to explore, only paused to determine the critter had probably been a walrus, and then we sped away, leaving behind the putrid odor.

In the weeks to come, we drove our four-wheelers up and down the beach to investigate, avoiding the stinky walrus. Our children were delighted in our new hobby of beachcombing. Trash of various types washed ashore, including massive stray logs, pieces of fishing gear, a torn life raft, and plenty of unidentifiable items. An occasional seal's head popped above the water and floated by checking us out. Bear prints followed the shoreline. Ravens, eagles, and seagulls created a continuous background of squawks and cries. There were no people in sight. With the sea on one side and lagoon on the other, water and nature surrounded us. It exhilarated me at first.

On one trip, eight-year-old Sutton screamed, "There's a fire on the water. Look!" We stopped the rumbling four-wheelers. All eyes watched the water. Waves rolled along the stretching shoreline, but we saw no flames.

We began our journey again. Sutton shrieked, "Smoke! Smoke!" A mist rose from the Bering Sea—then emerged the whale. Cheers broke out at our first spotting of a whale in the wild. It mesmerized us by spraying mist into the air and then slipping out of sight below the surface. We waited with anticipation for each of his returns above the water, spraying his mist of "smoke".

Humpback whales frequent the Aleutians in the summer months. They live to be forty to fifty years old and reach forty to sixty feet. To attract mates, they sing long, complex songs underwater. It was not unusual to spot them launching their entire, immense bodies out of the sea. Once I saw a humpback clear the water and splash on its side. When the water consumed it, I stood mesmerized for a moment, and then a second and third whale followed.

Nelson Lagoon was a drastic change from the desert of Wyoming. The school sat on the edge of the lagoon. From the school window, I expected to see everything on the treeless spit. Not so. Thick, tall grass covered the land from the lagoon to the Bering Sea and hid the dunes underneath. The treeless backdrop made it easy to believe we knew what was out there. We didn't.

They elevated most homes and buildings in the village; we assumed to accommodate the surging sea. High tides flooded the spit, especially during storms. Decks, large porches, and windows gave residents views of the village and beaches. Four-wheelers and pickup trucks rumbled by on the road while aircraft buzzed overhead.

Abundant wildlife lived on and along the seashore. Seals checked out the beach from the water. Whales breached for a breath of fresh air while birds circled overhead. Periodically, a curious Alaska brown bear appeared searching for an easy meal, leaving enormous prints in the sand beside homes and on the roads.

Russians ruled the Aleut people from the mid-1700s–1867, which resulted in some light-haired, blue- and green-eyed people with fair skin. The traditional Native skin tones, brown eyes, and black hair were also present in the community. They spoke English but had a distinct accent with an abrupt ending to each word.

On the first day of school, excitement filled the building. Nine village children greeted their three new classmates with enthusiasm. Elgin's room had eight elementary students while my classroom included one middle school student and three high schoolers.

Eager to begin the first day, I led secondary students through introductions. Kids told stories from summer break during their time to speak. A blue-eyed, blond Aleut teenager, Cilla, told me her story with enthusiasm. "This summer, we had warm weather and I was out sunbathing on my deck. My two younger cousins played tag by the house. I could hear them laughing and screaming, so I watched them play. Then I saw him in the grass, creeping up on the kids. He was stalking them like prey! I started screaming, 'Bear! Bear!' The kids stopped to look. I screamed for them to run upstairs. Then my uncle came running with his gun, but the bear had disappeared into the grass, and I couldn't see him anymore. It was scary!"

What does a teacher say to that? No student ever surpassed the first summer story shared with me on my initial day of teaching. The Alaska brown bear was common on the Alaska Peninsula. They weighed between eight and twelve hundred pounds and stood up to ten feet or four feet when walking on all fours.

After school, the classrooms filled with community members and parents standing around in their socks. Bush etiquette included removing your shoes at the door. Shoes carried in floor-damaging sand, which scattered by the backdoor instead of throughout the school.

The villagers welcomed us to Nelson Lagoon, and then several warned, "Beware of the bears. You can't be too careful." We heard one whopping bear tale after another! I won't lie. The stories scarred me for life, causing me to be on high alert for bear signs ever since that day. Do you blame me?

That night, I headed to bed after attempting to read the teacher manual for each class I taught—an impossible task. The day's events haunted my sleep. I dreamed of an Alaska brown bear stalking my children through the eerie grass and awoke in a sweat.

TWELVE

Abandon Ship

Those first days of the school year left us falling into bed exhausted. The endless summer sun was maddening at bedtime. I cuddled into a blanket, pulling it over my head to block out the undesired light. Troubled, Elgin squirmed, "I can't stand this! Look at it out there—it's daylight!"

"I noticed," I mumbled from beneath the covers. "Why don't you get some sleep?" He tossed. He turned.

"How am I supposed to sleep? It's as light as the middle of the day!" He rolled over in frustration. I peeked out to see his eyes were as wide as an owl's on its nightly hunt. He glared at the ceiling as if it were the reason for his torture. I returned to my makeshift cave, crafting a breathing hole through the edge of the blanket.

A few minutes passed. I was on the verge of sleep when suddenly the bed jerked, and Elgin raised his voice, "I can't stand this!" Did I dare peek out? I peeked.

Elgin rummaged through his camera bag. "What are you doing?" I inquired, watching his odd behavior.

"I can't take it anymore. It's daylight at eleven. Do you see that?" He pointed toward the window in irritation.

Pulling the camera from the bag, he snapped up the blind. Standing there, he checked his light meter. "I can take a picture, no problem. That's daylight!"

"What will the people think of the teacher standing in the window at midnight pointing his camera and waving his arms?"

Defeated, he dropped the blind, "I don't care."

After stuffing the camera bag under the desk, he dropped his tired body back into bed. The blankets pulled as he yanked them over his head and muttered as he rolled over, "It's daylight out there." Silence fell over the room. In a few minutes, Elgin was sound asleep while I lay there awaiting darkness.

The next day, we covered the bedroom windows with tinfoil which would not come down until we retired and moved away. The slightest light coming through the foil kept us awake. We fiddled with it nightly until the room was pitch-black, which we accomplished by pressing a towel to the door blocking out light from the living room windows.

We spent our first Saturday working at the school and overheard an emergency call come over the marine radio. "There's a bear on the boat!" a commercial fisherman bellowed. I was not sure I had heard that right. *A bear on the boat?* "We are abandoning ship. Someone bring a gun and shoot him before he wrecks everything!" the man begged. And that they did! A nearby fishing vessel answered the distress call, killing the uninvited guest. They dumped the bear's body into the lagoon.

The gigantic creature washed ashore a week later. The villagers inspected the bloated carcass, and so did we. It was a sorrowful sight, with patches of bulging, black skin and clumps of beautiful auburn fur. Its enormous paws had frightening claws extending out like human fingers. The mouth gaped open, exposing its black lips and large, white teeth—a heartbreaking sight. A bear willing to fish an easy meal from a fishing vessel's haul poses an extreme danger to the entire community. Accomplished swimmers, North American brown bears can surprise you anywhere, including on a boat in the middle of a lagoon.

We mentioned the death of the bear to the school maintenance man. "Bears will also break into your house, so don't keep any fish guts or smelly trash inside. Last year, one broke into the little house down the road. They had finished processing salmon in the kitchen but hadn't cleaned up yet. Be careful. If they decide to come in, you can't stop them. They're powerful *and* intelligent." Management of trash rose to a top priority for me after hearing that. We stockpiled garbage waiting for the next dump run on the back porch, a short distance from our living quarters, but that was as far away as I could store it without running to the dump with it every day.

Everyone had a bear story to tell. Nelson Lagoon bears were amongst the largest in the world. To control my paranoia, I did some serious reading on the topic. Four types of bears roam Alaska. The polar bear was a favorite topic when strangers discovered where we lived. Fascinated, I read about this white, man-eating, Arctic ice-dwelling predator which can weigh fourteen hundred pounds and stand eleven feet. These super bears of the north live along the Arctic Ocean and number close to twenty-six thousand. I discovered the Kodiak brown bears were equal in size and weight to their polar cousins. Their twelve thousand years of isolation on the salmon-rich Kodiak Island in the Gulf of Alaska accounting for their larger size and greater density. With one per square mile, that added up to thirty-five hundred bears roaming Kodiak Island.

Our new neighbors in Nelson Lagoon—you know, the ones who might show up in my kitchen—were the North American brown bears, also known as grizzlies. They are intelligent, curious, adaptable, exceptional swimmers, and have lived in Alaska for over a hundred thousand years before our arrival. They eat a variety of food and have a population of thirty-two thousand. The Alaska grizzlies are also called coastal brown bears. Their huge shoulder muscles allow them to run at speeds of up to forty mph. It also gives them impressive digging abilities. At eight hundred pounds and nine feet tall, the Alaskan grizzlies are the largest of the North American grizzly bears.

Alaska is also home to a hundred thousand black bears statewide. The smallest of Alaska's bears weighs two to six hundred pounds and ranges from coal black, brown, and white to bluish for those living near Southeast Alaska's glaciers. These bears are opportunistic eaters with a love for vegetation and salmon. Most bears hibernate seven to eight months of the year in caves, trees, and holes. Coastal bears living in more temperate climates on the coastline come out of hibernation after two to five months, depending on the weather. Prince of Wales Island's black bear population of one per square mile was once a mecca for trophy hunters. When all totaled, Alaska had one bear for every four people.

Lana had warned us on our first day, "The front door locks automatically. Before closing it, be sure to look around the outside of the house for bears." It took a few months to master checking for bears, and there were times I forgot.

One Saturday afternoon, I made a quick trip to the school to retrieve a book. Sutton, our third-grade son, asked, "Can I go too? I left my bag by the door." It was a beautiful day when I opened the door to our duplex. Sutton ran down the steps, and I followed. When the door shut behind me, I remembered the "check for bears" rule.

Darn it! Fear ran through my blood as Sutton reached for the Suburban's door handle. I glanced swiftly around the yard when my foot took the last step off the porch. Two huge black animals hanging around the back door caught my eye. My head jerked in a panic to identify the critters as a blood-curdling scream escaped me. Sutton was climbing into the vehicle when I gave him a hard shove and slammed the door to save him. No time to think; I grabbed for the driver's handle with my heart thumping in terror. Poor Sutton must have wondered what the heck was happening.

"What's going on?" a voice boomed from behind the house. I eyed over my shoulder while pausing mid-air, feet inside the vehicle, and body still hanging out. There stood the maintenance man with a concerned expression on his face and two oversize black dogs by his side.

Embarrassment washed over me. I fell back to the ground and stood there with no decent excuse for my shriek other than, "I thought your dogs were bears." He laughed. It was kind of funny, from his perspective. As for me, it took my heart a while to slow down.

THIRTEEN

Sucked Out to Sea

On our eleventh day in Nelson Lagoon, the Sand Point high school biology teacher arrived by bush plane to help Elgin harvest salmon eggs from a nearby stream. He planned to leave the eggs in a fish tank for the students to watch hatch and develop in the spring. I packed their lunches before they roared out of sight on our four-wheelers. An experienced beach rider and all business, the biology teacher headed out to the destination fifteen miles down the spit. Substantial Bering Sea waves rolled onto the beach and Elgin stayed clear of the water's edge. A stream of receding water backwashed on the beach. Elgin reduced speed to cross the water when his front wheels bogged down in the saturated sand, bringing him to an abrupt stop. Standing on the footrests, he threw his weight back and forth, rocking the ATV to break free. A rogue wave took him by surprise, crashing onto the beach and engulfing him in cold seawater. When the water receded, it pulled him out to sea, four-wheeler and all. Elgin stood in chest-high water as he fought being sucked further out to sea. The ATV rolled as the waves crashed around him. The tires floated above the water while the rest hung suspended underneath until the next wave rolled it again. Working his way over to grab it, Elgin took hold of the back end. A bungee strap kept the 30-06 rifle tied to the rack. He unhooked and held it above the water with one hand while grasping the four-wheeler with the other. The camera bag broke loose from the tie-down and washed away in the waves.

Bobbing in the Bering Sea, Elgin struggled. The biology teacher, oblivious to the situation, sped off down the beach. Elgin could not bring the ATV ashore by himself, and he sure as heck wasn't letting it go out to sea. Waves tossed him around as he battled to keep his grip on the rack. The four-wheeler tumbled and rolled in the wave action which made holding onto it grueling. Endless minutes passed as a half-frozen Elgin watched desperately until the teacher finally noticed his absence and headed back. He threw Elgin a rope, and together, they pulled the ATV to shore.

An hour after their departure, I heard a four-wheeler pulling into the driveway. I peeked out the window to see one machine pulling the other. A drenched, shivering Elgin stood at the door when I opened it. After changing into dry clothes and warming up, they worked for hours to get the four-wheeler running. Then they headed back out, a little less enthused.

Years later, I quizzed Elgin for more details about being swept out to sea. "*You* hold on to a rifle while fighting the waves and clinging to an upside-down four-wheeler rolling in the sea. No, I didn't just wait to be rescued! I tried to pull it to shore. And I may have said a few choice words while I was at it."

The decision to bring the four-wheelers to Nelson Lagoon was fitting because the boys loved the beach. *Cannot get enough of it,* I wrote home in September 1995. We found many treasures beachcombing, albeit most of it was trash. A few gems washed ashore with high tide and hid amongst the debris, including our lost camera bag. Salt water bathed the new 35-millimeter Minolta camera; it would not survive. Dang it!

We never knew for sure what we might discover when beachcombing on the shores of Nelson Lagoon. Tall grass lined the edge of the beach. I, without fail, kept my eye on the dunes because bear prints were as prevalent as tire tracks and shoe prints.

One stormy day, we discovered giant jellyfish scattered here, there, and everywhere—from the water's edge to the beach grass. "Their body acid will eat your shoes," one parent advised us. Those stunning stranded jellyfish grew to the size of Frisbees and had transparent bodies with brown stripes.

Tree-size logs littered the beach from the water to the shoreline. They floated across the Bering Sea from the Yukon River. "The logs are lost from the timber industry," a student explained. A few villagers used this wood to heat their homes. The journey across the Bering Sea to the Aleutian beach stripped the logs of their bark while the rough wave action during high tide semi-buried them in the sand. Violent storms rearranged the logs or took them away altogether.

Speaking of violent storms, the first month we lived in Nelson Lagoon Elgin left me alone with the kids to survive the worst storm we had ever encountered out there. To be fair, he had no idea how awful it would be when he flew out on Friday afternoon for his first administrator meeting in Cold Bay. Dreadful phone service with a two-second delay meant we could not hold a decent conversation, let alone a long meeting. Besides, the administrators enjoyed getting together to shoot the breeze at the bar.

A fierce storm raged throughout the night. I awoke Saturday morning to a storm with hurricane-strength wind. The boys piled into the Suburban, and we drove to the school to storm-watch from the large windows. During high tide, the ocean spray covered the village. Seawater swelled to the beach road entrances.

Ring. Ring. "Nelson Lagoon School."

"Hi Melissa, this is Tom Ryan. How are you doing out there?" He was weathering the storm in Cold Bay, eighty miles away. Nelson Lagoon was on a tiny spit, and this was my first frightening storm. The wind howled through the school. The mammoth waves crashed and battered the beach loud enough for us to hear from inside the building.

"It looks like a hurricane outside, and high tide is flooding the roads. What should I do? How high will the water get?"

"Take the Suburban to the highest point. Stay there until the water recedes," Tom instructed.

I wasted no time ushering the boys to the vehicle. Seawater flowed down the road much like a river. I drove the Suburban off-road to the highest hill in the center of the land spit. The additional ten feet of elevation made for a better view and added a margin of safety from the frightening storm. There we sat in silence, watching in awe while the storm surrounded us and roared.

One resident had long ago erected a barricade surrounding their house near the water's edge. We wondered why someone would obstruct their view. Now I knew. Monster waves collided with the wall, splashed seawater straight up into the air, where the ferocious wind carried it over to rain down over the house!

That afternoon, Elgin phoned. He was stranded in Cold Bay and staying at the Weathered Inn for a second night.

The brutal weather took its toll on the area. It tore up the beach, and the high winds and tide cleaned up the village of any unsecured items. Clumps of grass the size of hay bales dotted the roads after the seawater receded. Surprisingly, the school appeared to be unscathed.

The next week, a loud *crack* radiated throughout the classroom and all eyes turned to me. "What was that?" a child asked with apprehension.

"Sounded like a gunshot in the hallway. Wait here." I peered out the doorway but discovered nothing. The first school shooting was years away, so though it alarmed me, I wasn't petrified. Students crowded in behind me. "I told you to wait there," I reminded them, pointing to their seats. No one moved.

I opened the door wider and stepped out into the hall, holding my hand up to keep students from joining me. Still, nothing. Another much louder *pop* practically sent me jumping out of my skin and the kids all screamed. I surveyed for the origin of the sound and immediately identified the problem. Cracks in the school windows high above the hallway revealed the source of the sound.

The secondary end of the hall had no overhead windows. Entering the hallway to survey the damage, we stared in disbelief at what had startled us.

Why did the windows break? They built the school on a dune. So, when the storm sucked the sand out from under the foundation during the recent storm, it caused the school to settle. The next time a window cracked, we instinctively jumped and then headed to the hallway to inspect the damage.

This storm became the root of my nightmares there. I dreamed of storms coming in while I tried to load my children into the nearest boat. Nightmares of my boys being swallowed by the sea as they screamed for help haunted my nights. Not growing up in this remote village and fishing environment meant everything was new for me and, at times, a bit frightening.

In the fall, the fishermen stored their vessels on top of four fifty-five-gallon fuel drums for the winter. The boats then towered over the roads below. *How will we board the boats during an emergency?* I didn't know. *It's pitch-black at night. How will I find a boat in the dark if we need to get on it?* I didn't know that either. The questions poured in like the sea rolled down the village roads. Thoughts such as this stole precious sleep from me on stormy nights and even a few calm ones.

One night, I lay awake, knowing the alarm clock would buzz too early in the morning if I didn't fall asleep soon. The nasty winds settled on this winter evening, and the house stopped creaking day and night. An unfamiliar noise replaced the constant howling. It was a continuous sound but changed in a rhythmic pattern. *What was that noise?*

My inability to ignore the sound hindered my effort to sleep. *Could it be the wind?* I listened. It sounded like a washing machine. I slipped out of bed and checked the laundry room. Silence. Then I figured it out. *It sounds like waves rolling on the beach!* And it was.

FOURTEEN

The Aleutian School Bus

Practice for high school basketball began in the second week of school. By early October, students traveled by bush plane to tournaments twice a month. In the Aleutians, the school bus turned out to be a bush plane, and the bus driver a bush pilot. Tom Madsen, also known as the *Aleutian Aviator*, flew his brown 1959 Beechcraft E18S out of Unalaska to transport the teams. The district policy required the more expensive twin-engine planes for transporting students.

Each school hosted one tournament per sport season. Teams arrived throughout the mid-afternoon to play Friday night and Saturday morning games. Tom Madsen flew the entire afternoon, shuttling students in for the games and then home again the next day, weather permitting. Hosting sites fed the visiting teams.

Our basketball team had one tall student, and she had one short coach —me. At the tournament, Cilla joined another school's team to play. During practice, she dribbled the ball under my nose and ran circles around me. At twenty-eight years old and five feet tall, no way could I keep up, but I tried.

A month into the season, we hosted our first tournament. The village scrimmaged on Thursday evening to provide a more realistic practice for Cilla. The half-court gym with three feet between the court and the wall gave spectators standing room only.

Tournament weekends exhausted the staff. Traveling teachers chaperoned day and night. The event taxed the hosting teachers with all the preparations. Students prayed for ugly weather to extend their trips while teachers groaned when weather socked in the teams for the entire weekend or longer. By now, I knew to pack my bag full of food when traveling between bush communities because I didn't know for sure when or where to expect my next meal. For that matter, I never knew *what* the meal would be. I became leery of eating at every school event after a hosting site served me fish heads for dinner, though most events had fish tacos, and even those were not so awesome for this non-fish eater.

On Friday evening, the community members supported their team by standing along the court walls to cheer. Accompanying the games, the host site sponsored a dance, which always led to students pleading for one more song at midnight. My head pounded after hours of loud music. No one ever danced, instead the handful of teens sat in a corner bobbing their heads to the tunes. Afterward, visiting teachers and students slept on the floor in the library and classrooms.

On Saturday morning, I asked a chaperoning teacher, "Would you mind handing out these sack lunches I packed for the kids to take back on the bus?" There was a short pause, and then we both burst out laughing. The teams were returning home by *plane*.

Bush communities relied on the schools to provide the lion's share of activities and entertainment. When most teachers headed home for the day, bush teachers chaperoned, hosted, or prepared for events. Our school had two teachers, but there were single-teacher sites scattered around the state. In the winter, teachers in these bush sites shoveled intense snowfall from the sidewalks and doors to open the schools. Fortunately for us, the wind blew away most of the snow in Nelson Lagoon.

Remote teachers faced many challenges besides the snow. Try to explain the value of an education to a high school student earning more commercial fishing in six weeks than I did the whole year. Shoddy student work, lack of enthusiasm, and motivation led to what I referred to as "bushanized" teaching. These teachers relaxed standards to pass kids. As a result, students fell years behind in achievement by the time they reached high school. These hurdles may explain the state's high dropout rate. Some teachers mentally checked out and only assigned worksheets to survive.

We arrived each day bright and early, forty-five minutes before the students pulled up on their four-wheelers. The state-of-the-art classroom technology thrilled our boys who preferred school days to weekends. After school, they had the run of the building. We routinely worked ten to eleven hours per day. Still, they cried when I announced, "Time to go."

Hiking on the black sand beaches with school children was not a routine field trip, though we did venture outdoors on rare occasions. Outings required the 44-magnum. Fresh fish guts and enormous bear prints in the sand made for brief excursions. Recess was an indoor activity 99 percent of the time. Bears, risk of high winds blowing young children away (not kidding), lack of light most mornings during the winter, and cold weather sure didn't make going outside appealing. Sometimes I caught myself gazing out of the enormous school windows at the playground equipment. Such a shame the students seldom played on it.

During the school day, we left the marine radio on in the library. It kept us up to date on what was happening in the village. People used it for announcements, such as incoming pilots.

Who wouldn't be excited to hear, "Freight, freight, freight," announced over the radio? Freight, for me, was synonymous with a trip to the grocery store. Fifteen minutes later, the plane flew overhead, and a line of four-wheel-drive vehicles headed down the airport road. We watched a convoy of rusty, old trucks (one tied together with a rope), new trucks fresh off the barge, and numerous ATVs pass by the school window.

Elgin shook his head at the line of ten to fifteen vehicles because we seldom saw anyone unless freight was coming in. It surprised us to see how many people lived in the village because we often felt alone.

One day, a pilot radioed, "Freight, freight, freight. Fifteen minutes out." The lively classroom grew quiet. The radio announcement for freight always changed the tone in the room.

"Why do the kids turn grumpy when the pilot announces freight?" I inquired of one student.

"You don't get it. Freight means alcohol. It's a party night, and we won't be sleeping tonight." The revelation stunned me. I had no idea. Words that brought excitement and happiness to my boys forecasted a sleepless night for the village children. I turned off the school radio, though the classroom aide and students continually turned it back on.

Despite the occasional moodiness, we had fun with the kids. Bush teaching added a unique twist to the humor found in working with kids. One day, the two kindergarten students wrote letters on student lap boards as I dictated them.

"*V*," I instructed and watched to be sure the children wrote their letters the correct way. One child made his *V* upside down. "What is that?" I inquired.

He stared at it and then, with a smile, answered, "It's a tree."

"A tree?" Hoping to add a little fun to their day, I suggested, "Why don't you erase your tree and draw a better one?" They erased their letters and drew trees while I assisted the older students. When they finished, I checked their work. They had both drawn Christmas trees.

"Have you ever seen an actual tree?" Both little heads shook no. Their replies didn't surprise me. Most children didn't leave the village until they were older unless they became sick enough to require emergency medical care. Nelson Lagoon had no trees—none. Not one. Floating stripped logs lost from the Yukon washed ashore, which summed up the extent of trees in the area.

"What's the name of this part of the tree?" I questioned, pointing to the tree trunk.

Running his hands on the trunk of his body, the student found himself at a loss for words. "It's the . . . the . . . the part holding up the grass!"

FIFTEEN

Death Flight Along the Sea Beach

Dangers from the fishing industry reached into the safety of our classroom one afternoon. "Listen!" A student thought he heard a helicopter approaching the school. The room grew silent as we listened for ourselves.

Whop, whop, whop, beat through the building. The sound grew louder as the aircraft flew right by the school, skimming the beach. Students tipped over their chairs, scrambled out of their desks, and lined the windows to look for the aircraft. We had a brief glimpse of the Coast Guard helicopter flying over the beach before it flew out of sight. The students spun in unison, dashing to the back door.

We gathered at the school's rear entry and watched while the helicopter flew along the shoreline and out of sight. The deafening silence that followed the interruption confused me. The kids returned to the classroom without prompting with their heads hung low.

A third-grader offered me an explanation, "They are looking for the dead crabbers, they are. Two crab boats rolled in the high seas a couple of days ago. The Coast Guard is combing the beach for their dead bodies." The students returned to their desks as I contemplated the risks their loved ones took to earn a living on the high seas that had already claimed scores of fishermen. My childhood in Detroit was a striking contrast to that of these children. My father worked as a business executive.

Years after we left Nelson Lagoon, the show *Deadliest Catch* began airing in 2005. It depicted the dangers found in the fishing industry on the Bering Sea. Sadly, the crab boat death toll that year was fifteen. These numbers did not account for those seriously injured. Fishermen fell overboard, became crushed by unsecured equipment, or were hooked and dragged to their watery graves. Injured, missing, or dead fishermen's stories became our new norm.

On a lighter note, during a lesson on government, I asked the third and fourth graders to define taxes. "A *big* bill," one prosperous fisherman's son answered. The lure of the sea was the money that could be made from it and many of the locals had little choice but to head out to fish if they wanted to make a good living.

While the crab boats brought in good money in the region, Nelson Lagoon's primary income came from commercial salmon fishing. A brief season in the summer sustained the community for the entire year. It was a lucrative business. The village was originally only a summer fishing camp for the Aleuts until residents permanently settled there in 1960.

SIXTEEN

Fourth Class Mail

"There won't be a mail plane today," I shared the news with a neighbor entering the post office. The post lady asked me how I wanted to mail my package, but another customer answered for me.

"Fourth class," she replied.

"Fourth class?" the shocked postwoman repeated.

"That means dogsled at the rate our mail gets out!" I joked, and we all giggled.

It was not always fun and games at the post office. One stormy evening, a loaded plane arrived after weeks of no mail due to the notorious Aleutian weather. On these occasions, the post office opened at night for fifteen minutes.

I hurried over in the storm and waited to request my mail. First names of residents, not numbers, hung on the wall above the boxes.

I would have rather been anywhere else. Water dripped off our coats from the storm outside. Eight or nine men crowded into the tiny building, the stench of booze filling the air.

A drunken man standing behind me wrapped his beefy fisherman's arms around me. Others turned to see my predicament. "When is Elgin planning on sharing you, my pretty? It's our culture to share our women." He slurred into my ear loud enough for the entire room to hear and laugh as he squeezed me so tightly I could not escape. I twisted in his arms to break free, but he held me fast.

"Let go of me!" I demanded. He swayed back and forth with me in his arms. My feet dangled above the ground when he leaned back on his heels. He and the others in the building laughed.

"We share our women here," he said as I squirmed until his grip loosened, and I broke free. Fire burned in my eyes when I whipped around to face him. My sudden movement and fury delighted him.

In a low, angry voice, I warned him and anyone else with questionable ideas, "My 44-magnum and I say otherwise! I shoot first and ask questions later. Do you understand me?" I was mad now and raised my voice with the firmness of a strict parent. "Keep your hands off me!" His amused grin changed to a frown, and his eyes dropped to my hands. He was unsure if I had a gun on me. The men took a step back as I won the stare-down with the idiot. I refused to step away. I lifted my five-foot height, tiptoeing to look him in the eye, pointed my finger into his chest, and stated adamantly, "Don't you ever touch me again!"

The room fell silent, all eyes and ears intently focused on me. I stepped by the gawking men, held out my hand to the postwoman while keeping my eye on the fisherman, took my mail, and marched straight out of the building. A young and naive woman, I possessed the fury of a madwoman when pissed off.

Rain smacked me in the face when I stepped out into the storm. The wind slammed the door behind me—a perfect exclamation to my exit. The breath I held rushed from my lungs, and courage drained out the bottom of my boots. Frightened, I dashed to the Suburban in the pitch-black night.

Bush planes and post offices turned out to be lifelines for isolated communities. They connected us to the outside world, mainly by mail plane. We left and returned by plane. Snake Eyes flew in his produce store monthly, weather permitting. The buzz of incoming aircraft drew a sea of eyes peering out their windows. The village was only accessible by air, except for the annual barge and seaworthy vessels. However, no one ever arrived by boat.

At eight years old, Sutton could identify each of the planes within a month of our arrival. The drone of an approaching aircraft caused Sutton to jump up and stare out the window with the rest of the village. Looking through the blinds, he'd announce "A green, low wing coming in," "A Navajo is flying in," "PenAir is here in a Cherokee Six," "It's a high wing," "A taildragger," or "It's just Theo in his Cessna 180 taildragger" when he saw the local villager overhead. As much as he disliked Alaska, the planes fascinated him.

Patience and learning to live without began on day one in the Land of the Last Frontier. No stores and sporadic, unpredictable mail service meant locals traded resources as a way of life. The budding industry of shopping online existed for camper trailers and vehicle information, but Amazon, Walmart, and internet banking were still years away. Catalog companies inundated the school while Fred Meyers and Walmart supplied remote shoppers through their bush order departments by phone.

Planes arrived three times per week from the hub of Cold Bay, but that did not always guarantee mailbags were on board. Weather delays bumped mail for freight orders, fish cannery workers, sportsmen, and local passengers. Not to mention, Nelson Lagoon took more than triple the airtime from Cold Bay as any of the other villages, dropping our flights to PenAir's lowest priority. To stay in the good grace of creditors, I paid bills in advance and mailed them in a package to my mother-in-law, Connie. I wrote a "to mail" date on the parcel to ensure timely payments.

It took a while to figure out how to get extra groceries in Nelson Lagoon. There was no welcome packet with instructions when we arrived. I described how we managed to buy fresh food in an email:

This weekend, Elgin flew to Cold Bay for an administrator meeting. I had the store deliver two boxes to the school plane. When he returned, I made a treat—tacos. Ethan was quite content sitting down to the unexpected meal. Halfway through dinner, he said, "I sure like it when we get new food." We all giggled at tacos being new food!

"What's my physical address?" I asked the post lady upon arriving in the village.

"You decide. We don't have street addresses here, only general delivery boxes," she replied, and she wasn't joking either. So, we made one up. When we forgot the address we were using, we changed it to a new one. Our official address was Elgin and Melissa Cook, General Delivery, Nelson Lagoon, Alaska 99571.

Nelson Lagoon's post office was different from any I had ever known. Packages were scattered everywhere on the floor. You couldn't tell if boxes were coming or going. The tiny community building served as a post office, a medical clinic operated by a first responder, and the electric company that sold electricity credit on something similar to a credit card, which we ran through a reader at home.

The elevated building had three or four steps similar to other village structures. The medical clinic occupied half the space. The post office used the other half of the first floor with open mailboxes hanging on the wall beside the transaction table. Dogs roamed inside the facility—some unaccompanied! No one kicked them out; they expected them to be there. I was no longer shocked at their presence. Patrons circled the perimeter of the room to inspect box labels before requesting their letters. Students and parents told us if a package arrived with our name on it, which did take some getting used to.

The post office in Anchorage was a far cry from Nelson Lagoon's, but it was unique just the same. The Anchorage airport post office stayed open twenty-four hours a day, even on holidays. Many nights over the years, I found myself surrounded by cardboard boxes, duct tape, and a trunk full of shopping bags. Freezing temperatures made packing a rough go. The tape didn't remain sticky in the cold, and you couldn't use it with gloves on. No complaints here, though. The extended hours meant we could finish shopping before spending the wee hours of the morning packing and shipping. We were not alone in the parking lot taping boxes either. Bulk shopping and shipping were a way of life for bush people of the time.

SEVENTEEN

A Letter Home

Writing became a way of life for me as I recognized the unique opportunity to document this unusual experience. It also served as an escape from the long evenings and endless weekends. *Bush Humor* turned into a collection of funny stories from Nelson Lagoon during year one. By year two, it evolved into *Bush Life*—the newness had worn off, and I could no longer easily spot the humor. When I discovered this letter years later, I wondered what my parents must have thought. The thing is, they probably assumed I was exaggerating. I wasn't.

October 28, 1995

Dear Family,

Living in Nelson Lagoon is unlike anything I imagined before coming here. The village is on a sand spit in the Bering Sea, where we live in a two-teacher duplex with a generator twenty feet from our bedroom window. Did you know generators can start brush fires in the winter and put out the most annoying noise? Our clocks don't run accurately either, so we use battery-powered ones instead.

Besides the constant generator hum, it is not unusual to hear fifty to sixty mph winds gusting against the house and windows. Hail and heavy rain compete with the wind and generator noise. Above this, music plays all hours of the night, especially on Fridays and Saturdays. There are no police officers in the village to prevent it.

One day, Ethan whined, "Why did we have to move to Alaska?" Then he cried, "I know the volcano out there will get me when I'm sleeping." Alaska Volcano Observatory monitors the volcano for activity and threat. Explain that to a five-year-old. I tried, but he didn't understand.

The volcano is probably not the most dangerous thing here. Tidal waves leave little to be desired in a village on a narrow spit. A high tide almost transforms this place into a tiny island, and in low tide, the sand spit is eleven miles long. It separates the shallow Bering Sea from a lagoon. The mainland is seven miles up the spit. To make matters worse, the highest elevation is a whopping ten feet above sea level. A tidal wave of freezing water would be deadly which means if we didn't drown, death by hypothermia would be a sure thing.

Twice a month, I travel to the surrounding communities for basketball games. Last Friday, we flew into False Pass. The wind was blowing fifty mph, with gusts reaching sixty-five. The plane took off sharply out of Nelson Lagoon with scary jolts as the plane rode the updraft, steadfastly pressing me to the seat. Then without warning, we dropped in a downdraft, dead out of the air, snatching the air from my lungs. Two students sitting in the back screamed and sobbed with each jar.

We flew four hundred feet above the land and water for an hour. A severe crosswind forced our pilot into a crab landing with a sixty-three-hundred-foot mountain on one side of the landing strip and the Bering Sea on the other. From the air, the runway appeared to drop off into the sea. My winter hat prevented my hair from standing on end!

The willy-nilly wind made the landing even more difficult, forcing the plane up, down, and sideways with significant force. I couldn't scream or cry in fear with the students. I wanted to, but I didn't. Instead, I held onto my hat.

The pilot maneuvered the plane in line with the runway despite the gusty wind. The aircraft bumped and tossed mid-air. None of us took a breath. Once the wheels touched the ground, our breath escaped our agonized lungs, and I released my death grip on my stocking hat. I had hung on for dear life, pulling it down around my head.

Nothing can prepare you for a severe crosswind landing. The wings felt parallel to the runway, though that could be an exaggeration.

On the way home, instruments buzzed and beeped in the stormy conditions. This time, my hands stayed in my lap. My face drained to ghost white, no doubt. This is Alaska! Don't people come here for adventure, danger, and to have the hell scared out of them by bush pilots?

I wondered if events in my future life will be as exciting. Do we not all quest for more than we have already known? How can we top the adventures found in bush Alaska? The wildlife, weather, isolation, lack of conveniences, Bering Sea, and the flying!

Speaking of flying, Elgin flew into Cold Bay for a meeting last week. The Weathered Inn rented the dinkiest room he had ever seen at eight feet by four feet in size, or so it seemed. And the room didn't even include a private bathroom! The price was over one hundred dollars per night. The name is appropriate, given people become stranded in Cold Bay waiting for a break in the weather.

He said the sign on the door read, No Wild Game in Room. For the hotel to post this warning, someone must have slept with a dead animal beside their bed. Elgin decided the freezing nighttime temperatures made storing meat in the hotel room possible.

The heater ran long enough to warm the room up in the evening and early morning. Then it automatically shut off. As the hours passed, the temperature dropped. With hesitation, Elgin threw off his covers, put bare feet to the icy floor, and laid his sleeping bag on the bed, covering it with the blanket. The grueling hours rolled on. It was too cold to consider hopping out of bed again to get dressed. His teeth chattered until six in the morning when the heater kicked on. It was a welcome relief that relaxed him enough to fall asleep.

The alarm clock rang less than an hour later. It was time to wake up. The chilly bathroom with an icy cold shower added to Elgin's misery. Hot or even lukewarm water is a luxury. In case you don't know, bush Alaska has no luxuries! It was a rude awakening for one chilled to the bone with so little sleep.

The challenge of winter nights stretching into daytime hours can drive a person insane. In Alaska, darkness takes on a whole new meaning. We go weeks without seeing the blue sky or nighttime stars. There is no famous Aurora Borealis or even streetlights here. Thick cloud cover shuts out a fair amount of daylight, and the nights are pitch-black even with a full moon.

Each morning, extreme darkness grants me the ability to put my hand in front of my face and not see it at all—not even its silhouette. I skirt beside the school's rusty old Suburban with my hands frantically searching for the handle. I say frantically because if I cannot see the door handle, how am I going to see a startled, hungry bear?

Last week it poured and blew for a week. Locals here refer to it as "ugly weather," which is an appropriate description. The gloomy days caused us to wonder if the sun was hibernating, then suddenly it appeared out of nowhere. A kindergartner spotted it first and let out a squeal. Within seconds, the young and old lined the school windows. Each person awed over the brightness of the lost sun. I grinned as we took a break to enjoy the moment.

It's as though we live in a ghost town. Each morning, we drive by house after house on the way to school, though not one has a single light on inside. In the afternoon, not a soul is out. We can go days without seeing anyone other than our students. When we encounter someone outside on the road, we wave to them, but they do not seem to see us. Sometimes, I feel unwanted and alone here.

When was the last time I drove above second gear? To think we may be too frightened to drive the Alaska Highway at any speeds greater than fifteen mph when we go home next summer.

We say a town is forty-five minutes away, not forty-five miles away. We relate distance in airtime, which makes sense since no roads exist except those of the sky.

I wonder, will I remember the taste of foods we don't have access to now after we finish this year of deprivation? How spoiled will I be to buy a loaf of bread instead of baking it in the bread maker? Thank goodness for that invention! Will crowds of people suffocate me? Will a city cause me to go madder than this darkness? When I shop in a grocery store, will I load my cart with everything in sight, or will overstimulation cause me to flee in frustration? Will the "Alaska Time" lifestyle hamper our ability to readjust to the hustle and bustle of our previous life? How many days will it take to counteract ten months without stores or services?

My students shopped at a tiny grocery store during our recent visit to the slightly larger village of False Pass. The unique bush store had no price tags. They displayed products on creative shelving, some in cubbyholes. They opened the freezer room for shoppers, so I stood there shivering while selecting cold goods. Fresh produce was practically nonexistent, and what fruits and vegetables they had appeared to be from last year. The store opened for an hour daily unless the storekeeper chose not to open at all.

The bush pilot, Snake Eyes, arrives with his monthly fly-in grocery store and buzzes the village three times. We know the routine and can identify his plane just by the sound of the repeated flyovers. Snake Eyes is a slick entrepreneur and venturous Alaskan bush pilot—a tall guy, but *not fat, rather brawny, dressed in denim from head to toe. He possesses the bushy hair and scruffy face of an old-time mountain man, wears thick glasses, and speaks with gruffness in his deep voice. He is a sourdough—a real Alaskan.*

The villagers drive the one mile to the airstrip in pickup trucks or on four-wheelers with laundry baskets tied to the back end. There are no cars here, not a single one. We seldom encounter anyone outside of school. We peek out the school window to see who lives here as they pass the building one by one. When Snake Eyes arrives on a school day, it's not a problem, we take an hour break to go grocery shopping. Snake Eyes lands on the remote gravel strip and unloads his plane in the parking area. A line of shipping boxes loaded with fresh produce stretches from the door past the plane's tail. The cooler near the door has specialty items such as eggs and ice cream. Then he uses the freed-up space in the aircraft to check out customers.

Last week, I took the school kids to the airstrip to meet Snake Eyes. Being first to arrive, I stocked up on a half-gallon of ice cream, three bags of Halloween candy, a dozen eggs, one bag of grapes, and a container of cream cheese.

Ol' Snake Eyes pulled out his food scale and weighed my items. The cost was $3.00 per pound for all produce, $3.50 for a fifty-cent bag of candy, $4.00 for cream cheese, and $7.50 for half a gallon of ice cream. I should have grabbed two! Most people spend $250–$500 each month at Snake Eyes Traveling Grocery Store, three weeks' salary at minimum wage back in Wyoming. He flies in because he can sell what he hauls to Nelson Lagoon, despite the outrageous prices.

I've been thinking lately, whose stupid idea was it to move here, anyway? Oh, that would be me.
Love,
Melissa

P.S. Can you send me twenty dollars in one-dollar bills? The Tooth Fairy is due for a visit soon. The other night, I asked Elgin if he had any cash in his wallet. He rolled over in bed, stared me directly in the eye, and admitted in all seriousness, "I haven't seen a dollar bill or even a dime in months." With that, he rolled back over, and I fell onto my pillow laughing. But seriously, we do need Tooth Fairy money please.

EIGHTEEN

I Shoot to Kill

Halloween had me out with the boys trick-or-treating by four-wheeler while Elgin stayed home to pass out candy. It was cold but not unbearable, and it wasn't raining for once. We lucked out. Ethan rode with me on the ATV's seat while Everett and Sutton sat on the rear rack as we rode along the village streets. The few neighbors generously dished out candy to the beggars.

"Trick-or-treat," the boys repeated in unison at the last house. We waited for a man who stumbled down the stairs with a bowl of candy. He reeked of alcohol and his eyes drifted from the boys and fixed on me. I felt uncomfortable in his stare. "Say thank you, boys," I said, now eager to be home.

The man reached past the kids and grabbed my upper arm. "Why don't you let the kids trick-or-treat while we party?" The drunk fisherman was older but still powerful.

"No, thank you," I declined in a bit of panic. "My boys are ready to go home." I attempted to talk him out of the party, but he was having none of it. No longer responding to my rejection, he dragged me up the carpeted stairs, his grip bruising my arm. I hung onto the railing. "Not tonight. I mean it! My boys are right there." At the top of the stairs, he reached over to the table for a glass, his grip shifting from forceful to unsteady, which allowed me to escape.

The boys stood in the doorway, watching in confusion as I flew down the stairs. "Let's go, boys!" The urgency in my voice spurred them to skedaddle with their treat bags to the four-wheeler. I didn't look back, relieved to be free. Fortunately, I had left the ATV running. The following year, we handed out candy during the school Halloween party, freeing us both to take our children out trick-or-treating though we refused to stop at that house again.

The next week, Elgin informed me, "The district has scheduled another administrator meeting in Cold Bay this weekend." The students had not arrived yet.

"*Are you out of your mind?* You can't leave me here after what happened in the post office and on Halloween!" I insisted. Aside from my two incidents, rumor had it three men accused of rape lived in the village. With no local law in the town, crimes often went unpunished. Travel time and weather hampered troopers' efforts to investigate crimes. There was no way he would be leaving me alone again.

"I'm not sure what to do. The district requires me to go." Elgin sighed, "Let's ask Tom for his advice." Tom Ryan, the superintendent, did not appreciate my situation any more than I did.

"We will have a locksmith out there this week to change all the locks. That community has so many keys out, it's ridiculous. That same guy hooked up with the teacher last year. He probably has a key himself. We have to fix this." And Tom did. In a day or two, a locksmith arrived on a chartered flight. He changed every lock at the school and housing units while the pilot waited on the runway.

"This is the farthest I have traveled for anyone to change the locks," he informed us. "This isn't cheap either. The district is paying my travel *and* overtime," he disclosed.

With the locks changed, I felt safer. It was no secret; Elgin was leaving for the weekend. I planned to pass the word on that you do not want to mess with me.

"You are looking at a crack shot," I enthusiastically shared with the secondary students on the afternoon the district had scheduled Elgin to leave. It thrilled the kids to drift off-topic. Somehow the discussion had turned to guns. *I wonder who instigated that subject?*

"You can shoot?" It thrilled them to discuss my shooting abilities, so I indulged them.

"Oh yes! I can outshoot Mr. Cook any day of the week with my 38-special. I also target shoot with a rifle and 44-magnum," I added for good measure.

"You're kidding! I can't believe it," one student responded in awe.

"Let's put it this way, when Mr. Cook and I have shooting competitions, I typically win," I bragged. "I shoot for fun, but also to protect myself and my family. If anyone ever enters my home uninvited, I will shoot to kill. I do not mess around," I warned. My revelation impressed the students, and I wanted them to be wowed. I wanted them to be so amazed that they ran home and told their parents, who would then inform the neighbors. I expected it to be clear; I meant business.

We lived in Nelson Lagoon for nineteen more months. I never had another problem with anyone treating me with anything other than respect. I wasn't kidding about my ability to shoot either.

NINETEEN

Snake Eyes—The Unbelievable Bush Pilot

When you live in the bush, the grocery store is a world away. My options for filling the pantry included calling the Cold Bay store with my shopping list and having them run a box to the plane. I may have done this twice during our first two years. Freight charges added to the expense of the already expensive groceries, pushing the price of the needed food into the *I can live without that* category. The bush departments at Walmart and Fred Meyers provided shipping but I used this service only when I shopped in town. Ordering by phone meant calling during school hours and waiting for someone to run and see if the items were in stock. Once a year, we could ship groceries by barge in Seattle, which we did the first year. And then there was the option of traveling with groceries. For twenty years, we flew with the maximum number of bags and filled each to the allowable weight capacity with perishable food.

These tricks all took time to learn. I longed for items no longer on our kitchen and refrigerator shelves. In one letter home, I wrote:

> *To eat the egg or not to eat the egg, that was the question. For two weeks, I asked myself, "Can I live one more day without eating the egg?" If the answer was yes, I did not eat the egg but suffered another day until I could no longer stand the temptation. The day finally arrived when my answer was no. It was then, I ate my cherished egg.*

Perishable items were always in short supply and though Snake Eyes flew in with a planeload of groceries each month, we were never informed of the schedule and could not plan on his arrival by any certain date.

"Snake Eyes is flying in today," Cilla announced one stormy November morning.

It must be for Thanksgiving, I thought and made a quick trip home for my checkbook.

The wind kicked up an hour before Snake Eyes was due to land. I sat at my desk, listening to the school building shake with the fierce wind that brutalized it from the outside. Eerie sounds whistled through the walls.

"I'll be on the strip in five minutes," Snake Eyes shocked me with his radio announcement during class.

"He should not be landing in this!" We stood at the window to watch the incredible, unbelievable act of this bush pilot's landing. A snow squall produced impossible landing conditions. The wind gusted with low visibility. We watched in awe as his plane popped out of the clouds and roared mid-air between the school and airstrip.

The wind stole the sound of his plane. Snake Eyes emerged from and vanished into a storm of flurries. Watching the direction of the landing strip, we never saw him touchdown. A few anxious minutes passed before a second radio announcement confirmed he had landed safely. Despite the weather, I loaded the older students into the Suburban and headed out to shop.

People, including myself, hovered close to the plane for protection from the bone-chilling, blustery wind. As I stood there, the plane rocked with each gust. It was blowing hard. A cardboard box half-filled with celery sat on the airstrip. It inched toward me on the gravel with the wind gusts, stopping when it reached my leg. I set a large sack of potatoes in front of it to block any further windsurfing. Other boxes overturned and blew away after customers plucked the contents and deposited them into waiting baskets.

The shopping carts were heavy-duty laundry baskets reinforced with metal plates screwed into the corners and handles. Baskets without reinforcements cracked and fell apart, revealing the heaviness of prior loads. New to bush life, I stood there foolishly with a cardboard box that would, no doubt, be difficult to manage if it became wet. People loaded the baskets into their trucks or strapped them to four-wheeler racks.

That evening, I received a phone call from Leona, the village grandmother. "How do I use a pumpkin?"

"Have you ever had a pumpkin before?"

The seventy-four-year-old grandmother responded, "No. Snake Eyes gave me one and said I should bake a pie with it. When I looked in my recipe book, it called for canned pumpkin."

"I have never made a pumpkin pie, but I do bake the seeds," I explained how to gather and bake them. Grandma Leona must have thought I was off my rocker. "They are similar to sunflower seeds. Have you eaten sunflower seeds?" She had not heard of them either. "Pumpkins make wonderful decorations from Halloween through Thanksgiving. You can set it out on the table for a holiday knickknack," I offered.

"That's what I will do with it." She seemed relieved at the simple solution to her dilemma of the pumpkin.

Snake Eyes flew groceries and supplies into twenty-five remote villages regularly and thirteen more on occasion beginning in 1982. When he flew into Nelson Lagoon for his last grocery stop in March 1997, I was there standing in his line.

I only knew Sam Egli of King Salmon as Snake Eyes, but in 2020, I contacted him about this book, and this is what he had to say about his prices. "It was a nonstop full-time proposition, between ordering the groceries, picking them up, taking care of the freeze, chill, and dry commodities once I had them, doing the aircraft maintenance, getting the fuel, doing the fuel truck maintenance, and then finally flying the loads to the villagers in the bush. That's what the high price per pound had to cover."

Over the years, Snake Eyes introduced the villagers to various holiday items, foods, and recipes. He hauled in ice cream, real milk, dairy products, candies, hamburger and hotdog buns, fruits and vegetables, and meats found at the Anchorage grocery stores, but not in the bush. When holidays rolled around, he delivered costumes and pumpkins for Halloween, turkeys for Thanksgiving, Christmas decorations, Easter baskets, and fireworks for the Fourth of July. In 1991, he expanded his business to include air taxi flights, cutting back the bi-monthly village visits to once a month. By 1997, he purchased his first helicopter for Egli Air Haul, ending the grocery flights altogether.

Given his intimate knowledge of the area, I asked Snake Eyes if he knew where the closest trees were to Nelson Lagoon. "My guess is that the nearest natural stand of trees is about 160 straight-line miles to the northeast of Nelson Lagoon, just south of Mother Goose Lake."

TWENTY

Relentless Wind

Nelson Lagoon's weather was "dramatic and irregular, with constant twenty to twenty-five mph winds," according to Wikipedia. On some stormy days, the wind reached over one hundred mph. It was intense, and at times, overwhelming.

"Is that the wind or an earthquake?" I seriously asked one night. Earthquakes, tidal waves, and volcanic eruptions struck the Alaska Peninsula and Aleutian Chain. But it was the never-ending sound of the wind in the background combined with the rolling waves and squawking seagulls, that I will remember.

Tap, tap, tap, tap, tap. I awoke to the sound of rain against the window. It sounded like someone dropped a bucket of marbles into the windstorm. The racket came in waves. *Intense tapping*—suddenly nothing—*tap, tap*—*intense tapping.* And so on.

Elgin and I lay in bed listening to the rain, unaware the other was awake too. I pressed the clock light—two in the morning. *Tapping, Tapping, Tap, tap, tap. Tapping. Tapping.*

"Banging," as Elgin recounted. Several times throughout the night, he and I wondered if the rain might break a window, or the wind might suck the roof off the house. It sounded as if one could bust out at any second. We pulled the covers over our heads to protect ourselves against the possibility of flying glass.

The boys' bedroom window faced a different direction, so I didn't question their safety. Tapping. Tapping. It continued until the alarm clock buzzed at seven—five hours of drifting in and out of sleep made for heavy eyelids the next morning.

The school district installed an anemometer on the roof connected to the library Macintosh Classic computer. The software allowed us to read the past and current wind speeds. Readings never dropped below eighty-eight mph, with gusts over a hundred for eight hours. Significant wind rates continued until six in the morning. The last blast of wind clocked in at 110, and that was the end of the anemometer. It blew away in the storm.

I will awake each day for the rest of my life knowing the sound of an eighty-eight mph raindrop against my bedroom window. Sleepless, frightening, yet unique, I wrote home.

Crashing waves ravaged the beach. Antique Japanese fishing floats commonly referred to as *glass balls* lined the black sand from the water's edge to the dunes' grassy crest. Upon discovering them, we grabbed trash bags from home and drove back to the beach on the four-wheelers to collect as many as possible before dark. The glass balls ranged from opaque greens and blues to browns and even clear. Worn netting encased some balls. We discovered one float with water inside, which probably slipped in through microscopic imperfections found in the glass when the ball was frozen in Arctic ice or cast deep into the sea secured to a fishing net.

Old skiffs scattered around the community overflowed with glass balls and various sizes, shapes, and colors decorated yards and homes. The oldest of them were handmade by glassblowers in Japan and the Mediterranean over a century ago. They preserved the old way of fishing and once served as buoys for fishnets.

The next day, the glass balls mysteriously vanished; the tide either recaptured or buried them in the sand. We don't exactly know. We only found one more, despite fruitless searching over the next eighteen months.

One winter night, wind gusts shook the house for hours when eighty-to-ninety-mph winds blew through the village. I dozed off. Elgin was awake most of the windy night. By morning, the wind died down to the forties.

On the way to school, Elgin asked. "Can you check the bedroom wall to see what smashed into it last night when you go home at lunch? I would look now, but it's dark outside." Unable to disguise my shock, he explained. "Last night, the wind slammed something into our bedroom wall."

That afternoon I found a fifty-five-gallon drum pressed against the teacherage. The wind posed a threat to everyone's safety when it could whisk away a fifty-five-gallon drum. That is precisely why we seldom had recess outside; young children could literally blow away.

The wind always kept the village clean as trash flew away in the gale-force wind. Unfortunately, items you wanted to keep blew away as well.

One day, the wind was whipping at fifty mph with gusts reaching into the seventies. Forgetting to park the Suburban into the wind, I managed to get the door ajar despite the gale pushing on it. I balanced myself mid-air against the wind-pressed door while jumping in. Suddenly, the wind ceased for a split second and my weight flung the door open, while my feet narrowly made it to the ground before the wind resumed slamming my body between the truck and its door. Ouch!

The next week, I flew into Anchorage for an appointment. Frank Milliman gave me a lift from the airport so I could use our Bronco. While visiting, a sound shook his house and radiated through the living room. "Wow! You have wind like we do!" I jumped from the couch to peer out the window. I expected to see the trees blowing wildly in the high wind; the Aleutians had no trees. Through the windowpane, the trees stood still causing me to glance over at Frank in confusion. "The wind isn't blowing," I pondered the situation.

"That's the sound of the Aleutian wind? I had no idea," a shocked Frank replied. "*That* was a jet airliner taking off from the airport!"

The wind. Oh, the wind. It was relentless, unforgiving, unmerciful, and a significant cause of a person's madness during the long winter months. Its strength, unpredictability, and ruthlessness were unmatched by anything else we endured in Alaska. Okay, the Tongass National Forest's rain was almost as maddening as the Aleutian wind, but not quite. I was never afraid of the Tongass rain.

TWENTY-ONE

A Flight to Remember

We had a simple Thanksgiving dinner that year. Canned food made up most of our diet, and the holidays were no exception. Canned beans. Potato flakes with boxed milk. Our daily homemade bread baked in the bread machine, which we no longer consider to be a special treat. But thanks to Tom Ryan, we had a turkey, which he sent to us by mail plane. The fall harvest passed with no fanfare. No pie. No extended family. But we had each other.

To pass the time, we played games on our new $2,600 Macintosh LC580 computer, a luxury beyond our means in Wyoming. With nowhere to go and limited television to watch, reading became a new hobby for each of us. Before we knew it, we entered the short stretch of school days between Thanksgiving and Christmas break. I broke out the mail-order catalogs to shop.

In the first week of December, as I prepared for my medical trip to Anchorage, a worsening storm left me wondering if I should fly out at all. The storm guaranteed no planes the next day. I rushed to meet the last flight before the ugly weather set in and prevented me from traveling.

Bundled up for the cold, I fought the howling wind to climb aboard the PenAir flight bound for Sand Point. I announced, "125," when the pilot called my name—a standard practice for bush aircraft. Weight limits and proper distribution were critical safety considerations the pilot factored in during the pre-flight checklist. I smiled at the oddity that we willingly agreed to break the social taboo of sharing our weight with the entire group.

Crossing the Alaska Peninsula from the Bering Sea to the Pacific Ocean meant flying over the mountains. They equipped the planes with IFR capability but, to be honest, I lacked confidence in its ability to detect all the nearby terrain. *If you cannot see it, you should not be flying by it,* I thought.

We flew into the cleavage of the snow-covered mountains with awe-inspiring peaks. The wind gusted, and the plane creaked. An air pocket caused the plane to drop elevation with a sudden jolt, smacking our heads into the windowpanes. *Air pockets are common. Besides, they wouldn't be flying if it wasn't safe,* I reassured myself.

The lady in the seat beside me flapped her arms akin to a helpless bird with every jolt. Her arms instinctively flew out from her body as if to catch her fall. I felt that way during my first flights. I know now that my optimism and confidence in bush flying revealed naiveness.

Inside the cabin, my earplugs muffled the engine's blare. Checking out the plane, I noticed broken plastic above each window and in the ceiling above the seats. *Collisions with heads,* I assumed. *How could passengers hit the roof if they had their seatbelt secured? That must have hurt!* Still, I had no concerns for my safety, yet.

We bumped along with up and downdrafts, throwing passengers around at will. Clouds closed in, immersing the plane. The new pilot tried to avoid them by increasing altitude. Before long, the storm engulfed the aircraft, dropping visibility to zero. We knew the mountains were out there, and I suspected the plane might not be clearing all of them.

Bump. Creak. The plane's engines hummed and then roared. It was a short flight distance-wise. We searched the clouds for an opening to the landing strip below. The pilot hesitated and then dipped the plane in a steep descent through the clouds. I hypothesized, *He's unsure of where the airport is.* The passengers held their breath in fear. On second thought, the pilot pulled the plane back up. What a relief!

A minute later, he took a deep breath and the rest of us with him. The plane plunged through the clouds toward Sand Point's airport as I envisioned a mountain abruptly appearing through the clouds in the front window. Instead, we broke through the heavy overcast skies with the runway ahead.

Whew! I guess he knew where he was after all or took a lucky guess.

"This is the worst flight I've ever been on!" a man with twenty years of Aleutian flying experience spoke into my ear after spotting Sand Point below.

A couple of hours later, I boarded the Reeve's Lockheed L-188 Electra four-prop passenger plane headed to Anchorage. I spent two days in town, which allowed for unplanned Christmas shopping time. To shop by catalog, I should have ordered by late October to accommodate the required bush mail time.

While standing in line at the airport post office with my packages, tape, and marker, I giggled to myself. A woman nearby gave me a strange look. "I haven't been in a line in months," I explained.

I had been fortunate to discover Walmart's bush department would box my in-store purchases and mail them to me for a small fee plus postage. By shipping most of my purchases, I freed my luggage space for fresh vegetables, fruit, meat, and a yummy box of Cinnabons. Now I prayed that the mail plane delivered the packages in time.

The Reeve Aleutian Airways jet flew from Anchorage to the windy hub of Cold Bay, a town of ninety. The former WWII airstrip was the fifth largest in the state, with relic hangars and buildings. Black sand left behind by passing footwear destroyed the pattern on the lobby floor. There were no comfort services of food, beverages, or reading materials available either. Many facilities were cabled to the ground to offset the predictable high wind.

All the villages in the region were short distances from Cold Bay except Nelson Lagoon. The village was the lone flight northeast eighty-one miles or rather, forty-five to sixty minutes one-way depending on the wind and type of plane, which made us dead last for departure. I understood it was better to serve several closer communities than one tiny, faraway village in case the weather socked us in.

Cold Bay airport had a lobby, a shelter from the elements for passengers waiting for flights in the region. None of the other villages had facilities to wait in except for Sand Point. Passengers sheltered in their vehicles near the airstrip waiting for the plane.

Severe high winds caused a weather delay in Cold Bay. An older woman approached me, "You don't seem too afraid to fly." As I had gained four months of flight experience, my fear of flying had unjustifiably diminished. "My daughter is deathly afraid to fly over to Sand Point tonight. Can you ease her mind?"

To her sobbing grown daughter, I suggested, "Think of the plane as a feather. When the wind blows the feather in the air, has it sustained any harm?" I slid over a step depicting the movement. She shook her head no. "Unless it hits a mountain," I added without thought. Her sobbing resumed with earnestness.

"Nelson Lagoon, Sand Point." At last, the pilot Kim Post announced our flight. The prospect of staying at the Weathered Inn sharing a bathroom and sleeping in a freezing room the size of a jail cell was less than appealing.

The passengers pressed through the bitter wind on the tarmac to the rear entry of the plane. Freezing, we scrambled into our seats. With the passengers seated, the pilot shut and locked the door. A whirling gust of icy wind blew through the plane when Kim opened his door and jumped in. A wind gust slammed it shut behind him, startling us all.

"Sit by me," a man comforted the frightened woman. The closest she could be to him landed her in a seat beside me.

Despite departing close to sundown, we expected to land in Nelson Lagoon by dark. It was blowing over fifty miles an hour in Cold Bay. Still, we took off in a Piper Navajo—twin-engine aircraft with a seven-passenger capacity. I held my breath and watched the altimeter until we gained altitude. One solid downdraft could drive a plane into the runway on takeoff. On a flight out of Cold Bay a few weeks before, we had a sudden drop in elevation on takeoff, so I knew the possibility was real.

The lady and I chatted on our way over to Nelson Lagoon, despite the overwhelming noise of the wind and hum of the plane's engines. Bundled up, I shivered to stay warm.

A headwind had substantially delayed our arrival, and it was now close to dark. Rumors of fifty-five to sixty-five mph wind gusts blowing across the airstrip turned out to be true. I desperately searched for something—anything—recognizable below. Nothing. Nada. Only faint, violent whitecaps were visible along the coastline. Realizing high wind causes whitecaps, the sight of them was not comforting. The sea was angry. Did I mention Nelson Lagoon's airstrip was an unmanned, unlit road of gravel on a narrow Bering Sea sand spit? *Eek*!

The lights of Nelson Lagoon were dimly visible in the distance. However, identifying roads, houses, or the landing strip was impossible. The airstrip was no airport; it was a landing strip by the sea—pure and simple. We made our descent. My breathing ceased altogether in sheer terror. *How can you land on something you cannot see?*

The woman received no comfort from the horrified gentleman in front. I half expected her to become hysterical, but she chose shock instead. The unrelenting wind tossed the plane around, similar to the feather in my story.

We watched out the windows, searching for the landing strip. Not a sound uttered from the souls on board. However, the thunderous fight of the engines forcing their way through the hostile environment toward the ground was deafening. The pilot rested his curly red head against the window. Was he lazy, bracing for impact, or did it provide a better view while crabbing through the storm? I didn't know. One hundred feet and descending. Hair-raising jerks, tugs, and pulls on the aircraft bounced us around inside the cabin. The plane crabbed toward the estimated location of the runway. Roaring engines, rattling, and banging luggage caused my vulnerability to overcome me, as I felt powerless under the circumstances.

Each jolt and jerk brought the landing strip closer, but I couldn't see the ground. A lone truck sat at the end of the runway with its headlights pointing down the gravel strip. Amidst the faint, white waves pounding the shore, we attempted a touchdown. On the crosswind landing, the plane pivoted near the ground. The wheels approached touchdown on the gravel strip when a gust of wind blew us off course. The strip, which had been below us, was now outside my window! I saw the entire landing strip lit up by the truck's headlights, and we were *not* landing on it! The plane continued descending as I screamed in my head. No one flinched, not even Kim. A horrific crash and our untimely deaths seemed unavoidable.

We are missing the runway! I should have warned the pilot. I did nothing. No one did anything. We watched motionlessly as Kim's bushy red head bumped on the window with jolts from the wind gusts. My jaw dropped, but no scream escaped. I had stopped breathing. The plane jerked, unforgiving in the wind. Engines blared as the pilot yanked the plane up in the nick of time. The airstrip was now behind us, one set of truck lights as its beacon.

"I jumped from the truck and landed on my belly with my head in the snow when the plane buzzed me. It sure looked like it was going to hit my truck!" the driver of the lone truck informed me later. He was not the only one wondering if a collision was imminent. By the time we made our second landing attempt, he was long gone, leaving behind his truck to light our way.

On our next attempt, we could see a second truck had pulled onto the far end of the airstrip. Two sets of headlights shone in the distance, signaling the location of the runway.

My feet subconsciously pitter-pattered on the floor. I could not stop them. I didn't want to stop them. I didn't care. The plane roared through the storm and over the Bering Sea. It banked sharply to turn while battling the harsh wind. No horizon was in view. My hands clutched my face. The woman seated next to me cried in agony. Okay, maybe that was me! The plane dipped from the sky, engines blaring. The pilot began another terrifying crosswind approach, but I was ready to go back to Cold Bay. Enough was enough! The Weathered Inn was never more inviting.

Time stood still. The headlights gave us an approximate location, but that did not mean the ground was visible, or the trucks for that matter. I held my breath; my feet pattered on the floor; my hands clawed my cheeks. The wind brutally beat the plane. A downdraft dropped us out of the air while an updraft thrust us back up, pressing me to the seat. A jolt here, a jar there. Touchdown! Extreme nausea washed over me as we taxied to the parking lot.

Don't puke. Don't puke. Please don't puke! I told myself.

Kim casually turned in the cockpit to face the passengers, merely stating, "Where else will you experience a thrill like that?" I picked my jaw up off the floor and pulled my fingernails from my cheeks before standing on my jelly legs. Pity, the other passengers' destination lay over the mountains in Sand Point.

At least Sand Point has an airport with runway lights, I reminded myself as I exited the plane into the cold, blustery night.

I opened the Suburban door without considering the wind. A sudden gust grabbed it from my hand and sprung the hinges.

"What a night," I exclaimed, jumping into the vehicle.

"What a flight!" Elgin concurred.

Pilot Kim Post's new home arrived on the barge that afternoon. That night, the high wind from this storm scattered its roof across Cold Bay's airport. They had not cabled it to the ground yet.

When Kim passed away in November 2009, his obituary quoted him as saying, "A story without embellishment wasn't worth the time it took to listen to." I assure you, no embellishment was needed to describe our flight into Nelson Lagoon on that particular night.

TWENTY-TWO

The First Winter

Winter arrived with a howling wind that whisked snow around the village. I lay awake half the night listening to waves crashing onto the beach. It was cold and dark when we loaded the boys into the Suburban each morning. Not an early riser, Everett grumbled, "Why do you keep waking us up in the middle of the night for school?" It genuinely resembled the wee hours with sunrise a few hours off.

The drive to school was short, but we always drove, always. Between the threat of bears, blowing wind, and freezing cold, I had no desire to walk, ever. However, Elgin did walk home on rare, pleasant days when I worked too late.

One morning, our headlights lit up fluffy snowballs covering the road. We wondered how they had formed. A short time later, an ecstatic student rushed into the classroom, asking, "Did you see the snowballs the fox left behind last night?"

"What?" I inquired in bewilderment. I had never heard of such a thing.

After school, a parent stopped in. "Did you see the snowballs this morning?" he asked. I shared the fox story and he laughed, "When the snow is just right, and the wind blows just so, snowballs appear everywhere. It doesn't happen often. Great snowman starters." And so we solved the mystery of the fox and the snowballs.

"Not many places on earth where the wind will start a snowman for you," Elgin laughed.

Before long, Christmas break had arrived, and we were ready. Ready to sleep in. Ready to stay home and play. Ready to do nothing. Teaching in a two-teacher site exhausted us.

During my trip to Anchorage, I had a single day to shop for Christmas presents and mail them out through Walmart and Fred Meyer's bush departments. It took two weeks for the boxes to arrive. What a nail-biter!

Christmas was almost late!

With little to do during the break, the boys yearned to beachcomb daily. After discovering the glass balls, five-year-old Ethan begged to go to the sea beach to search for more treasures. On the first day of winter break, I encouraged him to, "Wait until a storm."

He checked out the sky and claimed, "A storm is coming." The wind was blowing and dark, low-lying cloud cover resembled a storm. It was typical Aleutian weather, but not downright stormy or ugly out. A dump run gave Ethan hope for a trip to the beach.

"Soon," I answered. We dreaded being outside in the cold any more than we had to. It took a big storm to expose glass balls, so I told Ethan with emphasis, "It is best to wait for a big storm."

In frustration and confusion, he insisted, "But Mom, there *is* a big storm out!"

The next afternoon, we gave in and took a trip to the beach. It turned out to be a chilly day but with only a light wind which meant playtime for the boys. They loved the water and ability to hunt for treasure. We figured it would not take long for them to grow cold and realize no glass balls had washed ashore. However, we found a deflated life raft mixed in with the logs and sand. I wondered what the story was behind its arrival.

I stood at the edge of the water and listened to the sea. It was freezing, with little bits of ice creating a heavy slush on top of the rolling waves. I closed my eyes and listened. The sound seemed familiar—acutely familiar. *What could it be?* A memory of a breeze whispering through a Michigan forest surfaced. The tide pushed icy water toward my feet. Peacefulness filled me as I stood on the shore and contemplated the sounds, smells, and beauty of both the past and present experiences. I grew to love being on the seashore.

"Ready to go?" Elgin asked. I stood there.

"Not yet." I listened for a few more minutes. White round pebbles of ice steadily sloshed at my feet as the waves tried to form crests despite the floating particles' weight. It was a losing battle.

The next time we brought the boys to the beach, it presented us with a surprise. Elgin drove to the beach's edge for us to survey the coastline from the warmth of the vehicle. Snow drifted here and there, but something new surfaced, an ice wall sprinkled with black sand. We hopped out of the Suburban crossing the exposed beach to climb the ice shelf and peek over the edge at the water below. A vast wall of ice built up at the water's edge and ran the shoreline's length. It grew close to ten feet high over the winter, and then one spring day, we arrived at the beach to find it had totally disappeared.

The two-week holiday break ended, and back to the grind we went. January turned into February and then March. Each day was the same. Dark. Lonely. I struggled to bring joy and excitement to the school children, who also felt winter's grip. Gray clouds hung over our heads as the wind blew, and the snow turned into rain.

To lift the spirit in the classroom, I asked the elementary students to draw an image of their best day. A kindergartener completed his picture first and proudly displayed it for me. "This was my best day. It's when the sun came out!"

One day, we received a care package from my mother-in-law, Connie. Our house filled with little ones oohing over the carrots. Everett even lost control with a "Yahoo" at the sight of the goodies.

By April, we heard the voice of Uncle Sam calling, and until now, had ignored it. Finally, we tackled the dreaded task of filing our income taxes with a new software program. Question after question strolled across the screen, from moving expenses to medical bills. One question on foreign income caused us to giggle. Had we received any foreign income?

I looked at Elgin with a grin and inquired, "Does bush Alaska count as foreign? We receive Siberia's weather on our news whenever RATNet (Rural Alaska Television Network) is on and refer to the Lower-48 as the United States." We both laughed.

Finding humor in our situation was essential to our mental health because some of us exhibited varying degrees of cabin fever or Seasonal Affective Disorder also known as SAD, which was most prevalent during Alaska's dark months. Winter depression affected 10 percent of Alaskans. Nelson Lagoon was in one of the most remote locations in the state, far away from our home and society. Plus, we lived through week eleven twice! Was it any wonder some of us were SAD?

What do you mean by week eleven, you ask? During Christmas break, we started counting the weeks until summer break. In March, I discovered an unfortunate error that forced us to live through week eleven twice! Talk about a rough week. Ugh. *Nineteen more winters to go until retirement,* we thought to ourselves.

TWENTY-THREE

Hang the Dog with a Rope

Nelson Lagoon residents used the VHS marine radio more than their land-line phones. Mounted emergency radios hung under kitchen cabinets, the library cupboard at the school, and within easy reach in outbuildings and shops. The villagers announced community events, hours for the post office, and when residents could purchase electricity cards even though the radio's intent was for emergencies, safety, and boating information. However, no one resisted the urge to contact the entire community in one sweep because people stopped to listen when someone spoke.

Some conversations made us blush as if we were guilty of eavesdropping on a party line. Typically, we turned it off to avoid distractions. Fighting, apologies, singing, and gossip flooded the airway too. Occasionally, something unusual aired, such as the *hang the dog with a rope* call.

"Help! Help! I need help!" I looked up from my work to listen.

"What's the problem?" a second voice chimed in.

"My dog was in a fight with a porcupine and has quills all over his nose, mouth, and face. He is bloody and swelling horribly. The pain is excruciating, and he won't let me pull the quills out! What should I do?"

"Where are you?" the second person asked.

"I'm the caretaker at the lodge." I stared in the radio's direction, confused. A lodge in the area was news to me, and I had never seen a porcupine here. According to the Alaska Fish and Game, porcupines do not live in the Aleutians. Still, they do live on the Alaska Peninsula.

"We radioed to charter a plane hoping to fly our dog to the vet, but the storm has us weathered in. We don't have access to a phone to contact the vet for help. All we have is this radio!" The man was frantic.

"I had that happen to my dog once," someone else chimed in. "Hang your dog with a rope around its neck until he passes out. Lay him on the floor and pull out as many quills as you can before he wakes up. Be real careful because he will try to bite you when he comes to, so be sure to wear leather gloves. When he awakes, hang him again. Keep hanging him until you remove all the quills. If you take him down when he passes out, he should be okay. It worked for me." My eyebrows lifted at the advice.

Hang the dog with a rope? I couldn't do that.

"Thanks, man. I'll give it a try." We did not hear how it turned out. I hope the distraught man didn't kill his dog. Researching it online now, nowhere does it advise hanging a dog until it passes out. I do not recommend it to any of my readers—vet or no vet.

I wrote home:

The people here share way too much. They share their conversations over the VHS radio. They share their music as they drive by our house in the middle of the night. They share their stories in the late hours of the evening. Above all, these people enjoy sharing their favorite tunes. Day or night, a short song is certain to play over the emergency radio.

During class, short twang solos on the guitar blared over the speaker and beat through the classroom. The students listened and smiled. Some villagers played rock-and-roll on their stereo, interrupting my lessons. Soloists screeched into the microphone. Can anyone blame them? It interrupted the otherwise dull moments.

In March, we listened to the villagers discuss a fuel shortage over the radio. They were in a pickle. One week of heating fuel remained in the reserve. The annual barge arrived in May but it was only March now, rationing would be necessary.

"Why won't they fly in the fuel tomorrow?" one person inquired.

"They require full payment ahead of time. The check must clear the bank before they bring in the fuel," another explained.

"Why not pay them when they bring it?" Everyone wondered this as we sat by our radios.

"Some villages didn't pay the bill after the company delivered fuel, so they changed their policy. We must conserve until the fuel plane arrives next week. I hope we don't have a storm blow in," was the final word on the matter.

TWENTY-FOUR

The Doctor Called It MS

"That's weird," I confided in Elgin one April evening while in the shower. I inspected the tip of my index finger.

"What's weird?" Elgin asked through a mouthful of toothpaste.

"My fingertip is tingling or asleep." I was not too concerned until the weird sensation continued into the night, the next day, and then for days.

Looking back now, I can guess what caused the tingling. I had been playing volleyball for PE with the four secondary kids that afternoon. Scoring a point, a large student and I went to slap a high-five in celebration. He knocked me to the ground with a sucker punch to my hand. Holding my throbbing hand while seated on the floor, I scolded the high schooler. "What were you thinking?"

Feet shuffling and head down, the student confessed. "I just wondered what would happen if I did it. I'm sorry."

"I should see a doctor in Anchorage," I told Elgin a few days later. A trip to Anchorage meant a forty-five-minute bush flight to Cold Bay and a two-and-a-half-hour flight on the Reeve Aleutian Airways jet. Then I had to rent a car and find my way around Anchorage, a city I didn't know yet, while searching for a hotel in a presumably safe area. The trip was not cheap either.

"I cannot teach the entire school by myself all day, and we have no one to substitute," Elgin replied as the lead teacher of our two-teacher school. Sick time was not an option. We crawled in sick rather than leave the entire student body to the other. "A doctor may see you over Easter break," he offered.

Chiropractor Dr. Dale Springhill made appointments for me on Thursday, Friday, Saturday, and early Sunday morning over the Easter weekend before my flight home. I required no classroom substitute by seeking help over the holiday weekend. No medical doctors planned on seeing patients unless I showed up in the emergency room, and urgent care clinics did not exist on every street corner yet.

Dr. Springhill was excellent. The adjustments failed to fix the tingling, though. He suspected multiple sclerosis or a pinched nerve and gave me the card of a neurologist in Seattle. It was the second time a doctor had suspected MS.

When I was fifteen years old, a language comprehension problem sent me in for an evaluation. Thirteen years had passed. MS symptoms waxed and waned, though no one ever mentioned multiple sclerosis again until now. *What was MS anyway?* With few resources and no medical websites available during the early days of the internet, I would have to wait until summer to figure this out.

Another symptom developed when I returned home. My arm began burning. I leaned against the cold classroom window to attain the only relief possible. My second bout of pneumonia forced me to sleep on the couch while struggling to breathe, which may have caused a pinched nerve, so I swept the possibility of MS under the rug. I was wrong.

In July, the neurologist identified one lesion in my brain with an MRI. "It may be multiple sclerosis, a degenerative disease. Schedule another appointment if you have more symptoms. I recommend not reading about the disease; it can cause you to believe you have symptoms you don't."

A diagnosis of multiple sclerosis was scary enough without considering the implications it might have on my career. A non-tenured teacher with skyrocketing medical bills and the need for sick days could cause an uncommitted school district to search for a better deal. For this reason, I kept the potential illness under wraps. Rather than using sick days, I pulled myself out of bed for years with the pep talk, *Get up. Tomorrow could be worse!*

In the not-so-distant future, recurring symptoms caused me to act peculiar for those who didn't know what was wrong with me. I struggled with confusion, vertigo, vision issues, balance problems, tingling, pain, cognitive deficits, and fatigue. I didn't always grasp language, which meant reading aloud or speaking with my students was difficult. Strange combinations of words came out of my mouth and in email, forcing my secret out into the open. When the time came to inform our employer, it caused me grave concern for my job security. Fortunately, our highly sought-after technology skills counterbalanced my illness.

But in 1996, all I knew was the doctor had called it MS.

TWENTY-FIVE

Ethan and the Whale Bone

"Let's go home!" I yelled out to the boys one late afternoon in May 1996. As the site administrator, Elgin was in Cold Bay or Sand Point for his once-a-month Friday night and Saturday administrator meeting so I was manning the ship alone in Nelson Lagoon.

The boys and I gathered at the backdoor to change our shoes when I remembered an email I had forgotten to send. "Just a minute," I returned to my computer. The boys knew when I returned to my desk it could mean a long wait. After finishing the email, I discovered another task and lost all track of time. The boys quit waiting and returned to playing. More than an hour passed. "Ready, boys?"

Sutton and Everett ran to the building's rear entrance to change out of their school shoes and into boots. Village etiquette included removing shoes at the door for everyone, no exceptions. Sand not only destroyed the carpet but also made a colossal mess. Chasing black sand with a broom was a daily chore at home and school. Therefore, we had the students arrange their street shoes neatly by the back door.

"Where is Ethan?" I wondered. The boys shrugged. "Ethan!" I hollered so he could hear me anywhere in the school. Nothing. With a questioning expression, I looked at the boys who raised their eyebrows in bewilderment. I began to search for my six-year-old son.

"Ethan," I hollered as I searched the tiny library's short bookshelves of mostly old books. "Ethan!" I raised my voice in the partitioned classroom, cutting across from the secondary end into the elementary. Nope, not there.

Concern rose within me as I yelled down the hall toward the bathrooms, front door, and gym. I peeked into the preschool room across the hall from our classroom, but he wasn't there either. Fear seized me. *Where is he?* I ran into the half-court gymnasium and threw open the equipment room doors. He wasn't there.

"Ethan!" By now, Sutton and Everett were rushing through the school with their sandy boots on to search with me. I didn't care. Sand could grind into the carpet for all it mattered. *Where is Ethan?* Then I realized how long he had waited for me.

"Is he outside?" I asked with hope. We raced to the windows to scan the beach and playground. Nope, no Ethan.

Bears! Bears roamed the beaches searching for an easy meal, and with it now being spring, we kept our eye out for them. Nelson Lagoon had two coastlines, the lagoon and the Bering Sea. The memory of a six-year-old boy killed by a bear in nearby King Cove drove me out of the school in a dash to the truck.

I hollered to my other children, "Get in!" Images of Ethan standing before a ten-foot, twelve-hundred-pound Alaska brown bear terrified me. I resisted the urge to announce his disappearance over the marine radio. *Check the house first before alerting the entire community!* I scolded myself. My alarm had reached the terror point.

My racing mind feared the worst. *Oh God, please don't let a bear have eaten Ethan. Please, God. Please!*

My heart pounded against my rib cage as I drove the short distance to the duplex along the black sand road. "Do you see Ethan?"

"No!" The boys replied in unison. Sutton cried. I saw Everett frozen in fear through my rearview mirror. Horrific visions of an enormous hungry bear chasing Ethan into the grass and tearing his tiny body into bloody pieces filled our wild imaginations as I drove home. No one said it aloud. Dread filled the old, rusty, school vehicle.

We pulled into the driveway, circling the teacherage, passing the village generator and jail before arriving next to our front porch. I flung the driver's door open and threw myself out. There stood my trembling child balancing a whale rib bone taller than himself in his hand. He cowered beside the locked front door.

"Just in case," Ethan whimpered and held out the large bone as I reached the top of the stairs and engulfed him in my arms. Holding my son never felt so good.

"I thought a bear took you!" Tears ran down my cheeks as I held him close. "What are you doing here?" He pulled back from our embrace to speak.

"I waited, *but you took so long*. I figured I'd walk home. Then I remembered the bears, but the school door locked when it shut. No one came when I knocked on it. So, I went home. I saw this whale bone in the grass and thought I could use it to fight off a bear if I ran into one. When I got home, you had locked this door too!" he cried. "What took you so long? I thought I was dead meat!" A little fire of anger burned in his eyes.

As a parent in the Lower-48, the fear of kidnappers stealing my children scared me, but once I was in Nelson Lagoon, my worries turned to hungry bears on the beach and tsunamis washing my boys away.

TWENTY-SIX

Return of the Endless Daylight

In the Land of the Midnight Sun, stars are nonexistent in parts of Alaska. The sun skimmed the horizon at sunset before promptly rising again. Living under a blanket of clouds in the Aleutians' overcast world and later, the rain-soaked Tongass National Forest, starlit skies became a long-standing rarity for us. We viewed the northern lights, also known as the Aurora Borealis, online or in photographs with the rest of the world. The gripping skies of the north, seen by most of the state, were never seen by us.

In the spring, the return of the endless daylight kept us awake at night. Despite the heavy cloud cover, the sun now refused to set. The return of the endless sun wasn't a horrible thing on some levels—unless you required sleep.

I felt slightly insane one night when I wrote:

We cannot run, and we cannot hide. It is there, watching us every minute of the day. We escape to the privacy of our home, but it peers in our windows. We close the blinds, but it finds its way into the room. We close our eyes but still feel its presence. The midnight sun has returned, and to think, we longed for sunlight throughout the winter. Now we curse it when we want to sleep at bedtime and again while grabbing one more wink before the alarm rings each morning. It is there reminding us— Alaska is the state of great extremes.

When daylight saving time arrived, we fought light creeping through cracks under the bedroom door at night. The tiniest bit of light sneaking through a pinhole in the tinfoil told our bodies the truth; it was light outside. Insomnia haunted our nights and not only ours. The boys struggled too.

As you no doubt know, a tired child can be so much fun. One evening,

Ethan responded to discipline in anger, "I wouldn't be so crabby if you would stop forcing me to go to bed in the middle of the *day*!" He stormed off to his room.

Spring presented one of my favorite stories from the Aleutians. One afternoon, I passed out a worksheet of a garden to the first graders. Students pulled out their crayons boxes and began to color. "What do you see in the spring?" I posed the question to the kids expecting to hear green grass, birds, and cubs since they recently emerged from hibernation. A kindergarten girl raised her hand.

"The polar bear," Michelle stated as she colored the garden soil black. Her answer surprised me.

"The polar bear is a large, white bear who lives up north," I replied. I waited a minute and repeated, "What do we expect to see in the spring?" Michelle raised her hand again.

"The polar bear," she said with no hesitation or explanation.

"The bears around here are Alaska brown bears. The white bears are called polar bears and they live up north. We won't be seeing any of those." She shrugged as if I was an idiot and continued coloring.

"Mrs. Cook," a high school student responded to the conversation from the other side of the partition separating the learning spaces. "The *Polar Bear* is a barge that brings our supplies in for the year every spring," he explained. I thanked him for clarifying, and he returned to his work. Smiling to myself, I realized I still had a fair amount to learn.

Speaking of the barge, it arrived at the end of May. With the first sign of salt damage on the four-wheelers, we tried unsuccessfully to sell them. Metal objects rusted quickly in the salty environment; nothing lasted out there. Destructive rust was a normal part of life for the villagers, but it was not for us. One guy offered $500 for both ATVs, despite the value being ten times that amount. We loaded the four-wheelers onto the barge heading to Seattle to pick up in June.

"I would rather push them into the sea before giving them away for nothing," Elgin rejected the man's offensive offer.

TWENTY-SEVEN

Bush Life

Living in one of the most remote villages in Alaska made me feel like a modern-day Tisha. *Tisha* was a story based on Anne Hobb's life as an Alaska bush teacher in the late 1920s. Alaska's bush was still the Land of the Last Frontier in 1996.

In April, I wrote home:

> *The bears are out of hibernation now. Someone spotted three near the dump two days ago. We ran our garbage out to ensure we didn't attract any surprise visitors in the middle of the night. While tucking Ethan into bed tonight, he said, "Mom? If a bear smells trash on the porch, couldn't it sniff me out in my bed?" He had an excellent point.*

Remote living does something to a person's mind. What was once comfortable became scary. For example, I grew up in Detroit and Tucson. Anchorage should not have overwhelmed me, but it did. For twenty years, I struggled the first few days of being in the city surrounded by unfamiliar people, traffic, buildings, and material items. It's strange, but true. Also, coming out of the heavy cloud cover into the sunny areas like Tucson gave me a throbbing three-day headache.

Let's imagine being a villager raised in the bush and then visiting the city. Now we are talking about a whole different kind of fear. Many of the villagers arrived at the airstrip to say goodbye to a community member heading to town. Tears. Hugs. "Please come back safe," they'd plead, maybe more to God than to the person leaving. The group waved as the villager climbed aboard the bush flight, excited for their week or two in Anchorage. The residents returned home to repeated tears and hugs. Having someone leave was a scary thing because the world was a vast unknown to many of the people there.

"Why do people come home early?" I asked the high school girl, Cilla, after someone returned who was not due back for a week.

"A lot of times, they run out of money," she replied. They stayed in hotels and ate out for all their meals. Shopping and shipping ran up the tab, as did the taxis. With no service fee to change a flight reservation, why not return home when the money ran out?

Once in Anchorage, most people relied on taxis for transportation. "It would save money to rent a car," I suggested.

"They don't have driver's licenses. And even if they did, they could never drive in Anchorage: they don't know how. It's worth the wait and money to take a cab," Cilla explained.

Some residents had lived in Anchorage, and a few stored cars in town. As for driver's licenses, with no law or roads aside from the few meandering around the houses, who needed one? And where could they have obtained one, anyway? Nelson Lagoon was an isolated village with no services, hours from the nearest DMV by plane.

License or no license, people still operated their vehicles. Though buying one in the village had its unique challenges. Locals bought their vehicles through newspaper ads. Dock workers strapped trucks and SUVs inside or on top of shipping containers in Seattle and Anchorage to be barged in on the *Polar Bear* once a year. The proud new owner did not bother to take off the Washington, Oregon, or Alaska plates.

Driving in the village was challenging too. The three miles of narrow, rudimentary sandy roads required a four-wheel drive. The bumpy, snake-like roads made driving comparable to an amusement park ride. Fishermen parked their boats in yards and along the roadside. Morning fog and darkness meant we crawled through the village with great caution to avoid rear-ending any vessels on our way to school.

I buried the Suburban in the sand right to the chassis one afternoon. "How did you do that?" Elgin asked as he pulled on his boots to check out the situation.

"I came into the driveway too slow. The tires spun and it sank." Driving around Nelson Lagoon was like driving on a sand dune. Wait, it was a dune! Elgin usually drove and increased his speed in the areas of loose sand to avoid sinking.

Someone knocked at the door. "Can I help you dig the Suburban out of the driveway? She's buried it pretty deep," the man informed Elgin. "Happens all the time here." I was careful to give it more gas before coming into the driveway in the future.

Trucks and SUVs ranged from brand-new to quickly rusting, to premature old age. The salt in the air cut the lifespan of a vehicle substantially. A low mileage truck may require a rope tied to the back end, securing it to the front. If a rope broke, the driver did not fret. He simply radioed for someone to fetch him another one. With no police officers in the village, there was no help for issues on the road.

The troopers answered the village council's request to send a VPSO or village public safety officer to live in Nelson Lagoon during our second year there. He lasted four months. Gung-ho, when he first arrived, he planned to install speed limit signs and thought the state should require residents to have a driver's license or at least an off-road permit.

"They need a law stating how close a vehicle can back up to a plane to unload freight," Elgin suggested instead.

I giggled at the thought of a speed limit in Nelson Lagoon. I seldom took the Suburban out of first gear. It had been months since I'd driven in a vehicle topping fifteen mph.

When the *Polar Bear* arrived in May, it provided a day of entertainment for the villagers. Groceries, fishing supplies, boats, four-wheelers, SUVs, and trucks drove off the barge onto the beach. The men examined the new vehicles. They wanted cruise control, mag wheels, and overdrive. Nelson Lagoon had three miles of bumpy, winding, black sand roads—one mile in town, one mile to the dump, and one more out to the airstrip. The lion's share of supplies for the villagers arrived on the annual barge. Most bush communities had a small grocery store, limited in selection but staples available, nonetheless. Nelson Lagoon was not one of those places. By May, we found ourselves low or entirely out of several food items.

I phoned the Cold Bay store to place an order for groceries. My list consisted of eggs and cheese. Putting an order together was difficult because I couldn't remember what was available on the shelf. Who would ever guess a person could forget Betty Crocker made the cake mixes, and Del Monte canned the vegetables? Those are easy. Name a few items without peeking in your pantry or refrigerator. The fact is, I probably could have just said I needed a can of corn, and it would have been fine, but I didn't know that at the time.

The store owner seemed surprised at my shortlist. "You don't need anything else?"

Embarrassed, I confessed, "I can't remember what is out there anymore. I haven't seen the inside of a grocery store in months."

"We have Jell-O, pudding, chips, pop, canned fruits, vegetables, meats . . . " I closed my eyes and imagined as she spoke.

"Wow! I forgot that cake exists. Please send one chocolate cake mix with a chocolate frosting." I was so excited. She went on to ask what kind of chocolate frosting I wanted because they had five different kinds. I had forgotten that too!

A grocery store was not the only place I had not seen in a while. I hadn't filled up at a gas station in the better part of a year. A personal gas station was inside the school cargo container. The fifty-five-gallon barrels stacked inside provided an ample supply of fuel. One barrel had a nozzle connected, which Elgin seldom used to fill the Suburban tank. There was nowhere to drive anyway.

To take a break outside, we headed to the airstrip, beach, or dump. There were no other places to go except to spend more time at the school, which would have thrilled our boys, but not us. We stored trash in an enclosed porch called a wanigan. When it filled the Suburban to the brim, we made a dump run. There, Elgin and I fought off the pesky eagles, ravens, and seagulls while throwing bags out the back of the vehicle while our boys kept a watchful eye out for bears.

Self-entertainer should be a required trait for anyone moving to bush Alaska. RATNet TV was sporadic, unreliable, limited in viewing hours, and the broadcast turned off for weeks without warning. The publicly-funded TV station broadcasted a different major network each night. Football aired on Monday nights, so we became football fans for the first time in our lives. Tuesdays offered nothing since it was the beginning of a miniseries with zero possibility of seeing how the show ended. Wednesday night was comedy night. For the rest of the week, we read while the kids took turns playing games on the computer.

Lana opened the Tides Inn kitchen to sell burgers and fries a couple of times each winter. She always phoned us to be sure we knew before she announced it on the radio. Gotta love her! Summer visitors, workers, and seasonal residents returned home during the winter, closing her tiny restaurant for months with the exception of these rare but welcome surprises.

One day, I was waiting for Elgin at the school door with the boys. I stuck my hands deep into my coat pockets out of boredom. Low and behold, I found a quarter! I held it up for the boys to see and we celebrated the find. Money had become a forgotten aspect of our former lives until that moment. There was nowhere to spend it in Nelson Lagoon, so who needed it?

We learned to be self-sufficient, being alone most of the year. We became our own doctor with no internet or WebMD, so I relied on *The Doctors Book of Home Remedies* to determine medical treatments. I also learned how to cut hair and cook from scratch. Every meal was homemade from limited ingredients.

At the job fair, we had focused solely on securing two full-time teaching positions. We gave little to no thought about what we were getting ourselves and the boys into when we decided to move to bush Alaska. The reality of day-to-day village life had never crossed our minds. It was as if someone had thrown us into the deep end of the pool, and it was a sink or swim situation. We were now dog-paddling our way through that first year.

TWENTY-EIGHT

The Corkscrew Pilot with One Too Many Screws Loose

Nick Sias was his name. Daredevil was his irresponsible game, or so it seemed if you had ever flown with him. He is missing now, lost to the Bering Sea in the fall of 1996. Nick routinely flew in challenging weather to get from Dutch Harbor to the village of Akutan. He nestled the plane into the trough between raging sea swells to fly below the thick cloud cover. Nick accomplished the job when no one else dared. But he paid with his life when the Grumman G-21 Goose plane's wing may have clipped a wave. No one knows for sure. The sea overtook the plane, swallowing it, Nick, and his unsuspecting passenger. Rescue flights flew for days—among the volunteer pilots was the *Aleutian Aviator*, Tom Madsen. They never found the wreckage, though a piece of his aircraft later washed ashore, confirming his demise.

A teacher had complained about Nick's flying the spring before he crashed. "He scares me to death flying so low, skimming the top of the water and hopping from one wave trough to another. It's impossible to see what is ahead in the fog. One day he is going to have a head-on collision with a fishing boat! And I'd rather not be with him when he does."

Chicken pilots, as the locals called them, refused to fly in risky conditions. Nick was no chicken pilot. Those who didn't mind the hair-raising flights cherished his willingness to fly in situations that caused acute anxiety and heartburn for other pilots. To the rest of us, he flew recklessly through the local mountains, cliffs, the turbulent Bering Sea, and ferocious weather. I know this firsthand, having been on several frightening flights with him.

On one trip, Nick had problems with the plane's engine. Leaving us in Akutan, he warned, "I have no idea when I'll be back." After days of sleeping on hard floors, it thrilled me to hear Nick was inbound. Right then, the state announced a tsunami warning following an earthquake near Japan.

The villagers left their homes and the school to climb the side of Akutan Volcano to reach safety. We expected to take off before the predicted potential tidal wave and strolled the boardwalk of the deserted Aleut village to the dock instead of joining the locals in their mountain hike.

Escaping the tsunami was perfectly fine with me. Akutan was a tiny village at the base of the volcano. There was no road, only a boardwalk that stretched the length of the bush community with one town four-wheeler to deliver packages and mail.

The floatplane struggled to get on step before lifting off the water. The plane's engine roared, crossing the bay with a heavy load of six passengers, baggage, and mail. We spotted the villagers climbing halfway up the side of the volcano.

From the passenger seat, I easily mistook the Akutan Bay for a box canyon. Nick flew toward a rock wall in front of us. *It must be a shortcut*, I thought, watching from my window. He was not gaining the required altitude to crest the top, which was clear to me. And I wasn't a pilot!

What is he doing? It was apparent he intended to have the lift necessary to breach the mountain. My heart raced. *This will be close!* The cabin grew tense as our deaths loomed before us. Come hell or high water, Nick was not veering off course. The engine's roar filled the cabin while we all focused intently on the wall of rock before us.

We aren't going to make it! Nick banked the plane at the last second, seeming to suck the loose gravel from the cliffs with its wingtips. I screamed in my head. The view outside my window was all rock wall and sky. It appeared as though we flew close enough to touch it. The students began shrieking in the back and rolled themselves into protective balls while they sobbed in their seats. The plane flew a corkscrew pattern, gaining the required elevation to fly up and over the cliff. Whew!

We sailed along the top of the volcano, no longer increasing in altitude despite our close proximity to the ground. Glued to the passenger window, I failed to look ahead to see what was coming next. Instantly, the view shifted from barely hovering over the mountain to a distant rolling sea far, far below. The abrupt elevation change sucked the breath from my lungs and tugged at my stomach.

Unalaska was up ahead. It was to be my last flight with Nick before he disappeared forever. Researching on Google Earth in 2019, I could see the area surrounding Akutan. Several flight paths would have taken us to Dutch

Harbor without having flown directly toward a rock cliff. He unnecessarily risked the lives of a full flight of passengers. It is no surprise this bold pilot never became an old pilot.

I had no idea when I might encounter another pilot like Nick, so I typically filled my coat pockets with emergency items before leaving on flights. I memorized the floatation devices and ELTs' location in each aircraft I frequently flew in over the years.

In 2012, the local Lions Club dedicated the Nick Sias Memorial Park in Unalaska, Alaska, honoring Nick's service to the city and the surrounding communities.

TWENTY-NINE

Leave Them at the Door

Week eleven turned into ten, which turned into nine, then six, four, two, and finally, we headed home for the summer. We couldn't wait. The countdown wore us out with seven days in a week for over twenty-six weeks. I insisted we not begin counting ever again.

We flew out with PenAir on a chartered flight to Cold Bay and on to Anchorage by way of Reeve Aleutian Airways at the cost of $6,500 for a round trip. Flying George Nathan in from Homer would have cost less, far less. The jet was a new experience for the boys who had never been on a large plane. The ride thrilled airplane-lover Sutton, but not Everett.

"I'm going to be sick," Everett didn't want to look out the window. The man sitting next to him refused to switch seats with me until Everett threw up after takeoff. Two hours later, the plane began its descent. Everett stared at the floor and gripped his armrest. His fingers turned white as his eyes grew wide with fear during the landing.

Frank Milliman, the man in Anchorage storing our Bronco, waited for us at the airport. Driving on pavement felt intense, more like sixty in a twenty. *Gees, he is a madman!* I thought as I watched the older man driving thirty-five mph through town. Wow!

We drove white-knuckled our first evening in the city. From then on, it was smooth sailing. And I do mean *smooth sailing*; pavement never felt as pleasant as it did that day. Relieved after a year of the bumpy village roads, I relished my time in our Bronco, listening to the radio playing songs I hadn't heard in a year. The next morning, we drove the Glenn Highway loaded with sleeping bags, a tent, coolers of food, suitcases, and three enthusiastic boys.

We made our way across Alaska and part of the Yukon Territory before we made our first camp. Driving late into the evening, we had hoped to find the rivers and lakes fully thawed. No such luck. Camping in the Yukon in

May meant freezing temperatures, snow, and ice.

The vivid colors along the way provided a striking difference from the greens, browns, and grays found in the village. The view of mountains, trees, pavement, rivers, lakes, colors, and people overcame me. Boy, had I missed the people and the color!

As I admired the scenery, a sudden shock burst through my body. No sea, and no lagoon. I glanced around in a double take, dumbfounded. In Nelson Lagoon, water was always in view from each direction. Now the water was gone, and *that* took some getting used to.

We set up camp in the Yukon Territory, being more mindful of the time. Having experienced the midnight sun, we knew the sunlight would not clue us in on the actual time. We didn't have to worry; few people camped in the snow-covered Yukon in May. We had the campground to ourselves. I felt vulnerable, not having neighbors. What if a bear wandered into camp at night?

With its streams, lakes, and glaciers, the Yukon inspired us to come out of the tent in the morning. Too bad we couldn't see the brilliant colors beneath the frozen water. The crunching of snow beneath our feet and the sight of our breath as we spoke proved it was frigid. Did anyone say adventure?

The third twelve-hour day of traveling had been a lengthy one, landing us close to Dawson Creek. The excitement for our first summer wore with each passing mile.

"Does this place look okay?" Elgin asked as we pulled into a lodge on the Alaska Highway. That night we drove too late to camp and decided to stay at a hotel instead. As extraordinary as the snow-covered ground outside our tent was that morning, I preferred a heater and soft bed. Plus, with us both working, we could afford the expense.

The kids piled out of the Bronco while Elgin and I handed them their backpacks and unloaded several suitcases. The sunset lit up the colorful sky despite the late hour.

The entry had two main sets of doors to trap cool air in an outer room where we now stood. Elgin held the door open for Sutton and Ethan to pass through into the lobby and then left when Everett lagged behind. I stood in the dark, windowless entrance waiting.

"What is taking you so long?" I couldn't see, but he was struggling with something. At seven years old, he tried hard to follow the rules. "Hurry. I'm exhausted."

"There." He scampered through the door into the lodge, where he stood in his stocking feet, eagerly searching for Elgin and the other boys.

"What happened to your shoes?" I inquired, puzzled at his shoeless feet.

"I left them at the door." We had ingrained the Alaska way of life into our son already. No self-respecting Alaskan stepped past the entryway with their shoes on. Why should the lodge be any different?

A week later, I noted in my journal:

My first trip to the grocery store in Wyoming was an expensive one. I refused to buy anything in a can. I filled the cart with fresh fruits and vegetables. Not one thought went into how long it would be until I shopped again. Mail time never came to mind either. No boxes or tape awaited me in the Bronco. It was a carefree experience that almost felt wild. How long had it been since I had shopped in person, without a list, no catalogs, no post office, no boxes or tape, and no suitcases? I walked right in and shopped! Whew.

NELSON LAGOON, YEAR 2

ALASKA BUSH LIFE

1996–97

THIRTY

I'm Not Going!

Our first summer break in Wyoming was an unprecedented twelve weeks long. With money in our pockets for the first time in our married lives, we lived it up. Our new feast or famine lifestyle had just begun.

We feasted on foods we hadn't eaten in months and devoted most of our time to family and friends. The boys saw all the children's movies in the theater. We went camping, fishing, hiking, swimming, and shopping. We crammed in as many activities and restaurants as possible, spending way too much because months of famine loomed on the horizon.

"I can't wait to get back to my classroom. Nelson Lagoon is a challenge but a unique one," I told my skeptical mother the night before we left Tucson, Arizona, for Nelson Lagoon. "How many teachers have elementary and high school students at the same time?" My mother shook her head and sighed. She was not happy with our new teaching location.

That night, I finished packing our luggage and climbed into bed next to Elgin. He informed me in no uncertain terms, "I'm not going!"

"What do you mean you're *not going*? We can't *not go*. We have contracts!" His out-of-the-blue statement shocked me.

"I can't take another year there. I just can't." He pulled the sheet over his shoulders and rolled over. His cabin fever symptoms from last winter were already creeping in, and we hadn't even left Arizona yet.

"No one will ever hire us if we break our contracts three days before the school year begins," I pleaded. "We won't be able to pay our bills."

"I don't care. I'm not leaving. The district can do whatever they have to; I don't want to go." With that, he buried his head in the pillow and didn't say another word.

I lay in bed half the night wondering what to do. If Elgin was not boarding the plane, then I certainly wasn't. Where would that leave us? With no work? No income? All of our belongings were in Nelson Lagoon. How were we supposed to retrieve them? I worried myself to sleep.

"It's time to get moving," Elgin said the next morning. I refused to ask what happened to, "I'm not going!" Why bring up those emotions again?

That evening, in Anchorage, we ran from store to store to fill our luggage with last-minute items. We selected meat, paid the butcher to freeze, and mail it in a fish box—a waxed cardboard container. We received the meat a week later, but it was ugly. The box contained mostly bones—not what I had picked out, that was for sure. I threw most of it away. Lesson learned, mail it yourself or bring it with you—not everyone was honest.

Elgin and the boys stayed at the hotel while I shopped at the twenty-four-hour grocery store. Then I headed over to the twenty-four-hour post office to mail the boxes. I arrived at midnight to discover many people with boxes, tape, and shopping bags spewed across the pavement. I listened to the sound of tape pulling off the rollers and boxes being filled until I stacked my packages on a dolly and rolled them into the building at 1:15 a.m.

Now, where was that hotel? Hmm. *Dang it!* I was lost. I searched the city for over an hour before finding the hotel again. In the future, I would know the Anchorage streets like the back of my hand, but not yet. Elgin was worried sick. I had no way of contacting him since I had forgotten the hotel's name. We had three hours of sleep before leaving for the airport.

The flight was not as thrilling as the one we had taken with George out of Homer the previous year. Then again, we didn't have to wait out a three-day storm either. Our two-hour jet ride landed us in Cold Bay, where we waited hours for the only bush flight to Nelson Lagoon. We flew almost an hour in a single-engine, six-seater bush plane, arriving by early evening. Lana Gunderson met us on the airstrip with the old school Suburban. Year two had officially begun.

A month later, I wrote home:

The first year, I loved it. When the wind blew over one hundred mph, the adventure thrilled me. My first white-knuckle bush flight caused my blood to speed through my veins like nothing else ever had. But that wind is still blowing. Standing next to the school windows watching them being sucked in and out with each gust is exhausting. Now, for me, bush flights have become real since one of the school pilots disappeared into his watery grave this summer. So, the Bush Humor newsletter has now become Bush Life.

THIRTY-ONE

Seal Throat Stew

We arrived in Nelson Lagoon loaded with luggage and ready to begin the school year. Boxes upon boxes of food and supplies I had shipped from Anchorage started arriving by mail. On our second day back, we flew into the larger village of Sand Point for a week of teacher in-service. The weather was terrible, blowing and pouring rain every single day of the trip. Did I mention it was cold? *Brrr.* The transition from Tucson's dry, intense summer heat to the Aleutians' damp and windy fifty degrees shocked our systems.

On the first day of school, the students rumbled up on their four-wheelers beginning our second year. They told plenty of summer fishing stories but no bear tales this go around. Nelson Lagoon fishermen harvested comfortable incomes from the sea and even children pocketed handsome salaries for their efforts in the catch.

The grueling first weeks of the school year caused me to drop into bed like a ton of bricks by mid-September. Despite my fatigue, an unusual noise caught my attention one night. *Is that a train?* I wondered, turning my sleepy head on the pillow for a better listen. *It sure sounds like a train to me.* A distant rumbling was faint yet audible.

That's impossible, I argued with myself. *There isn't a train for hundreds of miles.*

What is it then? I sighed. It was cold, and I dreaded leaving my warm covers, but the rumbling was real. *Could it be the washing machine?* Now awake, I listened intently to the rumbling. I entered the other apartment, flipping on lights to inspect the bathroom and bedrooms. *Hmm,* I thought. *What is that noise?* Puzzled, I figured it was village nightlife and climbed back into bed, pulling the covers over my chilled body. Odd noises at night were par for the course in Nelson Lagoon.

The next morning, a student ran through the door, yelling, "Did you see Pavlof Volcano?" The one place I hadn't thought to search for the mysterious noise was outside my window. We missed the chance at front row seats to a volcanic eruption in our backyard. Of course, I could have died from shock or a heart attack too.

We all stepped outside and observed the volcano. A narrow, steady stream of ash rose straight up from the mouth of the now active volcano, similar to chimney smoke. The jet stream caught the ash and blew it toward Dillingham, away from us.

Despite the fascinating turn of events, we returned to the classroom to prepare the high school students and me for a field trip to one of the four volcanic Pribilof Islands. Students from the surrounding communities were attending eight days of Aleut cultural education.

There were no canceled flights that day because the pilot flew around the active volcano. A twin-engine Piper Navajo landed on the airstrip by mid-morning with False Pass students and their teacher already on board. Akutan School attendees flew by floatplane from their village to Dutch Harbor and by wheel plane to the island.

"The district requires you to wear insulated boots, winter coveralls, hats, and gloves at all times during the flight. The superintendent was clear in his travel expectations." I stood in the center aisle of the plane while I spoke to the students. They grumbled. "What you're wearing in a plane wreck is what you will have to survive until someone comes to rescue you," I explained, but the students rolled their eyes. They knew if we wrecked into the sea, no one would be there to save us in time.

The twin-engines blared outside the plane during the long 350-mile flight over the Bering Sea to the Aleut village of Saint Paul in the Pribilof Islands. I saw endless seawater in every direction through each window, and boredom quickly set in. I drifted into doomsday thoughts of crashing into the icy cold sea. Scaring myself, I searched for a possible rescue boat. Seeing none, I wondered, *how long could I tread water?* So much for the hat and gloves!

It was a relief to land in St. Paul, a treeless island of volcanic rock hidden under tall, thick grass. Upon exiting the plane, the chilly breeze carried with it the familiar and unpleasant fish cannery smell. The overcast sky hung barely overhead, and the ground was damp from recent, and I suspected relatively constant, rain.

A waiting bus shuttled our group to the school, where the host expect-ed us to camp on the cold, hard floors for a week. Ouch. The girls slept in the music room with me while the boys made camp in another room with the two male teachers. Local high school boys waited outside the door, hoping to entice the girls to sneak out each night. For seven nights, the girls waited for their break. As a new teacher, I stayed awake half the night to prevent their escape. In hindsight, sleeping in front of the door would have effectively blocked their exit and given me better sleep.

We started the first morning with cereal and milk and then loaded onto a bus for an island tour. The sightseeing schedule kicked off with the beach masters or bull seals. Hundreds of black fur seals crowded the sandy beach below us on the hillside. The bus driver peered through binoculars at the seals and then grabbed the radio.

"One seal on the beach with a net embedded in his neck," she announced. We waited several minutes for another vehicle to arrive and then headed down the road to the beach. "The fishing industry leaves debris in the sea that entangles marine life. Today we will cut away a fishing net from a seal's neck. He probably swam through it when he was younger and couldn't escape it. The net embedded into his flesh as he grew. If we don't remove it, he will die from starvation when he can no longer swallow food."

The bus stopped in the drizzling rain. We stepped out to watch the spectacle of several Aleuts sprinting toward the beach, two with snare poles. The seals spotted the ambush and raced to escape. Barks filled the air as hundreds of seals used their flippers to lift their bodies and rush toward the Bering Sea. Splashing white water mixed with hundreds of black bodies amidst the roar of barking. A single snared seal protested loudly.

Hundreds of black seal heads with inquisitive eyes stared from the safety of the water. Students and teachers gathered to observe the volunteers strapping the seal to a board with a cradle on one end. They secured his head to avoid an undesired bite. The fishnet was embedded deep into his open flesh, causing terrible suffering. Volunteers cut deeper into his tissue to reach and sever the material while the seal bellowed. After removing the netting, they released him from the board. Springing to his flippers, he hurried, as fast as a seal could hurry, back to the sea to join his companions. Seeing his mangled neck free of the net inspired us.

We drove to a nearby rookery to view fur seals through a blind built at the edge of the beach. The wind picked up and waves crashed onto the shore, but the seals were no fools. Who could miss the chaos of a busload of fifteen high school students, three teachers, and two local tour guides? Wet and chilled to the bone in the wind, I stepped up to the blind for my turn.

A mass of black bodies mingled from the edge of the water to the beach grass. Fur seals pointed their noses to the sky and barked, cried, and even roared depending on their size. A sea of teeth, beady black eyes, whiskers, and bodies filled my view. The black mass was in continuous motion, with seagulls squawking overhead and then landing within the rookery. The seals paid little to no attention to those of us watching. Never again would I see anything remotely similar.

Back on the bus, a local woman spoke to the visiting Aleut students. "We are one people. You are Aleut; we are Aleut. We are the People of the Seals, which makes us responsible for protecting the welfare of seals that come to our beaches. About 80 percent of the world's fur seal population spends time here in the rookeries and on our beaches. For many decades, the U.S. government forced our people to slaughter hundreds of thousands of seals for their pelts. We were not free people but wards of the federal government. They paid us for our labor with food and meager supplies but no money. In 1979, our people received a government settlement for forced labor and unfair treatment. In 1983, the government released its control of the declining seal industry. Today, we harvest seals for subsistence and take only non-breeding males." She returned to her seat, and the bus took the students to the school for lunch.

That afternoon, we met in the science room. An Aleut woman stood before the students with a plate of seal throats. "Our ancestors carried water using seal throats as water bags because when wet, they are soft and malleable." She held up a seal throat for the students to watch her remove the inner lining. Then she strung it out to dry. "Nothing from the seal harvest goes to waste. We even use the ear bones for jewelry." Tiny bones circulated the room. They gave each student a throat to craft their own water bag.

The community members served seal throat stew for dinner, to my shock, along with fish tacos and an assortment of other seafood dishes. Not a seafood fan, I ate a peanut butter sandwich from my suitcase.

We fought the bitter morning wind crossing the village on foot to the dock where we boarded a fish tender. The large vessel received the catch from the local crab boats and processed it. The ship had lengthy, tight hallways with narrow, steep stairs and had no heat as far as I could tell. The workers endured harsh conditions in freezing temperatures for long shifts. They wore thick rubber over clothing and boots while standing beside a giant basin. Fishermen dropped ice-covered king crab through the window into the large tub. Ice water splashed the workers, leaving a puddle on the floor.

"If the king crab arrive dead, we discard them to avoid disease. The workers process live crab over here," the guide informed us.

A steady flow of bright orange and red Alaska king crab of various sizes filled the stainless-steel basin with long legs and claws. They attempted to escape, cluing workers as to whether they were dead or alive. I froze throughout the tour and had sympathy for the laborers.

The fish cannery even had a cafeteria for their workers. Our group hurried across the village most evenings through the wind and rain to join the workers for dinner. Saint Paul High School kids visited our students to socialize during their meal. An Aleut teenager voiced her displeasure about the white people in the room. Following a loud hate speech, she berated a white fisherman for eating his dinner and demanded he go home. He ignored her and continued to eat without saying a word.

Alarmed, I could not wait to leave the building. Being white, I had no desire to be the angry student's next target. I understood her outrage over the Aleut people's treatment by the U.S. government. However, I did not appreciate the spite dished out toward innocent people who were there to learn and help her community.

Each day began early and ended late. The students listened to Aleut and Russian history lectures. We visited the Russian Orthodox Church and took walking tours of decrepit buildings used in the former seal industry. The tour guide explained the rat prevention program and efforts to keep the island rat-free. Two hundred species of birds nested on the island, with millions passing through each year. Residents checked the rat traps daily because a predator from a fishing vessel or barge could destroy the world's bird populations.

Clear weather allowed us to spend time on the coast for our last activity. Rugged, volcanic rock covered the shore. It was a strenuous hike out to the edge of the Bering Sea. Pools of water gathered in the crevasses and pits of solidified lava. The cold made it a quick stop for the students and other teachers, but not for me. A brisk wind on my face and chilled to the bone despite my coveralls and insulated boots, I spread my arms as if flying with the birds overhead. I soaked in the extraordinary sense of standing alone on those rocks, being at peace with nature, and awed by the sheer adventure of it all.

It was a once-in-a-lifetime trip. The people's story, seals, and precautions to care for the wildlife were educational. The fur seal population has diminished at an alarming rate since my visit. Researchers continue to search for the cause. In the 1800s, four million fur seals visited rookeries in the Pribilofs. In the 1990s, that number was scarcely under a million. Today, scientists estimate the entire world population of fur seals is 1.1 million. No one can explain why.

THIRTY-TWO

Pass Me a Drink

September rolled into October while Pavlof Volcano huffed and puffed a constant stream of ash into the jet stream. Elgin set a spotting scope on the dining room table, pointing it through the blinds for us to view the activity. Passing through the kitchen, we stopped to peek at the lava flow and magma shooting out of two vents. One vent bubbled lava with full force, died down, and then the other vent revitalized to toss more globs out into the air which then oozed down the mountainside.

"The volcano is spitting chunks the size of cars and semi-trucks," one pilot reported over the radio. Strong winds carried the ash toward Dillingham, opening the air space for travel from Cold Bay to the village. Looking through the scope, I tried to get an image of it, although its size was deceptive at forty-eight miles away. The view of spewing hot lava at night was spectacular.

Active volcano or not, life in our bush school continued as usual. With volleyball season upon us, Nelson Lagoon hosted the first games for the district's small schools of False Pass, Akutan, and Cold Bay. The teams arrived two hours apart as the school plane made round trips between the villages to bring in the staff and students on Friday afternoon. The villagers provided dinner for their guests, something with fish, I can assure you. Then it was onto the games with parents and community members standing along the three feet of sidelines in the tiny gym.

When the games ended, the gym transformed into a dance floor. As a courtesy, I chaperoned the evening alone to allow a break for the other teachers who had the students the rest of the night. To the students' disappointment, I closed down the event at midnight.

After an early breakfast and the second round of games, the weather held out long enough to transport two teams home by mid-afternoon. Then heavy fog rolled in.

"Tom probably won't land in this weather," I predicted.

"Don't say that!" the Akutan teacher scolded. "I need to have a day at home this weekend."

Fog blanketed the airstrip as a plane's engine buzzed overhead. We could see nothing but thick clouds. If we couldn't see anything, we knew the school pilot Tom Madsen wasn't seeing much either. I sat with the Akutan teacher and team in the Suburban near the runway. Tom only had to be off course by mere yards to collide with us.

We rolled down the truck windows to listen for the plane's location. The hum filled the air, indicating Tom was coming in. We watched in every direction. Finally, he broke through the clouds giving us a glimpse of his airplane between the airstrip and our vehicle. Suddenly, Tom sharply banked away and disappeared, engulfed again by the fog. The buzz of the plane faded into the blustery wind. Thick cloud cover hovered over the ground.

Time ticked by as we waited. What had happened to the plane? Concern for the pilot grew. Did he crash into the runway, the dunes, the sea? Did we dare drive down the strip to investigate, given the possibility of an unexpected plane breaking through the fog? Oddly, the thought of Tom returning to Cold Bay had not even occurred to us. We simply waited.

Minutes passed. Two trucks hesitantly inched to the runway to determine the pilot's fate. A faint figure of a plane taxied down the gravel strip, and it was *not* Tom's, but Theo Chesley, the local pilot. *You've got to be kidding me!* The school pilot was still coming in and could land any second. Visibility from the ground was near zero, creating a potential for a head-on collision. As Theo taxied in, we sat on the edge of our seats, minds willing him to *get off the runway*!

Once Theo safely pulled into the parking area, a man knocked on the Suburban window. "Tom radioed, he turned back. He's not landing today." What a relief!

I returned the team and their teacher to the school for another round of camping out. "The weather may clear up tomorrow," I tried to encourage the teacher.

Tom called the school to inform me of his hectic flight and inability to safely approach the strip. "Sorry, Melissa. I tried, but the weather closed in. On my approach, Theo's plane broke through the clouds right in front of me, so I veered away and flew back to Cold Bay. Man, that was a close one!"

As soon as I landed, my passenger and I headed to the bar. I seldom do that, but 'pass me a drink' was all I could say to the bartender after that near miss!" Mid-air collisions were not uncommon in bush Alaska.

"Please take us to the beach," I begged Elgin on our way home from school one late October afternoon. With no other entertainment options, we could at least watch the wave action.

"The tide is coming in, and the wind is blowing fifty to sixty mph. That means the waves should be huge," I continued to present my case. The boys were always game for a trip to the beach, and I welcomed a brief break between teaching and cooking dinner. Elgin passed our driveway and continued down the road.

"The Nelson Lagoon windsock could be replaced with an anchor," Elgin joked as he drove the one-lane road. The vehicle stopped along the edge of the beach. We peered out the Suburban windows at the roaring sea. Thick, frothy foam rode on the tips of the curling waves and gathered at the water's edge.

"Could you roll down your window for me to snap a picture?" I asked Elgin as I opened my camera bag. Gusting winds sprayed the foam off the rolling waves into the air above the sea. Seawater rose to the beach grass. The raging wave action walloped the shoreline.

Elgin fussed, complaining the salty air could blow onto the camera. "Just a quick snapshot," I begged. He gave in and reached for the window handle. *Splat. Splat. Spppllaatt.* Silence fell over the Suburban as we stared in disbelief at the driver's side windows. The slimy, brown foam coated the vehicle, obstructing any view of the furious storm outside.

Needless to say, I took no snapshot. Ethan cried, "Now people will think our truck looks like a dork!" The boys washed away their embarrassment with a pan of water and a snow brush upon our return home.

The truck wasn't the only embarrassing thing to happen that fall. When Elgin returned from a trip to Anchorage with kites in hand, we headed for the sea beach to our favorite spot. Hopping out of the vehicle, Ethan and I attempted the first flight of his new kite. He giggled with anticipation as I ran down the beach with the kite in hand.

"Here comes a plane," Elgin warned. The wind was whipping, and waves crashed onto the beach. It was impossible to hear. "Hey, Melissa! Don't let go of the kite. Theo's plane is right there!"

"Huh?" As I looked over my shoulder, the wind snagged the kite from my grip. Too late! The kite flew into the sky above me as I found myself suddenly face-to-face with the low-flying Cessna 180. It must have startled Theo as much as me. He sharply banked away, creating a roar of the plane's engine in his wake. I stumbled over backward at the abrupt sighting of the aircraft buzzing fifty feet overhead. A few choice words escaped me. I am glad no one could hear me in that wind.

Though it was fall everywhere else in the country, winter was ready to settle in for the long haul on the Alaska Peninsula. Scarce entertainment in the bush made the ability to self-entertain a requirement for remote living. So, if we weren't flying kites in windstorms, beachcombing, or working long hours at the school, we stayed home and read or took turns at the one desktop computer in the kitchen.

Elgin read books on flying in Alaska. *Glacier Pilot: The Story of Bob Reeve, Flying Cold: The Adventures of Russell Merrill, Pioneer Alaskan Aviator*, and *Bush Pilots of Alaska* kept him busy. I hooked the boys on the new series, *Goosebumps*.

The Alaska history books captivated me. I read multiple tales of ancient Alaska people living in perilous times. *Two Old Women, Bird Girl and the Man Who Followed the Sun, Mother Earth, Father Sky*, and the *Alaska Bear Tales* series sat on the school bookshelves waiting for me to find them.

THIRTY-THREE

You Call Yourself a Dentist?

In the fall of both school years we lived in Nelson Lagoon, the Native Health Services sent a dentist to the community. His unannounced arrival in the first year surprised us. He showed up at the school door, expecting to use and stay in the building during his weeklong visit.

"Any chance you could fill a cavity for our son?" Elgin inquired.

"Sorry. No can do. The clinic does not allow me to provide services to non-Native people." The scruffy and unimpressive dentist chatted about his flight to the village while we hauled in his equipment and luggage. He transformed the preschool room into his provisional office in less than an hour. The school kitchen, shower, and couch became his quarters for a week.

The next day, community members and students began receiving their dental checkups. One student couldn't wait for his turn. "I haven't had my teeth cleaned in three years. I can't wait for that smooth feeling." He ran his tongue across his front teeth and imagined the expected sensation.

"How do your teeth feel?" I asked when the student returned from his quick appointment. Delighted, he reported that the dentist had told him his teeth were fine—no cleaning was necessary. He was doing a great job on his own. My jaw dropped as the student resumed his studies, content not to have the smooth feeling he had looked forward to, and unaware of the unacceptable dental care he had just received.

The constant classroom interruptions made for one tough week. Students left one-by-one for appointments. Community members visited while waiting for their turn. The dentist hung out in the classroom, interrupting our day when he wasn't busy. With all the commotion, keeping kids on task was like herding cats.

"I don't bother fixing their teeth. It's easier to pull them," the dentist bragged. This practice may have explained why the Alaska Native population had so many missing teeth.

Remote villages had severely limited dental care. Periodontal disease affected three times as many Alaska Native people and a shocking sixty percent of their children under the age of six suffered from severe tooth decay.[1]

Of the one-hundred-twenty-five thousand Native Alaskans, seventy percent live in one of the two hundred villages cut off from services by mountains, glaciers, lack of roads, and extreme temperatures. Bush travel was time-consuming and difficult, meaning a quarter of the rural dentist jobs with the Native Health Services remained unfilled.

"Let's squeeze your little man in before I leave," the dentist offered at the end of his last day.

Sure, I thought. *As if we would allow this poor excuse of a dentist to treat our son after watching a week of malpractice. No way!*

The next year when the dentist arrived unannounced ready for us to haul in his luggage, Elgin blocked the door. "The disruption to the classroom last year was too much. Find somewhere else to provide your services this year."

The change in accommodations angered the dentist. He begrudgingly checked in as the only guest of the Tide's Inn Motel with Lana. The post office transformed into his new workspace, though it was not as convenient as the school, it was far less distracting for the students.

It stunned me the next morning when the dentist phoned the school and told Elgin that I had to bring over specific children for their appointments. I checked with my principal. Yep. It was my responsibility to escort the children to the dentist. No parental consent, supervision, or notification was required. Really?

I chauffeured and acted as a substitute parent for the village children. It was undoubtedly a demanding situation for the dentist with no elbow space to function or privacy for patients. Post office patrons picked up their mail and packages by stepping over the patient's feet in the chair while dogs sniffed the packages on the floor. Kids joked with the current patient while the dentist worked on them.

We had no guilty conscience though. A dentist willing to pull savable teeth from the mouths of babes out of sheer laziness deserved to have it rough—at least we thought so.

---

[1] Sekiguchi, E.; Guay A.H., Brown, L.J., and Spangler, T.J. Jr. Am J Public Health. 2005 May. "Improving the oral health of Alaska Natives." 95(5):769–73. https://www.ncbi.nlm.nih.gov/pmc/articles/PM-C1449253.

THIRTY-FOUR

Children of the Aleutians

You might assume Alaska's frontier children were like nineteenth century kids with no access to modern-day trends or fads. Nope. Satellite television and VHS movies provided plenty of material to keep our students informed about what other kids around the country found popular. Though teacher housing only had RATNet television, ten-foot satellite dishes sat in the yards of the wealthy fishermen. In 1996, the boys wore pants without belts exposing their underwear, and girls danced around the classroom on break to the *Macarena*.

Satellite television only compensated for the outside world to a point, though. We found ourselves sidetracked one day when the kids discovered there was such a thing as bubble gum ice cream. Seven-year-old Michelle eagerly raised her hand, "Mrs. Cook. I had bubble gum ice cream once when I was in Anchorage."

"Once?" I questioned in surprise. Michelle nodded with pride. Ice cream was a rare commodity in the community, a treat flown in by Snake Eyes in a cooler. Vanilla was the best seller, but he brought various types and flavors.

Bubble gum ice cream wasn't the only foreign topic for the village children. Michelle diligently worked on an assignment pondering a picture of a gas pump. She studied the image with a puzzled look on her face, "What's that?"

"A gas pump," I answered.

"That doesn't look like a gas pump to me," she shrugged. To her, a gas pump was the fifty-five-gallon fuel drum with a hand pump stored in the container out back.

Nightmares were different too. One morning, a boy came to class upset. "I had a bad dream last night. First, a seal bit me, and then I fell off my dad's fishing boat, and a bunch of seals tried to eat me!"

A discussion in health class uncovered student distress over using restrooms. These kids had little experience using public bathrooms. Cilla commented, "I was in one once when I was in Anchorage, but I didn't use it."

Reality was in the eye of the beholder. Correcting Michelle's schoolwork, Elgin smiled when he graded, "_____ land at the airport." Her answer was cubs. Piper Cub airplanes landed in Nelson Lagoon all the time, so he accepted her answer as correct.

The uniqueness of being raised on a sand spit meant students understood the ground to be sand. No dirt, soil, or rocks of any considerable size existed there. The vegetation was beach grass. I contacted a few teachers highlighted in an educational magazine from Ohio, Alabama, and Kentucky who mailed dirt, clay, and leaves of various sorts for the students to see. In return, we shared Aleutian black sand and Japanese glass balls we had collected from the local beach, enough to give one to each of the students and staff working in these classrooms. We might have thought twice about sending all those glass balls had we known we would only find one more.

Once I asked the high school students if they had ever seen trees. "Oh, sure." One student shared his experience of seeing a forest along the roadside while driving from Anchorage to Kenai. The others had never seen a tree prior to them floating ashore as barkless logs on the beach.

Buying shoes in Nelson Lagoon was not easy either. Locals often wore poorly fitting shoes and ordering a new pair from the catalog did not mean relief arrived in the mail. It was a crapshoot. "How many of you have shopped at a shoe store?" Not one elementary student raised their hand, so I turned to include the secondary students in the discussion. No one raised their hand.

"What's a shoe store?" one first-grader asked what the others may have wondered.

"It's a place where you buy shoes. A store filled with shoes of all sizes and colors displayed on shelves." The kids started giggling and fed off each other's laughter until it became a slight roar.

"What's all the laughing about?" Elgin asked, entering the classroom.

One student volunteered a response as he held his stomach in laughter, "A store full of shoes!" The kids giggled.

Teaching in a remote village with no stores or traffic, I had a huge learning curve to overcome when it came to my students' background knowledge. Only a few students had been to town, and those who had, totaled their time in days or weeks.

One elementary health lesson on safety reviewed street signs. No signs existed in Nelson Lagoon, so I started with a Stop sign, which all the students knew. Then I displayed the Do Not Enter sign and allowed the kids time to consider it. A hand rose, "It means the store is closed." That was a reasonable guess.

On a more serious note, it was challenging to explain the dangers of drunk driving on the freeway to students with only three miles of black sand roads. My attempts to describe on-ramps, driving on the wrong side of the highway, the draw of oncoming headlights turned out to be a meaningless discussion. With the students' limited driving opportunities, they stared at me in confusion as though I was speaking Greek. I should have taught them about the dangers of drunkenness while captaining a boat or driving a vehicle at top speed on the beach. More than one student from this village would die or become seriously injured in drunk driving wrecks on the black sand beaches of Nelson Lagoon. I think of the lost kids involved in crashes—remembering the fun times we spent together in their youth. Death arrived earlier than expected for far too many community members in bush Alaska.

"Do you eat radishes?" A middle school boy was examining a radish in his textbook. The high school student looked confused.

"What's a radish?" Cilla asked. I realized I hadn't ever seen radishes at Snake Eye's Flying Grocery Store.

And then I had an idea. "Let's take the kids to Anchorage in December and show them the city decorated in Christmas lights. We could visit a shoe store, the mall, a larger school, ride on a bus, eat in restaurants, visit museums, and go sledding on an actual hill. While we are at it, we could visit the grocery store to see the radishes and other vegetables not available at Snake Eye's store," I suggested to a parent.

In a little less than a month, I raised $9,000 to take four third- and fourth-grade students, a parent, and myself to Anchorage for a week. It doesn't sound like much to you or me, but for elementary school children from the bush, a week in the city was a rare opportunity.

Thinking back to my teaching in Nelson Lagoon, I taught about the society I knew. Instead, I should have adapted my instruction to the bush world and tried to see it from their perspective.

THIRTY-FIVE

The Ring of Fire

When we moved to the Ring of Fire, we were aware of the occasional volcanic activity in the Aleutians. However, when I thought of an eruption, I envisioned Pompeii with bodies frozen in time and in positions of hiding, escaping, and dying from the 450 mph pyroclastic flow from Mount Vesuvius.

The story of Pavlof Volcano began for us with the middle-of-the-night eruption on September 16, 1996. It erupted again on October 22. I detailed the event in an email home: *Today, the Alaska Volcano Observatory or AVO called to say Pavlof was shooting ash and debris as high as 25,000 feet into the air. Wow! This is as close to the real thing as we want to be!* Unfortunately, the thick cloud cover prevented us from witnessing the eruption.

The color codes for volcanic activity include green, yellow, orange, and red. Green meant a dormant volcano. Yellow indicated a restless and somewhat active volcano, while orange alerted residents of a possible upcoming eruption. Then there was red, or the strong possibility of a full eruption. The volcano had been bouncing between yellow and orange with an occasional red since September. It was now mid-November. We debated leaving several times, wondering if we were complete idiots for not evacuating. The AVO wasn't issuing evacuation warnings, causing us a terrible dilemma. It's not like we could get into the Suburban and drive away if necessary; we lived on an isolated spit. Pompeii was only five miles from Mount Vesuvius. We lived forty-eight miles from Pavlof. Did the additional forty-three miles mean the village was safe? We didn't know for sure.

In an email, I updated our family: *Pavlof has been hidden behind a cloud of ash and heavy overcast weather. It died down to a code yellow, but it was code red for two and a half days!*

While shopping at Snake Eyes' Flying Grocery Store, Cilla borrowed my camera and snapped a picture of me. The flash caught everyone's attention.

Several people thought it was lightning. That surprised me, given the time of year and its rarity in the area. Later, I discovered an active volcano can create lightning.

On November 4, 1996, at 9:35 a.m., we received a call from the AVO stating they thought Pavlov was erupting. A newsletter home described the experience:

We jumped from our seats and ran to the front door to witness, once again, the "burp" from Pavlof. When I say burp, I mean it spat out a cloud of ash that rose above the volcano, resembling an atomic bomb explosion. A large mushroom cloud gathered high above the volcano as it spewed its ash and debris.

Then, one quiet mid-November day there came a point in my life when I instantly thought I was going to die. No hope. Seconds to live. Or so I thought, when the voice of the local school board member Paul Schaack screamed over the marine radio, "Pavlof is blowing its top, and it's heading our way!"

Suddenly terrified, my husband and I made eye contact from across the room. We could hear the rumbling outside. Images of the Pompeii people flashed through my mind. I ran for the front door, wavered a second with Elgin and the boys by my side, and flung it open to watch the volcano explode into a full eruption a mere forty-eight miles away. I chose to witness the blast even though I believed it was the last thing I'd do in this life.

The students, our children, my husband, and I stood in front of the school and watched the volcano erupt. Explosive gases and steaming hot lava shot through the volcano's mouth, filling the surrounding area with large, rolling clouds of gray ash. The Aleutian sky merged with the debris six miles above the volcano. Though ash headed in our direction, the pyroclastic flow of hot gas I feared did not accompany it. We would live to see another day.

Elgin quickly assembled the equipment the AVO had sent out in September. The students gathered outside the school to watch as he explained how the instrument measured the height of the volcanic ash in real time while I made a beeline for home.

Sand scattered all over the apartment floor from my boots when I rushed to grab the camera and tripod from the closet. I heard a constant rumble as I sprinted up the hill beside the teacherage and perched myself at the top to capture the most awe-inspiring moment of my life.

How long does a volcano erupt with such velocity? I should know. I honestly don't, and Elgin doesn't remember either. However, I can tell you I sat on the beach until I grew tired of taking photographs. Then, I remained on the grassy edge of the sand and allowed the extraordinary circumstances to consume me until guilt forced me back to the Suburban. I had left Elgin alone with the entire school—all twelve children.

With the students watching, Elgin measured and remeasured the rumbling blast, documenting a distance of six miles from the mouth of Pavlof to the visible top of the mushroom cloud. We realized we would survive, had seen all there was to see, and returned to the classroom.

We watched Pavlov huff and puff throughout December. It spewed, flowed, rumbled, and blew chunks of lava the size of vehicles down its mountainsides for two more months. Then, without warning, it ceased all activity on January 3, 1997, ending the saga.

In the spring of 1997, the AVO sent us a copy of the magazine *Popular Science* with one of my photographs of Pavlof Volcano on the front cover. Elgin was mistakenly given credit for the image, probably because he was the lead teacher and the contact for the school. Since then, the Smithsonian Institution's Global Volcanism Program, Geology.com and other websites have published the photograph.

Another nearby volcano became active that year. In March 1996, Akutan Volcano shook violently from rolling earthquakes for days. The teacher at the site told us the entire village had been evacuated. Only he, his wife, and two other residents had stayed behind. "It is comparable to driving across Wyoming sagebrush at forty to fifty mph. Rough." The volcano settled down without a full eruption.

THIRTY-SIX

Cabin Fever

In January 1997, a notice from the State of Alaska printed out on the school fax machine. An arrest ended in the murder of Trooper Bruce Alan Heck in Glennallen. In the memory of the heroic officer, Governor Knowles ordered flags lowered to half-staff.

"Elgin, do we have a flag to lower?" I realized we did not have a flagpole at the school.

He looked at me as if I was an idiot. "Can you imagine the condition of the flag after being on a pole out here? Even for a week!"

The dark days of winter were upon us again. It wasn't unusual for me to work while singing to the tune, *Let It Snow! Let It Snow! Let It Snow!* And snow it did, month-after-month during the long winter. When it wasn't snowing, it was raining. Endless, pouring, sprinkling, blowing rain with heavy overcast skies. It could drive a perfectly sane person mad. They coined the term *cabin fever* in 1900 to give a name to the psychological experience of being isolated indoors for extended periods.

When left unchecked, cabin fever resulted in depression, irritability, and a severe case of loneliness. Today some call it Seasonal Affective Disorder or SAD. It arrived in January and lingered until March or April. We fought it off by staying busy, eating protein, traveling, exercising, and being outside even if it was cold and dark out there. When cabin fever raised its ugly head, we experienced a rigorous period of soul searching.

Wintertime blues, cabin fever, SAD, or whatever you want to call it, was common for those enduring isolation in the far north. We developed camaraderie with those sharing the experience with us.

The Aleutian winters proved exceptionally difficult. For all intents and purposes, we were alone out there. Sure, a tiny village of people endured the winter with us. Still, we found ourselves submerged in a *fishbowl*, which essentially meant—alone. And when you are alone, you become lonely.

The first winter, Elgin fell into depression and saw bush Alaska as miserable, hopeless, and dreary. By the time mid-winter arrived the second year, I was no longer holding him up; he was supporting me. It required a team effort to outlast the winters. Everything we knew in life was gone. Our extended family, culture, society, hobbies, and lifestyle changed drastically, replaced with an isolated village on a spit where most people seldom left their homes.

At times, I found it exciting despite the struggles:

Can you believe we moved to the edge of the world on the shores of the Bering Sea? I get a kick in the shorts over the whole thing! Living amongst volcanoes, the changing tides, hundred mph wind, Alaska brown bears, bush flights, and wolves certainly has become an adventure. I never dreamed of living by the Bering Sea, and I will say it is extreme here. Shouldn't everyone weather a radical period in their lifetime?

Most of the winter, it was a daily struggle to keep my head above water. As a second-year teacher, I instructed multiple grade levels at one time. As a wife and mother, I maintained our home and made every single meal from scratch with little food variety. Elgin had his hands full with teaching and administrative duties while learning to manage the school's budding educational technology.

Email became our temporary salvation from cabin fever and was often our only connection to the outside world. We ate breakfast to the modem dialing and squealing each morning, hoping for news from home. Then we watched as the load line worked its way across the screen for a few minutes before revealing in a friendly voice, "You've got mail!" I won't even begin to explain how our day proceeded if we didn't hear that message. Only a few family members owned a computer or had email at this point in time.

An internet speed of 9,600 bps (bits-per-second) is unimaginable today. We turned off images in the Netscape Navigator web browser, downloading only text to ensure we received the coveted data.

In an email home, I shared: *I have adjusted to bush life, for as much as a person from the city can adjust to such a life. No screams of insanity have come from our house this week, anyway.* Another one said: *Some days are just so much lonelier than others.*

The school district used FirstClass for communication between staff, which auto-dialed twice a day. Out of desperation to hear from anyone, we forced internet connections throughout the day to check for email. My heart jumped with glee to see the little red flag indicating a new email. To be clear, a forced connection meant an additional long-distance call for the school district with a pricey phone bill. They never said a word when the bill arrived each month. Not once. It was a small price to pay to keep teachers floating in bush Alaska.

Fellow bush teachers in the other tiny sites scattered along the Aleutian Chain understood and suffered from cabin fever right along with us. We counted on a daily email with a splendid joke to bring a smile to our faces and laughter to our lives.

We were among the last group of people to endure the extreme isolation in bush Alaska. We relied on ourselves to pull through each day despite the challenges we faced. Technology has forever changed life in the bush. Today, videoconferencing, email, and social media ease the loneliness. People can now shop online and even obtain career training.

THIRTY-SEVEN

Alone and Lonely

The creak of the rusty Suburban door disappeared in the wind, but my husband's voice radiated across the beach as he stepped out into the storm. "Come on!" Elgin worried. Was I losing my grip as he did last winter? He knew the signs of cabin fever.

I turned my back on the sea. The wind pressed my red coat against my body. Rain pelted my backside, drenching my final dry spots as I made my way from the beach up the hill to my waiting family. They were all I had out there. We spent every waking hour together. So why did I feel so alone?

Elgin was clearly unhappy with me for staying out in the cold. As I stepped beside the Suburban, it blocked the relentless wind, and my body trembled from the cold. A sense of sadness overwhelmed me. I couldn't explain how I felt or why. I just felt it, like a gray cloud following overhead. Wait, gray clouds always hung overhead. Thick dark clouds the sun could not penetrate hovered less than one thousand feet above us—a constant in this godforsaken place.

I opened the passenger door; grateful the wind was directly blowing on Elgin's side. It took strength to open his door, battling the ferocious wind when he called out to me. I lifted my heavy, insulated boot to get in; my icy-wet pants stuck to my leg, and I shivered.

"What took you so long? It's cold out there!" Elgin put the Suburban into drive with our three young boys bouncing in the backseat. There was no need for seat belts driving ten mph on the isolated beach road surrounded by water on both sides, and besides, we seldom passed a single moving vehicle.

"We're hungry. What's for dinner?" My children had had enough of storm watching and begged to go home.

We bumped down the road for a few minutes as the wind pounded the vehicle's windows and howled. The storm was growing worse. What else was new?

"Are you okay?" Elgin asked, looking at me with concern. I forced a smile.

"Yes," I half-whispered with little conviction.

"What do you say we go home and begin our job search?" Elgin suggested. I knew how difficult this teaching assignment had been for him too. My mood easily affected my family, so I sat up a little straighter, ignoring the pain I felt inside. My face burned from the bruising, freezing rain, and my legs turned numb in my freezing pants.

"Where do you want to look for a job?" I inquired with as much enthusiasm as I could muster.

"Wyoming!" Sutton interjected. He never stopped dreaming of returning home.

The two years in Nelson Lagoon proved to be intriguing, productive, frustrating, lonely, scary, lonely, lonely, and lonesome. I once expressed my loneliness in a January email:

> *People . . . I miss you. World . . . I miss you. I am suffocating here with the sea closing in on me. I see water wherever I look, but not a single tree. The skies are gray, with storm clouds ready to release their snowflakes or raindrops upon my head and ready to increase the size of the frozen pond in our front yard. Oh, how my heart would skip a beat to see a sunset through the branches of a tree. It must be winter in bush Alaska.*

I cried while writing this email because I couldn't put into words the depth of my loneliness. I knew people existed out there, somewhere. But standing on the edge of the Bering Sea made me feel as though nothing else existed. It was as if my memories came from a dream of another world. The loneliness became excruciating.

Bizarre highs and lows swung minutes apart. The wonder and awe turned on a dime to desperation, restlessness, and uncertainty—even fear. What if something happened in the world, leaving us stranded there forever? The swings between sadness at being alone and the sheer delight of living on the edge may have left one speculating the possibility of being bipolar.

Diving into a book helped to escape our reality with so few other distractions available. I wrote to document our story:

It is the simple things I miss from my urban life. A trip to the grocery store. Seeing people pass by on the street, in a hall, or while shopping in a store. Even waiting in a line and overhearing a conversation not meant for me. I should close my letter before I reveal any more secrets in my state of loneliness on this late Monday evening.

People laughed when I said I missed pavement, yet it was true. The smooth ride through busy streets gives a person the satisfaction of belonging to a society. This was to say nothing of the rush one has driving at speeds above first gear.

A restaurant. The mall. A video store. A movie theater. Church. Fast food. A gas station. Book stores. Seeing the headlines of current magazines as I wait in line at a store. Having a stick of gum in my pocket from a spur-of-the-moment purchase. Daily mail service. Comedy TV available every night. Walking into a store after not shopping in months.

I longed for the life I had left behind while living in Nelson Lagoon, and honestly, during all of our years in Alaska.

It was lonely. There was no way around it. Some moments truly felt as though no one else lived on Earth, leaving us as its sole residents.

At the beginning of the second school year, my mother-in-law Connie had inquired, "How many weeks until you come home?" I refused to count given the nightmare we experienced the first year living through week eleven twice. But by the time we reached the end of each school year in Alaska, we couldn't help ourselves and counted again. It was impossible to avoid it. Someone always started calculating.

In late March 1997, I wrote:

We have eight weeks until we leave. Fifty-six days. We have seven weeks until our last week here. 1,344 hours left. Thirty-seven school days. 80,640 minutes remaining in Nelson Lagoon. We have . . . Another tangent, you say? You'd go on one too if you lived out here!

In early April, I asked Everett if he was ready for summer. His response, "I can't take another day here!" And he meant it too. The boys also suffered, lonesome for family and old friends.

And yet, despite the trials and tribulations, I began experiencing a sense of loss at leaving two months before our departure. I noted: *The entire second semester has slipped by; it's as if the blink of an eye could snatch away my last days here. Despite the isolation and daily struggles, I have enjoyed my time in Nelson Lagoon.*

Anyone who survives two years in a small, bush school with only their children and spouse as reminders of their home and society has earned the title of *adventurer*.

THIRTY-EIGHT

And Then They See Your Boat!

I leaned against the door of our apartment storage area, gossiping with Curt, the district maintenance man, who'd flown in from Sand Point to fix our heater. "Thank you for flying in so quickly." And I was grateful too. Curt gave me someone to talk to other than Elgin and the kids and he brought news from other schools in the district that was not being announced in our email.

"I don't mind jumping on the first plane to help you guys. We can't have you freezing." Curt was on his knees working on the heater. He would have to work fast to catch the mail plane in an hour. "I resigned effective at the end of this school year," he stated after sharing which teachers had quit from the other schools.

"No! The district will be lost without you." That was no joke. Curt knew all the schools and their issues. "Why are you leaving?"

"The wind and scary flights have become too much for me. I have this feeling that if I stay, I will die in a plane crash. Too many close calls over the past five years. Too many sites desperate for a plane and willing to give false information about the ground conditions."

"It is crazy how people lie about the weather to get their supplies in," I agreed. An unspoken struggle existed between villagers who wanted the planes to land and pilots who were unsure of the weather below. People desperate for supplies lied about the weather to convince pilots to fly out. Yet, the pilots put their lives on the line if they landed based on bogus ground reports.

"I was on a flight that landed in Port Moller a few months ago," Curt continued. "We flew over to check the runway but could only see that it was snow-covered. On touchdown, we sank deep into the snow. The pilot cussed them out, but it didn't change the fact we still had to take off. The plane barely pulled up just when we ran out of runway. And do you know what is at the end of their runway?"

"No, what?" It shocked me to hear his story. Lying about wind speed was one thing but snow depth?

"The Bering Sea, that's what! The plane's tires stuck to the snow so we couldn't lift off. We were moving too fast to abort, forcing the pilot to commit to the takeoff. We could have died! That was it. I knew it was time to quit then and there. My contract ends in June, and then I'm out of here." He kept working while sharing details of his other horrific flights in all kinds of weather. "I'm the maintenance guy; I fly to each of the schools. Flying is part of my day. I can't escape it without quitting." He paused and looked at me, "So I quit."

Curt, I don't remember his last name, was always a breath of fresh air and entertainment when he flew into our site. The mail plane arrived as he finished the repair and I rushed him to the landing strip. The pilot was unloading the mail into a villager's truck when we arrived.

When I returned to the classroom, first-grader Michelle was writing words to match pictures on a worksheet. She stared at one image without recalling it. "Mrs. Cook, what's *that*?" I glanced at the picture; it was an ant. There were no ants in Nelson Lagoon.

That afternoon, a parent phoned the school. A frightening, foreign insect had stowed away in a shipment of supplies. She asked if she could bring it to the school for us to identify. Upon her arrival with a friend in tow, she presented a mason jar with a large black beetle hopelessly attempting to escape the slippery glass. Elgin identified it as a beetle, but that was not sufficient.

"Is it poisonous? Will it sting? Does it lay eggs? How many more of these bugs could there be?" she wanted to know. I unscrewed the lid. "No! No! Don't open it! It might escape!" The ladies became hysterical at the thought of the freed beetle.

Nelson Lagoon was close to bug-free during the winter, though summer meant giant mosquitoes and a few other bugs. The consequence of having few bugs hanging around was ignorance of the critters. In fact, the students never saw a spider, or so they claimed. During science, I presented a book on arachnids and grossed them out. A fourth-grade boy could not stand the sight of the creepy, crawly bugs. He was sick at the idea and refused to look at the pictures, feeling faint throughout the lesson. He glimpsed a tarantula and bolted from the classroom in disgust.

The eighth grader hung out to watch the beetle commotion. "I hate when spring comes," the student shared his dread. "When we are fishing, swarms of flying and stinging bugs come out. First, you hear the buzz and then you see the monsters coming through the thick fog. They skim the water, searching for a place to land. *And then they see your boat!*"

THIRTY-NINE

No Coffin Sniffing

Grandma Leona passed away in Anchorage during our second school year. The people in Nelson Lagoon considered her to be their grandmother, even if she wasn't. The Alaska Native culture highly respects their elders. She arrived home on a bush flight in a plywood box. VHS radio announced the final arrangements to the village.

"Grandma Leona is here. We have her stored outside in the boat shed," someone informed the community.

The next day, a surprising announcement aired over the marine radio. "A bunch of dogs are sniffing around Grandma Leona's coffin. Please keep your dogs locked up until after the funeral at three o'clock today."

Another conversation perked Elgin's interest. "Grandma's favorite color was purple. We could use spray paint and color her box purple."

"Sounds good. Meet you there in a few minutes," a man responded.

Elgin raised his eyebrow and told me, "You do realize they nailed the plywood box shut in Anchorage? If they use spray paint, some will go through the cracks and onto their grandmother's body." I couldn't help but imagine the end result.

The entire village attended Grandma Leona's funeral except for our family; we were unaware the villagers expected us to attend. In our culture, we do not go to funerals of people we don't know. The community noticed our absence, which we heard about by phone call later that day.

They held the funeral in an outdoor work area and buried the village grandmother at the top of the children's sledding hill at her request. She loved to look out the kitchen window and watch the kids sledding. No cemetery existed there, so they buried the dead wherever they preferred. A white cross marked an old grave on the hillside beside the teacher housing, which we saw out of our living room and master bedroom windows.

With the increasing daylight hours, we found ourselves busy with school travel. Elgin flew out for several administrative meetings. He chaperoned students from across the district on a weeklong trip to Anchorage for the Alaska Federation of Natives conference, known to the locals as AFN. I traveled with sports teams to other remote schools twice a month for weekend games. It was exhausting being on the road with students all weekend and managing our home and school by myself with Elgin gone so much that spring.

During one call home from an administrator's meeting in Sand Point, Elgin told me there had been a 4.5 magnitude earthquake there. It shook the whole school building and the table he was sitting at. He wanted to know if it had shaken the buildings in Nelson Lagoon. It hadn't. I was jealous because I wanted to feel the earthquake too.

The isolation became unbearable for me in April of 1997. I sat at my desk one Saturday afternoon, lonely with Elgin away. He called from the hotel room using our phone card or sent an email if the internet was available at night. The events in town kept him busy, making calls short and emails few and far between.

Tom Ryan, the district superintendent, invited us to call anytime to chat. He had warned of the fishbowl sensation after hiring us. I dialed Tom at the Sand Point district office. "Hello, Melissa! How are you?" Hearing his friendly, upbeat voice gave me a sense of relief. It was almost like he knew why I was calling, and the truth is, he probably did. It was late spring in bush Alaska.

"I'm living in a fishbowl as the lone fish!" I said, making light of my situation, but Tom understood exactly what I meant. I was alone, and nothing has ever compared to the hollow feeling the fishbowl gave to me at that moment in my life; I truly needed a lifeline. It didn't matter what we discussed over the phone. I believe the topic of discussion turned to the major events in the life of Tom's mother. The conversation provided a connection with someone who totally understood my situation, which made all the difference in the world.

As the days drew closer to leaving Nelson Lagoon, the emotional swings continued from the fishbowl feeling to writing an email saying:

It has occurred to me to enjoy each day and moment here because there will be a time I cannot smell the sea, watch the waves, walk on the beach, feel the sand falling through my fingers, have the comfort of sitting in this classroom preparing for my students, and being a part of these children's lives.

Job Fair 2.0

We intended to transfer into Sand Point after we finished our commitment in Nelson Lagoon, but life didn't work out that way. Chuck Coons and Tom Ryan planned to retire by summer. Chick Beckley was changing positions, and a year earlier, Bob Robertson had accepted a superintendent position on Prince of Wales Island in Southeast Alaska. Aleutians East Borough School District had significant changes on the horizon. The incoming New York City superintendent had not been in Alaska before his interview. *Sigh.* It was time to move on, but that meant another grueling job search.

Around this time, I wrote home: *The pain of loneliness hasn't bitten so hard with the constant rush of preparation for the upcoming job fair.*

Leaving nothing to chance with plenty of time on our hands, we hammered out a list of acceptable school districts. First, we determined where we could live for the next eighteen years. It was time to settle down. No more villages. Nothing as remote as Nelson Lagoon. We prioritized a store for groceries and the ability to travel with greater ease and less expense. Seward on the Kenai Peninsula made the top of the list, followed by Cordova, Kodiak, Valdez, and Fairbanks.

Second, we rose above the competition through our multimedia skills. It broke the bank, but we purchased fifty CDs at ten dollars a pop and developed an interactive CD to present our application materials. The professional cover blended images of Elgin fly-fishing and me sitting on a hill. The back cover displayed an old-time western family photo. A technical job application of this quality did not exist in Alaska's schools at that time.

Three weeks before the job fair, we mailed the CDs to the principals, human resource directors, and superintendents of the top five districts on our list. Within a week, the principal of Seward called to schedule interviews for the first evening of the job fair. To say it thrilled us would be an understatement.

My mother-in-law, Connie Cook, arrived to babysit the boys. She flew in two days early, in case the weather turned ugly, as was often the case in Nelson Lagoon. Our trip took six days, though we had Connie stay for a two-week visit. Until her death in 2018, she reminisced about the Aleutians and the kindness of Frank and Kathy Milliman who showed her around Anchorage and put her up for the night between flights.

We arrived in Anchorage for the Alaska Teacher Placement Job Fair in mid-April 1997. The first evening, I found myself overwhelmed. Nelson Lagoon had a handful of houses, a few storage sheds, the school, and a tiny two-story community building that housed the post office, clinic, and the village council office. Anchorage was a far cry from the village. There was so much to see. Sidewalks, streetlights, garbage cans, gas stations, buildings with endless windows, people, pavement, automobiles, signs, storefronts, and on and on. Everything called my attention at once, and it took my breath away.

"This street corner has more junk on it than the entire village of Nelson Lagoon," I noted, sitting at a red light downtown. The city mesmerized me each time I flew in from the bush. "Someday, I'll probably laugh at the thought of a street corner overwhelming me, but not today."

We stopped at the grocery store to grab breakfast and lunch basics. Storing food in the hotel room allowed us to eat on the run without waiting in line at restaurants. Starving, as we'd done at the last job fair, was not on our agenda this time.

A whiff from the bakery startled me as I stepped through the front doors of the grocery store. "Do you smell that?" The aroma of fresh bread felt like a drug went up my nose, bringing me to a dazed standstill. Elgin shook his head in disbelief. A few minutes later, we rushed by the dairy section in a hurry to prepare for the upcoming *meat market* at the job fair. Gallons of milk lined the shelves. I had not seen a gallon of milk in a year, let alone a cooler filled with them. I stopped and stared; I couldn't help myself. I soaked it all in.

"What are you doing?" Elgin asked impatiently from two aisles away. "We have a list of things to do before tomorrow." I enjoyed basking in the moment. The milk represented what I had missed the past couple of years and symbolized my lost civilization. Whatever it was for me, it wasn't for him.

"Can you remember the last time you saw a gallon of milk?" I questioned him. The funny thing was, I didn't even drink milk!

"It's been a long time; now let's go," he replied. In Nelson Lagoon, we had powdered, canned, and boxed milk. My family complained that none of it tasted like real milk. What else did the store have lurking in the next aisle? I could not wait to see, though I did so on the run as we rushed to gather peanut butter, jelly, bread, and fruit.

FORTY-ONE

Count Kenai Out

The state of Alaska was enormous, but its small population made it ripe for gossip. Networks were alive and well. This tight network could make or break you depending on who you knew and what they thought of you. Chuck Coons, Tom Ryan, and Chick Beckley pounded pavement to help us with our job search.

We entered the Captain Cook Hotel in April 1997 with far more confidence, knowledge, and patience than we had in 1995. Friendly faces of coworkers and friends made it less daunting, despite the fifteen hundred (yes, *fifteen hundred!*) other teachers joining us. Hordes of educators desperate for jobs filled the conference room. This time only a few districts found us standing in their lines. We hoped to relocate to an urban area of the state, and Alaska did not have many of those.

By early afternoon, our names popped up on many interview lists. Teachers inquired as to what we had done to attract the attention. A North Slope administrator recognized us from our circulating CD and waved his fist full of papers across the enormous district map on the wall behind him. "Wherever you want to go. Say the word, and you are there."

"Sorry. We aren't applying for jobs with the North Slope this time around. We have three boys in elementary school and hope to move them into a larger town not so far away from services," I informed him.

"I understand," he conceded. We crossed paths a few more times throughout the job fair. Each time, he offered us jobs.

"Cooks!" the same pesky Lower Yukon administrator from the last job fair hollered across the room and scurried out from behind his table. Applicants holding résumés watched him run toward us. "Cooks! I have jobs for you. Step over to my table, and we'll sign you up! We'd love to have you join our team this year." We kindly rejected his offer. "If you change your mind, you know where to find me," he reminded us over his shoulder as he returned to the waiting teachers.

"There's Tom and Chick. Let's ask Tom what's going on," I suggested. The attention we received from districts we hadn't contacted confused us. We headed over to the Aleutians East table to speak to Tom Ryan, our superintendent.

"We are only accepting applications right now. If we select you for an interview, your name will be on the board tomorrow morning," Chick said to the crowd.

We handed him our packets the last time we were here. I reminisced for a moment as I watched Chick accepting résumés.

"Hey there. Have you received contracts yet?" Tom asked with sincere interest. We told him of our surprising reception coming into the conference room.

"Your CDs were a big hit! The administrators who received one last month have shared them with their friends and are talking. It's being copied and passed around. No one has ever applied for a job using a multimedia CD, but times are changing. You are leading the pack." We thanked Tom and left the school district table to allow him to work. The job fair was a meat market with a mass of teachers vying for jobs and districts competing for the few quality applicants who could cut it in Alaska's bush.

We had earned the praise and support of our administrators. We stayed two long and lonely years, which Tom and Chick respected.

"I hope you have me on your interview schedule," Bob Robertson was a friendly face amongst the chaos in the room. Last year, he accepted a superintendent position in a district with a reputation for difficult teaching assignments, but how could we tell Bob no?

We met with him and a few board members that afternoon. They clipped a school picture to a packet someone handed to me when I entered the room. Beautiful blue skies with puffy white clouds made the school look tempting. I laughed.

"What's so funny?" Bob wondered with a smile.

"Isn't your district in the Tongass National *Rain* Forest?" I held up the photo. "You shot this on the only sunny day of the year, didn't you?" We laughed at the truthfulness of my questions.

"I'll admit, it is rainy there but with a few more sunny days than Nelson Lagoon," he informed me. Despite the enjoyable interview, we set our sights on a larger community. Bob understood.

In high spirits, we prepared to leave for Seward in the late afternoon. Tom Ryan caught us at the door. "The Kenai human resource director is not pleased with you. Their hiring process begins with her. Principals have no say in the hiring until she approves an applicant. I would count Kenai out. The other school districts are not listening to her complaints, though. You should be okay." Tom attempted to lessen the blow.

Seward was on the Kenai Peninsula and at the top of our wish list. We planned to skip the job fair's opening event and the following meet and greet to interview with the Seward principal two and a half hours away. Kenai's internal hiring process was news to us. It was disheartening to know the human resource director had blackballed us. However, we had committed to an interview with the Seward principal. Skipping it meant absolutely zero chance of securing a job there.

The drive through valleys with glacier ice still protruding down the mountainsides was awe-inspiring. We stopped at Portage Glacier to see mini icebergs floating like islands in a lake. Now, a visitor center sits close to where the glacier used to be, but the glacier receded beyond view many years ago.

Upon arriving at Seward Middle School, the interview committee took Elgin right in. I wandered the school's halls while I waited for my turn. A teacher can learn a fair amount about the staff, principal, and district by visiting a school. Our interviews began at eight in the evening on a weeknight. Strolling along, I noticed half the teachers sat behind their desks, still working in their rooms so late at night. None of them, not even those walking in the halls, spoke to me. No one smiled; they had their noses to the grindstone. I wondered if they had waiting families at home. Exemplary student work covered the walls. For a middle school, it was too neat and organized. The thing is, perfection wasn't realistic. It worried me.

I entered the interview room as Elgin exited. The principal informed me of the district hiring process. He should have told us about that *before* requesting an interview. Now he designated the meeting as an "off the books" meet and greet instead of an official interview for open positions. This principal was not impressive. Who in their right mind skips meeting administrators from all over the state to greet just one?

A committee member laid out the expectations of their teachers. They required each to sponsor at least one after-school sport or club quarterly, which was merely the beginning of their demand list. I now understood the tired teachers at their desks so late. We were interviewing for a sweatshop of educators.

We drove in silence along the dark highway back to Anchorage. Seward was our dream location, the top pick on our wish list, and I hated it. *How do I tell Elgin?* Skipping the opening event at the job fair had been a mistake. Anxiety and fear ran through my blood.

Fifteen minutes passed before Elgin finally asked the inevitable, "So what do you think?"

I grasped for the right words. There weren't any. Our dream school turned out to be a torture chamber for teachers run by a shifty principal. What could I say? "If I had to teach there, I'd rather quit teaching altogether and find something else to do with my life!"

With a sigh of relief, Elgin responded, "I am so glad to hear you say that!" Seward was off the list. Now what?

FORTY-TWO

You Scare Me Every Time You Say That!

On the second morning of the job fair, more districts were requesting interviews with us—many who were not on our list. There was no hiding from them. Copies of our CD now floated between school districts. *Elgin and Melissa Cook* filled the board. Our wish list was not panning out though. Cordova and Valdez had no openings. Kenai had blackballed us. Kodiak requested on-site interviews, but the exorbitant, last-minute airfare for the possibility of two jobs was out of the question. Fairbanks swiftly became the only viable district on our list. They preselected a handful of candidates for interviews. It did not look good, despite the hoopla surrounding us.

Cole Lehman, the former teacher from Nelson Lagoon, bounced into the conference room ecstatic. "Number twenty-three!"

"Number twenty-three? What does that mean?" we asked him. Cole had been one of our first friends and a tremendous support to us by phone in Nelson Lagoon.

"It means I am the twenty-third person hired to work in Fairbanks for this year. If the district pink slips people next spring, anyone hired after me will go first." Pink slip practice was a genuine concern. The larger district's hiring practices included pink-slipping all non-tenured teachers in the spring and waiting until late summer to rehire them. And not everyone received a contract months later, leaving loyal teachers who waited in the lurch.

"Let's fly to Fairbanks and meet the principals," I suggested after Cole left to sign his paperwork.

"We can at least introduce ourselves," Elgin replied. Another couple lingered close by, listening to us.

"After meeting the principal and seeing the school in Seward, it's worth checking out the district," I agreed. Our time in Seward saved us from the monumental mistake of pursuing jobs there.

"May we travel with you?" The couple jumped into our private conversation. An hour and a half later, the four of us tightened our seat belts for an Alaska Airlines flight to Fairbanks. The round-trip tickets set us back an affordable one hundred dollars each, and we shared the cost of a rental car. We drove from one school to the next, introducing ourselves to each of the principals.

"Elgin and Melissa Cook," we introduced ourselves, shaking one hand after another. We gambled canceling interviews with districts we lacked the enthusiasm to hire on with in lieu of the slim possibility of connecting with a Fairbanks principal. With eyes wide open, we ignored the hiring protocols and did it anyway.

The principals still had our CD on their desks. One shared with us, "I used your CD application during in-service last week to show the teachers their competition." He offered us chairs for an informal interview. "The HR people offer a few teacher contracts in April. Then we wait to see how many students enroll before we interview in August. It's late, but if you can hang on until then, I would sure love to have you on my staff."

August? August was four months away and days before the school year started.

"August is late. We have three children. It would be a tremendous risk waiting that long and then having to move within days if your district did hire us. Darn." The principal could not hide his disappointment either. HR tied his hands. He encouraged us to go through the process anyway and see what happened.

The candid information made this the last school we visited. The human resource department of Fairbanks Schools left much to be desired. Hiring in mid-August was absurd. Pink slips were common in the district, just like Mat-Su and Kenai. And remember how Cole had secured number twenty-three? That year, the teachers' union put names in a hat and drew for tenure spots; Cole became number ninety-two. Boy, was he mad!

We returned to the airport to jump on the next Alaska Airlines plane back to Anchorage. Our flight took us close to Denali National Park allowing us to be awed from the air by Mount McKinley, North America's highest peak at 20,310 feet. In 2015, the federal government finally returned Mount McKinley to its former name of Mount Denali.

We returned to Anchorage and hung out in the Captain Cook lobby, visiting with old friends and making new ones. Social networks played an essential role in finding a preferable job in the state. A young couple sat on a nearby couch, looking as stressed as we had been at our first job fair. I left the group to offer them some comfort.

"We haven't had one interview. We spent all our money coming here, and we both need jobs." I saw myself in them and took pity.

I spelled out life in rural Alaska and asked if they could manage the task. They sat up straighter and enthusiastically claimed to be ready for the challenge. I asked if they had a healthy marriage and explained how Elgin and I had grown together during our isolation in the bush. We immersed ourselves in the budding technology age mastering photo editing, creating music videos, writing fun stories and newsletters, and developing websites. Still, we were the exception, not the rule. The couple before me claimed to have a stable marriage.

"Meet me right here at eight o'clock tomorrow morning." I stood and rejoined Elgin.

"What can you do for them?" he asked as we walked away.

"Just because we don't have jobs doesn't mean there aren't jobs available," I replied.

The next morning, we met in the lobby at eight sharp. "Now, you're sure you want this?" They nodded with enthusiasm. "Okay, follow me." I entered the conference room with a bewildered Elgin and the unsure couple following me. Applicants surrounded the Lower Yukon School District table as the pesky administrator spotted me heading his way.

"Cooks!" He jumped from behind the table. "You've changed your minds. Outstanding! Where would you like to go? Anywhere! Anywhere you want!" Elgin dropped back instantly when he realized my destination.

"Good to see you." I shook his hand. He smiled in anticipation and stepped to the end of the table.

"I have a contract for you to sign right here." His eagerness spilled over.

I placed my hand on the stack of papers he was fumbling with to catch his attention. "I am not here for a job." He looked confused. "However, your team missed a couple who applied two days ago." I took a step back to usher the couple closer for an introduction. (I have forgotten their names after all these years.) "This young couple reminds me of Elgin and myself when you had hoped to hire us. I'm sure you didn't mean to overlook them with so many teachers here this year. Can you give their applications a second look?" I kindly pleaded.

"Oh," he said. I could tell this was far from what he had hoped. I smiled and tugged the arm of the young woman to situate her in front of me. The administrator turned to his assistant, "Put them in for an interview today." Then he stepped to the side to talk to me privately. "We'll put them on the schedule. Thank you for bringing them to our attention, but we'd prefer to hire you."

"I have three boys to get into town. Thank you for agreeing to interview them." My gratitude was sincere.

The elated young couple caught up with us in the hall after their interviews. Both had received teaching contracts with the Lower Yukon. I smiled and asked, "Are you sure this is what you want?"

"You scare me every time you say that!" exclaimed the husband, who tried to hide his smile when he said it.

"It should scare you! The life you have now won't be what you have in the bush. You're leaving everything behind for this harsh reality. Some teachers don't make it and go home. You'll remember I warned you of this next winter." I smiled and shared their joy with them a moment longer. For years, we have wondered how it turned out for them.

It was time for us to buckle down. *We* still did not have jobs, and it was the last day of the job fair. Our day quickly booked solid with interviews, the final one being with a small district that had one K-12 school on Prince of Wales Island—Craig City Schools. We had canceled this interview the previous day to fly to Fairbanks, but Chick encouraged Superintendent Nancy Billingsley to reschedule the interview and hire us. Eager to secure tech-savvy teachers and requiring a technology director, she agreed to an evening interview for two jobs coming open later in the spring.

We left the job fair unemployed by choice, and that was unnerving. We were holding out for a better life for our children.

FORTY-THREE

Falling into the Past

Jobless with six weeks remaining in the school year, we found ourselves back in Nelson Lagoon. We taught by day and packed by night and were still unsure of what address to put on the boxes. Job or no job, we were leaving. The district hired our replacements at the job fair. As proof of our departure, boxes for the incoming teachers arrived in the mail by early May, and life was moving on.

One Saturday afternoon, beautiful weather attracted the boys' attention. After checking the yard for bears, Sutton and Everett ran out to play—a rare treat for them. Ethan refused to go outside, fearing a bear hiding in the grass.

Minutes later, the front door flew open. Eight-year-old Everett ran into the dining room, tracking black sand everywhere. He screamed in terror as he ran. "Sutton disappeared!" His body shook from fright as tears filled his eyes and streamed down his cheeks. I immediately thought an Alaska brown bear had eaten Sutton. They frequented our driveway and nearby beach at night.

"What do you mean Sutton disappeared?" We rushed to Everett's side to calm him and find out what had happened to Sutton.

"He jumped up," Everett raised his hands above his head and jumped in place with an exaggerated landing, "and then he was *gone*!"

It took some convincing for a distraught Everett to go back outside to show us exactly where Sutton had gone missing. Whatever happened out there had scared Everett half to death. He inched his way around the house, pointed across the yard, and exclaimed, "He disappeared over there." Then he, too, vanished—hightailing it to the safety of our home.

Baffled, I scanned the dunes and out along the beach but there was no sign of Sutton. Everett insisted Sutton had vanished into thin air. That wasn't possible. Was it? And yet, Sutton was missing.

We walked along our driveway and approached the front yard with caution. Faint cries for help rose from the ground. Inspecting the area with trepidation, we crept through the beach grass on our hands and knees. Elgin discovered a rotten trap door broken in the middle. He cleared away chunks of wood and grass to expose our son in an empty, black hole below. Sutton had fallen into an abandoned bunker—a leftover piece of World War II history.

Before the war, the United States government realized the strategic location of Alaska. Between 1939 and 1941, they built military bases in Anchorage and Fairbanks and naval stations in Sitka, Kodiak, and Dutch Harbor. Within eighteen months, the military presence in the state grew from one thousand to thirty-five thousand. The United States firmly controlled the Pacific Ocean and Bering Sea, though Japan had other ideas.

The Japanese planned to invade Dutch Harbor on June 3, 1942, similar to Pearl Harbor's attack. This time, however, the United States military was waiting for them. Warding off a disastrous attack, the Japanese shifted the battle twelve hundred miles down the coast, away from Alaska's mainland to Kiska and Attu Islands. On June 7, 1942, the Japanese Imperial Army invaded Kiska Island on the western end of Alaska's Aleutian Chain. They imprisoned forty-two Aleuts and a non-Native couple from Attu. The white man died during the invasion. His wife and the Aleuts spent the rest of the war in a prison camp.

The U.S. military swiftly responded to the Japanese invasion. They installed barbed wire fences throughout the Aleutian villages and implemented blackouts and checkpoints, frightening the people. War had arrived at the Aleuts' front door.

With only twenty-four-hours notice, the military evacuated 831 Aleuts to internment camps, forcing them to live in abandoned gold mines and logging camps in Southeast Alaska. The cold rain forest was a far cry from the treeless Bering Sea beaches. Each family carried one suitcase, leaving pets and the rest of their worldly possessions behind.

The Aleuts from the Aleutian and Pribilof Islands suffered a similar fate as the Japanese in America, with one exception, a news blackout kept this dirty secret at bay for decades. The U.S. government considered the Japanese Americans the enemy. The Aleuts did not pose a threat, yet the U.S. military devastated many of their villages before departing in 1945.

Fifty-two years later, nine-year-old Sutton ran outside to play. He strolled along in the front yard and noticed a piece of wood hidden in the grass, something perfect to jump on.

He jumped and landed squarely on the old, rotten plank with both boots. To his surprise, the wood gave way, plunging him below ground into utter darkness. Stunned, he sat for a second and then clambered to his feet, squinting to see. The grass covered the hole above his head, severely limiting the light. He searched his surroundings, running his hand along the wall, and determined he was in an underground room. *This might be a bear's cave,* he thought. A tinge of fear struck him.

It could be a dried-up well, he tried to reassure himself. He feared a potential bear entering the dank room. *What if no one finds me?* Minutes passed, he tried not to worry and continued to explore. More time passed. The sound of faint voices came from above him. *Someone's looking for me.*

He hollered, "Down here!" A hole in the ceiling opened, and his dad's head poked inside.

"Sutton! Where are you?" Elgin called into the darkness.

"I'm here. I fell in," Sutton replied as our eyes adjusted to the hole's darkness. His fall left him dirty, and he stood shocked by the sudden light but relieved at the sight of us.

As we peered deep into the room below, log pillars became visible when our eyes adjusted to the low light. The large bunker could hide the entire population of the village. Lying on the ground, Elgin reached into the hole and pulled Sutton from the bunker below.

The neighbors had seen us huddled on the ground, looking down at the grass and pulling Sutton out. They appeared on the scene to investigate our odd behavior.

"Why is there an underground room in our yard?" I inquired of the men, relieved to have Sutton back. One elder knew the history.

"During World War II, our people feared being captured by the Japanese. Back then, Nelson Lagoon was only our summer fish camp. We used the Yukon driftwood from the beach to build bunkers to protect ourselves. When we returned at the end of the war, we demolished the rooms for safety. We must have missed this one," the old man recounted. That spring day in 1997, the village men made a plan to cave in the last known escape bunker from World War II in Nelson Lagoon.

FORTY-FOUR

A Heartbreaking Goodbye

We have looked forward to leaving Nelson Lagoon for so long. It hardly seems possible the day is almost here. I know it sounds strange, but I will miss this place. The sound of planes overhead. The school children I have grown to know and care for personally. The isolation from the rest of the world. The windsock flying straight out, more often than not. The black sand incessantly underfoot and following us to every nook and cranny of our living space. The howling sound of the endless wind. The grocery boxes piled up outside the post office waiting to be picked up. The four-wheelers buzzing down the road . . .

– M.Cook, May 1997

Superintendent Nancy Billingsley from Craig City Schools contacted us weekly after the job fair. She hoped to hire us for jobs she expected to open in her district: a technology director and middle school generalist. As difficult as it was, we held on tight while declining multiple incoming job offers from other school districts.

After six highly stressful weeks and two days before our departure, Ms. Billingsley offered us both full-time positions. Our fortitude had paid off. We finally had an address to label all the moving boxes piled up in the living room. Craig had a grocery store, decent housing options, and they would allow our children in my classroom before and after school. The town was on Prince of Wales Island in the Tongass National Forest, forty miles from Bob and Neva Robertson.

With one day left to go, I wrote:

What will I remember and what will I forget when we leave Nelson Lagoon? What part of our lives here will go unremembered? Will it be the buzz of the planes? The sound of the waves? The shaking of the house in eighty to ninety mph winds? Will it be the buying of electricity on pur-

chase cards? Or will it be the fresh produce lined out on the tarmac with Snake Eyes, rain or shine—more often rain and wind? Will it be the grueling preparation for fourteen to eighteen lessons per day? Will it be the joy of watching a twelfth grader tutor his kindergarten cousins? Will I remember the oddity of glancing around the building and seeing the entire student body in one glimpse? Will I remember waiting for the sun to rise during third period? Will I forget how normal it felt to have everyone in the village inspecting my packages at the post office? Will I forget the red sunrises over the magnificent snow-covered mountains with the lagoon in the foreground? What will I remember? What will I forget?

The last day of the school year arrived at the end of May 1997. We were excited about leaving, however Cilla was especially upset by our departure.

"Couldn't you stay one more year?" Cilla pleaded. "Next year, I'll graduate. Then you can go." It was a bittersweet moment for me. She wasn't the only one feeling insecure. As a new teacher, I gained confidence in my ability to manage my class in Nelson Lagoon. Moving to the larger school in Craig was nerve-wracking for me too. Change is scary no matter what age, for me anyway.

For Cilla, a parade of teachers had come and gone through her life— more than one in a year now and then. The bond between a one-room schoolhouse teacher and their students grows stronger than with hourly rotating classes of forty students found in urban classrooms. It was as if losing a friend every year or two for these kids.

"We've taken new positions in Craig. This district has already hired new teachers for Nelson Lagoon, and their boxes have arrived in the post office. I'll miss you dearly." I now realized I had missed a meaningful piece of my being here.

Nelson Lagoon was my first teaching assignment. I reflected on my growth as a teacher in a letter home:

In my years in the village, I focused on myself. I noticed what affected me, such as the flights, the food, the mail system, and the weather. Each day, I noted what a student understood about what I naively referred to as the real world. What does that mean anyway? We aren't simply doing a job here. We do not just show up to push papers. We work with children who absorb what we say, do and express.

Early the next morning, Elgin wandered through the duplex, checking for stray items we may have forgotten. "Hurry, boys. The plane will be here in a few minutes. It's time to go." Winter coats rustled against backpacks as the kids loaded into the vehicle. "What are you doing?" Elgin looked at me as though I was crazy.

Broom in hand, I responded, "Sweeping. I don't want the next teachers to come into a sandy house."

"We have to go," Elgin urged as I dumped the sand into the trash can one last time, set the broom against the wall, took one final long look over my shoulder, and left what had been our home for the last two years.

Lana stood beside the Suburban. She had come to give us a ride to the airstrip and to say goodbye. It surprised us to see a few villagers had gotten up early to say farewell, including Cilla, who still hoped we would stay. I heard the plane approaching. Elgin unloaded the boys and luggage and then joined the rest of us to say goodbye.

The single-engine plane taxied on the runway and pulled up to the parked vehicles. The red-haired pilot, Kim Post, jumped out and loaded our bags while Elgin helped the boys board the plane. At the door, he turned to see if I was coming.

"I wish you would change your mind," a teary-eyed Cilla said hopelessly. We embraced as I tried to hold back my emotions to say one last goodbye to her. I turned to board the plane, choking back tears. I squeezed past the boys and into my seat. Kim was already running through his flight check. "Elgin."

"Yes," he replied.

"Weight?" Kim asked.

"155."

"Melissa."

"Yes," I managed to say. "125," and so it went until the rev of the engine filled the cabin, and we taxied down the runway. The aircraft made a U-turn at the end of the strip, paused a moment, and then the motor gunned as the plane gained speed on the gravel until the wheels lifted from the ground. Cilla stood at the end of the runway, waving long, drawn-out, whole-body waves of goodbye as we flew over her head. The plane dipped its wings in a farewell, giving us one last view of the village by air and Cilla. Tears fell down my cheeks as I turned and looked through the window. I watched Cilla waving until she disappeared in the distance—my hand still resting on the windowpane as my last goodbye to her.

Goodbyes grew in number and difficulty in the years ahead. Friends and coworkers took jobs elsewhere while our students and children grew up and moved away. For twenty years, we second-guessed living in Alaska as we left Wyoming each summer, not knowing who would be alive the next year. The fact was, we lost several essential family members while we lived far away from home.

The Aleutians East Borough School District took this photo of Elgin (29) and me (27) during our interview at the Capital Cook Hotel—*Anchorage, Alaska 1995.*

The village of Nelson Lagoon on a spit of black sand with the Bering Sea on one side and the lagoon on the other. Image by Lee Anne McDermott—*Nelson Lagoon, Alaska 1994.*

This was our home for two years in the Aleut village of Nelson Lagoon. The school district teacher housing had two apartments. We lived in the left side apartment which was slightly bigger—*Nelson Lagoon, Alaska 1995–97.*

PenAir flew Cherokee Six or Piper Navajo (pictured above) airplanes to Nelson Lagoon to transport people, mail, and freight. This was the plane Kim Post flew on that stormy night we missed the runway—*Nelson Lagoon, Alaska 1995.*

We discovered hundreds of Japanese glass fishing floats on the beach after a harsh storm. The glass balls had been used to hold up fishing nets. A quarter is included in this image for scale—*Nelson Lagoon, Alaska 1996.*

On occasion, we found frisbee size jellyfish densely scattered from the water's edge to the beach grass in Nelson Lagoon—*Nelson Lagoon, Alaska 1995.*

We flew with Tom Madsen in his 1959 Beechcraft 18, the *Aleutian Spirit*. Sadly, Tom died in this plane when it crashed near Juneau on April 10, 2002—*Nelson Lagoon, Alaska 1996.*

Santa did not arrive by reindeer and sleigh in Nelson Lagoon, he came by chartered flight. Ethan (5), Sutton (8), and Everett (7) at the airport as the sun set—*Nelson Lagoon, Alaska 1995.*

The *Polar Bear* barge arrived in Nelson Lagoon annually in the spring to deliver supplies, vehicles, four-wheelers, and groceries—*Nelson Lagoon, Alaska 1996.*

I'm (29) standing on the rocky coast of the Pribilof Islands on the Bering Sea, where I took the secondary students to learn about their heritage in September—*St. Paul Island, Alaska 1996.*

I'm (29) instructing the elementary students in the Nelson Lagoon School. The secondary and elementary were separated by rolling dividers—*Nelson Lagoon, Alaska 1996.*

Pavlof Volcano is located 48.3 miles from Nelson Lagoon. The volcano continually huffed and puffed sending ash into the sky for four months. The wind blew the ash toward Dillingham on most days. The village did not have a common graveyard so markers could be seen around the community—*Nelson Lagoon, Alaska 1996.*

In November, Pavlof blew ash six miles high—*Nelson Lagoon, Alaska 1996.*

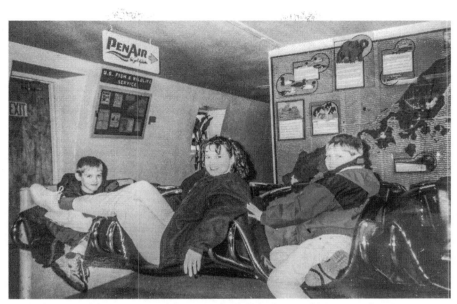

Me (29), Sutton (9), and Everett (8) waiting for a flight from Cold Bay to Nelson Lagoon on the way home from a week-long scouting trip into Anchorage in December—*Cold Bay, Alaska 1996.*

Me (29) and Elgin (31) standing behind Ethan (6), Sutton (9), and Everett (8) for a family photo after the Nelson Lagoon School Christmas program—*Nelson Lagoon, Alaska 1996.*

Elgin & Melissa

Cook

1997

CD—front and back cover—for our job search in 1997 we created a browser-based CD to present our job application materials. The top photo was take in Wyoming in 1994. The bottom photo was taken in Alberta, Canada in 1996—*Nelson Lagoon, Alaska 1997.*

Snake Eyes (Sam Egli) flew into Nelson Lagoon every month with a planeload of fresh produce, ice cream, dairy products, holiday decorations, and more during our years in Nelson Lagoon—*Nelson Lagoon, Alaska 1997.*

Every Alaska ferry had a car deck. Vehicles drove onto a ramp to board the ferry and then passengers rode upstairs. All of the ferries served hot food. The larger ferries also offered overnight guest cabins and a heated solarium—*Bellingham, Washington 1997.*

Elgin (31) & I (30) sitting on the back of the *Malaspina* ferry between Bellingham, Washington, and Ketchikan, Alaska in August—*Inside Passage, Alaska 1997.*

Everett (9), Ethan (7), and Sutton (10) riding from Bellingham, Washington to Ketchikan, Alaska in August—*Ketchikan, Alaska 1997.*

We traveled on the *Aurora* ferry from 1997–2002—*Ketchikan, Alaska 1997.*

This is the north side of Craig's harbor. A road passed between the two sides of the Craig docks. There were bathrooms with showers available to the public and the grocery store was just up the hill—*Craig, Alaska 1997.*

Sandy Beach was a favorite place to go after school and on the weekends to walk and play with the boys and dogs. I'm (30) standing on the coast of Clarence Strait which is part of the Inside Passage for the first time—*Sandy Beach, Prince of Wales Island, Alaska 1997.*

Sutton (10), Everett (9), Ethan (7), and Elgin (31) visiting Sandy Beach six miles from Thorne Bay—*Sandy Beach, Prince of Wales Island, Alaska 1997.*

Sutton (10), Everett (9), and Ethan (7) catching salmon on Duke Creek in August 1997— *Prince of Wales Island, Alaska 1997.*

This is a typical clearcut on Prince of Wales Island. The water in the distance is Clarance Strait, which is a section of the Inside Passage. Cruise ships, fishing boats, and barges use this waterway—*Clarence Strait & Prince of Wales Island, Alaska 2015.*

Sutton (10) caught a red snapper with Brian Castle in the background—*Craig, Alaska 1998.*

Ethan (7) holding up a shrimp Brian Castle caught in his crab pot—*Craig, Alaska 1998.*

A barge with shipping containers docked in Ketchikan as a commuter bush plane (upper right) flies down the Ketchikan Narrows—*Ketchikan, Alaska 2012.*

Elgin (33) & me (32) posing on the back of an Alaska Marine Highway ferry on our way into Ketchikan—*Inside Passage, Alaska 1999.*

Thorne Bay's welcome sign was a huge claw used by helicopters to log during the logging heydays—*Thorne Bay, Alaska 2013*

Thorne Bay, Alaska, taken from a floatplane—*Thorne Bay, Alaska.*

Sutton (12), Everett (11), and Ethan (9) canoeing on Sarkar Lake—*Prince of Wales Island, Alaska 1999.*

A de Havilland Beaver taxiing to the dock in Thorne Bay—*Thorne Bay, Alaska 2012.*

Connie and Kenny Cook touring the fishing vessels at the dock in Craig—*Craig, Alaska 2000.*

Kevin Castle, Elgin (35), Everett (12), Kenny displaying king salmon and halibut from their fishing trip—*Craig, Alaska 2000.*

Elgin (36) walking the boardwalk of McFarland Floatel near Thorne Bay. He installed wireless networks for many businesses and community members as a community service—*Southside Thorne Bay, Alaska 2001.*

Sutton (15), Elgin (37), Ethan (12), and Everett (14, holding Sampson as a puppy) resting on a log at Sandy Beach in the spring—*Sandy Beach, Prince of Wales Island, Alaska 2003.*

I (37) stopped for a photo with a soaked Sampson and Josie while on a walk—*Sarkar Lake, Prince of Wales Island 2004.*

Everett (16) and Erik Robertson (by the window) challenging Ethan (14), Stewart Robertson, and Sutton (17, by the window) to a game on the ferry ride to Ketchikan in December—*Southeast Alaska 2004.*

Neva Robertson climbing aboard the sailboat to inspect the damage from it turning on its side during low tide—*Ketchikan, Alaska 2004.*

Bob Robertson standing beside his sailboat after it was towed into Ketchikan for repair. It became swamped during high tide when it ran into an underwater high spot—*Ketchikan, Alaska 2004.*

Alaska's House of Representative, Don Young posing with Ethan (14) at his desk—*Washington DC 2005.*

Me (38) instructing teacher in-service in Thorne Bay in the spring—*Thorne Bay, Alaska 2005.*

184

Sutton (17), Ethan (15), and Elgin (40) displaying their catch on a fishing trip in 2005—
Thorne River, Prince of Wales Island, Alaska 2005.

Me (39) climbing the ramp during low tide. My office window was to the right of the ramp
on the first floor of the former J.R. Gildersleeve School—*Thorne Bay, Alaska 2006.*

J. R. Gildersleeve School turned into the school district office in 2000 after the logging camp closed down permanently. Notice the ramp is not too steep at high tide but it dropped about fifteen feet with the low tide—*Thorne Bay, Alaska 2013.*

Thorne Bay dock on a nice day—*Thorne Bay, Alaska 2015.*

I (40) flew out to Port Alexander to attend the graduation of the community's one senior. The photograph was taken by Jim Nygaard—*Port Alexander, Alaska 2007.*

903 Beaver Street, Thorne Bay, Alaska. We always parked our cargo trailer beside the teacher housing unit. We fenced the front yard for Sampson and Josie, though they often watched the neighborhood from the top step to avoid being rained on. We lived here for seventeen years—*Thorne Bay, Alaska 2014.*

The students wrote messages for me (43) on my final day of teaching before retiring on medical disability due to MS—*Thorne Bay, April 2011.*

Meliah (2) gathering Easters eggs on the back porch of our Thorne Bay teacher housing unit—*Thorne Bay, Alaska 2012.*

Ketchikan airport (with an Alaska Airlines jet in the background) had a seaplane dock. The commuter airline workers drove passenger vans down the ramp and onto the dock where they unloaded and loaded luggage and mail for the floatplanes. Once loaded the float-planes taxied into the Ketchikan Narrows for taking off—*Ketchikan, Alaska 2012.*

I (45) am showing our exchange student from Europe how to shoot a 22-rifle—*Prince of Wales Island, Alaska 2013.*

The view of Thorne Bay from where the floatplanes arrived and departed at the dock. The meters regulated utilities for the boats parked in the slips—*Thorne Bay, Alaska 2014.*

Evey (5) playing on the Thorne Bay dock wearing her Alaska tennis shoes and a "Kids Don't Float" life vest which she borrowed from the box at the top of the dock—*Thorne Bay, Alaska 2015.*

Me (48) and Becky Welton reminiscing about the old days with Elgin over lunch during Becky's last visit in September 2015. We were best friends for years. She retired to West Virginia in 2009—*Thorne Bay, Alaska 2015.*

The barge waiting for high tide before docking in Thorne Bay to unload supplies for Prince of Wales Island—*Thorne Bay, Alaska.*

Everett (27) riding his skiff from Thorne Bay across the bay to Southside Thorne Bay where he was building a house—*Prince of Wales Island, Alaska 2015.*

Moss grow on a Forest Service sign—*Prince of Wales Island, Alaska 2013.*

Me (48) decorating the Christmas tree with Auron (4)—*Thorne Bay, Alaska 2015.*

Erika taking her first Alaska bush flight in a de Havilland Beaver floatplane overlooking the Southside Thorne Bay—*Prince of Wales Island, Alaska 2015.*

Left: Shrimping with Joel & Deidre Jenson—*Thorne Bay, Alaska 2007.*
Right: Joy Weber standing with her quilt at the quilt show—*Craig, Alaska 2016.*

A float plane taxiing across the bay with an incoming barge being pulled by a tug boat during a snowstorm—*Thorne Bay, Alaska 2014.*

Me (48) taking a walk on the boardwalk at Eagle's Nest Campground in April. We took the boys, Sampson, and Josie here hundreds of times over the years—*Balls Lake, Prince of Wales Island, Alaska 2016.*

Evey (6) keeping Solomon in his place while she sits on a log—*Sandy Beach, Prince of Wales Island, Alaska 2016.*

Meliah (6), me (48), and Auron (4) posing after the kids finished their final visit with their great-grandmother (Patricia) in early May—*Thorne Bay, Alaska 2016.*

Me (48) and my mother, Patricia O'Flaherty (76), visiting Sandy Beach. I hopped up on a log to be taller than my mom in the photo which made us both laugh—*Sandy Beach, Prince of Wales Island, Alaska 2016.*

Elgin (50) strolling on Sandy Beach with Josie and Solomon until sunset on his last evening in Alaska—*Sandy Beach, Prince of Wales Island, 2016.*

Prince of Wales Island disappearing behind the low-lying clouds on our final ferry ride to Ketchikan—*Southeast, Alaska June 3, 2016.*

* Color versions of the photographs in this book can be found at www.MelissaCook.us.

THE TONGASS, YEARS 3–14

TONGASS NATIONAL FOREST
PRINCE OF WALES ISLAND

1997–2010

FORTY-FIVE

Unexpected Detours

"Welcome to Southeast Alaska, where residents grow fins!"
— Melissa L. Cook, 1997

We underwent drastic changes in 1997. Nelson Lagoon, a treeless spit covered in tall beach grass, withstood hurricane-force winds regularly. Eleven hundred miles away in the Tongass National Forest, trees surrounded us by the millions, *and I do mean millions*. We measured rain in feet, not inches. Prince of Wales Island was remote but not as isolated as Nelson Lagoon, so it seemed less lonely and somewhat easier to get to. Despite the constant rain and low clouds in both places, Bob Robertson had been right; sunny days were more prevalent.

Days before we were scheduled to leave Wyoming for Craig, Alaska, the Fairbanks principal was true to his word and called. Dang! Fairbanks had been at the top of our list. Integrity prevented us from reneging on our contracts with Craig City School District. The principal contacted us again the next summer with the same timing and result.

We received another call that caught us by surprise. "We have canceled your ferry reservation. Please contact the Alaska Marine Highway for further details," the recorded message stated. The drive to meet the Prince Rupert-to-Ketchikan ferry was sixteen hundred miles from Wyoming, and we expected to leave in two days.

"It may have something to do with the angry fishermen in Canada I saw on the news," my father-in-law, Kenny, commented.

I immediately contacted the ferry office in Juneau. "We can reschedule your trip out of Bellingham, Washington. You will arrive in Ketchikan on the originally scheduled date," the representative offered. The change meant we would ride the ferry for thirty-six hours through the Inside Passage at no additional charge. Who could be upset about that?

We arrived in Washington with a fully loaded Bronco for our first ferry ride to Alaska. It would be the only time we sailed through Bellingham. Each summer and several winter breaks we repeated the four-day trip from Alaska to Wyoming through Prince Rupert, British Columbia. We can only guess that we drove this route at least twenty-two times round trip.

"We have three hours until we sail. I hope they let us board early," I wished aloud. No such luck. The ship arrived an hour before our departure.

The ferry system required a three-hour early check-in with the risk of losing a reservation for late arrivals. It could be days until the next ferry, so we always arrived as instructed. That meant a long wait sitting in a cramped vehicle with cranky, restless kids eager to escape. We watched people walk their dogs, chatted with other travelers, slept, and read. People arrived by truck, car, motor home, motorcycle, bicycle, and on foot.

Finally, the ship began loading. Vehicles drove onto the ferry through an open doorway and parked in rows on the bottom deck. We piled out of the Bronco with blankets, pillows, and three ready boys. The sound of vehicles boarding the vessel echoed through the parking area. An enclosed metal stairway led to a long hallway of cabin doors. Filled with excitement at being on our first ship, we checked in at the purser's desk and unloaded our bags into the tight cabin. The room had a bunk bed and a tiny bathroom with a shower. It was time to explore the ship.

All ten ferries in the system sported names of Alaska glaciers. This ship was the *Malaspina*. A month earlier, the Canadian fishermen had blocked this boat in Prince Rupert for three days to protest overfishing in the area. A framed article hung on the wall explaining the event. The Alaska Marine Highway canceled sailings into Canada for the rest of the year as a result of the incident.

Passengers crowded onto the main deck. They staked out corners, reserved benches, loaded chairs with sleeping bags, luggage, and personal items, and then headed outside or to the cafeteria. Heat lamps hung above lounge chairs in the solarium for those sleeping outside. Tents taped to the deck flapped in the wind. We stood outdoors to enjoy the warmth of the Washington air and watched the city turn into wilderness along the shoreline as we proceeded north to Alaska.

At the rear of the ferry, we found the cafeteria. The short dinner line tempted us into eating early. We watched the incredible beauty of the Inside Passage passing by the large dining room windows while we ate.

Our exploration wasn't over yet. We moseyed single file through the narrow passageways from one end of the boat to the other. We changed floors and walked back again, repeatedly. As the ship rocked in the waves, our bodies gravitated from one side of the hall to the other. We giggled as the floor moved sideways under our feet while the ship rolled slightly back and forth in the waves.

We found a bar near the cafeteria and a movie theater on a lower deck. The ship offered a fantastic viewing room with tables scattered around for passengers to play cards or work on puzzles. The Forest Service displayed a schedule of guest speakers by the door. Others watched for wildlife through binoculars or read while taking a peek at the scenery now and then. A map pinned to the wall showed the routes of the Alaska Marine Highway. The ferry system stretched from Bellingham, Washington, to Dutch Harbor, Alaska, connecting thirty-five communities along thirty-five hundred miles of waterway.

Seasickness in the middle of the night prevented me from sleeping in the hot, stuffy cabin while sailing through Queen Charlotte Sound. Leaving my sleeping family, I slipped outside to cool down. The moon reflected off the ocean water and illuminated the shoreline. Waves washed into the ship, creating a constant background noise of moving, splashing water. In its wake, the vessel left behind a white, frothy trough in the ocean. The peacefulness filled my soul with excitement for our new home and teaching positions in Alaska.

We arrived in Ketchikan in time to have one last McDonald's breakfast. Afterward, Elgin and the boys perused the stores while I shopped for last-minute groceries. Outside, cruise ships passed by the mall, docked downtown, and let off thousands of tourists.

Stuffing groceries into every nook and cranny of the already packed Bronco, Elgin complained, "Why did you buy so much food with so little room left?"

"We need to prepare for the grocery store not being well-stocked in Craig," I defended my large purchase. With plenty of bush store experience, I knew it could be slim pickings. I was wrong. The Thompson House Supermarket in Craig and Klawock Market had an ample supply of food, but I didn't know that then, and I wouldn't call them supermarkets by any stretch of the imagination.

At that moment, seven-year-old Ethan stuck a long pin into a straw and pretended to be the jungle boy with a blow gun from the latest Tim Allen movie, *Jungle 2 Jungle*. Instead of shooting the long straight pin out of the straw at the front passenger seat, he sucked it in instead. We spent the rest of the day in the hospital, waiting for him to recover from emergency surgery. To our relief, Ethan was okay, and we were able to catch the afternoon *Aurora* ferry to Prince of Wales Island despite the unexpected detour.

We ferried for three hours and drove forty-five minutes down a bumpy, winding road from Hollis to Craig. Arriving at 7:30 in the evening, we had an hour and a half until dark, which gave us a chance to check out the town. We found the two-story house where we were renting the second floor for a jaw-dropping $1,200 per month—$800 more in rent than we had ever paid. It had an unobstructed view of the bay, mountains, and boat harbor. Eagles and seagulls blanketed the trees and beach directly across the narrow street.

"Welcome." Shane Westfall showed us to the door. "Remember when I warned that you were moving to the bush?"

"Bush? There is a grocery store here!" I replied with a smile.

A fishing village near Klawock Inlet on the Pacific Ocean, Craig was a traditional summer herring fish camp for the Tlingit people. With a population of 1,350 people in 1997, it felt like we had moved to the city. Though not nearly as far out as Nelson Lagoon, traveling to the isolated community proved difficult, time-consuming, and costly. The small town had no movie theaters, grand shopping malls, or traffic lights. Still, Craig had a couple of restaurants and limited shopping, so who was complaining? Not us. Okay, maybe it was a *bit* rainy and excessively windy, but the eagles camped on the nearby beach by the dozens made up for it.

FORTY-SIX

Function Over Fashion

Waiting in line at the bank in Craig, a rough-looking character around forty years old caught my attention, and I couldn't help staring at him from head to toe. His clothing shocked me, beginning with his hat. It was tan, stiff, leathery, somewhat dirty with a wide brim, and tied securely under his chin.

The heavy coat he wore was ripped, stained, and leather-like, while underneath, suspenders wrapped over a blue and white, narrow striped hickory work shirt. His grease-spotted pants with a wedge in the pocket appeared to be in worse shape, with the bottom seams missing and denim fraying above his ankles. I stood there, unable to take my eyes off him, and wondered if his pants could stand on their own.

Where had my life taken me? I wondered. The rain forest weather demanded waterproof, quick-drying clothing. It did not take long to realize my fine clothing would not cut it here. *Function over fashion* was how some explained it. In the future, I bet a newbie stared at me while standing in line and wondered what on Earth they had gotten themselves into by moving to Alaska. Okay, so I wasn't a logger, but I was Alaskan, and years later, I looked like it.

As for the man in the bank, he was a logger. The first logger I had ever seen in my life. A typical Tongass logger's day meant being awake before dawn to arrive at the current cut location by sunrise. He returned home for a late supper before being the first in bed. Most loggers valued hard work, discipline, fairness, and family. Their clothing was the epitome of function over fashion; safety and weatherproofing came first. Loggers were thirty times more likely to die on the job than you or me, a small mishap could end with a devastating crush injury from a tree. Donation cans for fallen or injured loggers sat at the end of the grocery store checkout line. Routine charity dinners paid medical and travel expenses for injured loggers and their families. A few of my students lived with fathers addicted to pain pills or worse, with the memory of a father who passed away from a logging accident.

I grew to admire the loggers themselves and their clothing's unique aspects that kept them safe, dry, and warm. The leathery, stiff hat with the wide rim was wax treated to keep a person's head dry in the rainforest. Wind, rain, and the physical requirements of the job made a secured hat and wax-coated clothing essential in an area with more than one hundred inches of rain a year. And those frayed pant legs? They were deliberate to save lives.

"When I buy new pants, the first thing I do is cut off the seams on the end of each leg. That begins the fraying process. It's all about safety. Trees don't always fall where we expect them to so I need my pants to rip if they catch on the underbrush. We don't call falling branches *widow makers* for nothing! It's dangerous in the woods. I also have spiked cork boots to stop me from slipping on wet logs," retired logger Harvey McDonald explained. He stood before me still dressed like a logger heading to work.

And the dirtiness? They could at least wash their clothes, right? Actually, no. "Waxed clothing can't go through the laundry without washing out the wax," Harvey told me. The worn aspect was proof of the job's difficulty, not the wealth of the individual.

Logging was the primary income for many families on Prince of Wales Island until the early 2000s. One of the world's largest logging camps was forty miles away in the town of Thorne Bay. When the Tongass National Forest timber industry shut down, these families struggled for years before moving to search for work. The island changed. The Forest Service blocked off hundreds of miles of old logging roads, allowing foot-only access to sportsmen, outdoorsmen, tourists, and others.

Logging trucks still rumble down the island roads, harvesting the Native and private lands with the help of a handful of old loggers. That said, the logger heydays were ending about the time we arrived on the island. The nearby Thorne Bay mess hall still served three meals a day until around 2000. Much like the rest of the old logging town, the mess hall eventually came down to make room for a new home.

FORTY-SEVEN

One Tough Year in Craig

On August 31, 1997, we awoke to the shocking news of Princess Diana's death. Charitable, beautiful, and now gone. Glued to the captivating story, I prepared a picnic lunch for our first outing on Prince of Wales Island. We planned to explore over by Thorne Bay.

"Time to go." Elgin corralled the boys out the door for a trip to Sandy Beach, forty-six miles away.

The peaceful, sunny day turned into a delightful break from the ever-constant wind and rain. The stench of rotting fish infiltrated the Bronco whenever the rugged road drove close to a stream. The wide-open beach, sandy as promised by its name, presented a grand view of Clarence Strait. Dead, smelly salmon dotted the beach where Slide Creek drained into the strait.

On the way home, we stopped at Eagle's Nest, a campground with a boardwalk along the edge of Balls Lake. Control Lake drained into Balls Lake by way of salmon-rich Control Creek. The boys played in the creek water—a big no-no as we later learned. Each step crushed the tiny salmon eggs into the rocks below their feet.

Lack of rain caused low water levels, which created large puddles in the creek bed. Nine-year-old Everett cornered a salmon in a pool and caught it with his bare hands—also a no-no. He proudly hung onto the feisty fish while I snapped a photo. We insisted he release the fish despite his disappointment. Having no fishing license or gear meant he ate no salmon for dinner, even if he had caught it with his bare hands.

Bob and Neva Robertson, who once lived in King Cove, in the Aleutians, now lived in a Native village an hour away. Many weekends, we watched movies and planned out our futures together. Their children, Eric and Stewart, became close friends with our boys, and they were all eager to play. Cold, windy days often accompanied by sideways blowing rain meant indoor visits. However, beachcombing across the street was a rare treat on the occasional beautiful afternoons.

It was a dream working with most of the staff at Craig City Schools. What a team!

"What are you doing after school? I'm going out to check shrimp pots in my boat. You can bring the boys and come along," fellow teacher Brian Castle offered. The chilly wind caused me to shiver when our families headed out that afternoon. The fishing vessel tossed in the waves while Brian winched in the large pots one-by-one. He dumped the shrimp out into a bucket and then tossed bait into the pots before dropping them back to the ocean floor. Brian showed the kids how to behead the shrimp while his wife, Ellen Hannan, waited to drop them into boiling water in the boat's kitchen. Preparing the squirming critters for dinner tickled the boys.

Principal Doug Rhodes also took us out boating and fishing. On one trip, Doug shared a memorable story. "Twenty years ago, I dropped a net and sat back to read a suspense novel. Out of nowhere, a whale breached the water next to me and jumped clear over my skiff! It scared me so badly, I threw the book overboard and never got to finish it."

We roasted marshmallows over a beach campfire surrounded by fun-loving teachers and their families. We took our kids sledding on snowy days while building friendships with coworkers that would last for decades. They became our family away from home.

Despite supportive coworkers, the Craig Middle School teaching assignment was close to unbearable. An angry boy assaulted me in the hall. A few obnoxious kids and their parents harassed me on the street and in the grocery store. A group of students took part in a year-long contest to see who earned the most office referrals. Kids bragged about running off all the new teachers while a bunch of kids surrounded the superintendent on the street and soaked her with mega squirt guns. I had sympathy for the good kids stuck in these classes from hell. Fortunately for Craig, only a few groups of students were this bad over the years.

The ongoing classroom stress took a toll on my health. The neurologist had suspected MS a year ago based on my tingling finger. My symptom list grew substantially when we lived in Craig. Debilitating fatigue, burning in my arm, loss of sensation in my hands and face, and balance issues pointed to the looming official multiple sclerosis diagnosis. Pain in my left leg caused me to walk with a limp. I required an immediate change if I planned to continue working.

One night, I walked into the bedroom to see Elgin's face drop in horror, "*What happened to your face?*" His concern caused me to dash back to the bathroom. A hot washcloth had scorched my face and hands, turning them bright red. I hadn't noticed the temperature due to numbness.

Elgin, on the other hand, was making strides in the new technology era. The position of technology director emerged in the schools around the time he accepted the Craig job. It catapulted his career since his technology skills surpassed most others and those skills were about to land us a new home. Despite our recent effort to secure a stable place to raise our children, it was time to move on. An Apple trainer offered us both contracts to work for TRECA as technology coordinators, which meant a job transfer to Marion, Ohio.

The barge dropped a shipping container in our driveway in mid-May 1998. Bob and Neva Robertson were also on the move. Bob hired on as the superintendent of Klawock City Schools, six miles away, while Neva secured my difficult job in Craig.

With a week remaining in the school year, Everett had a medical emergency that turned our world upside down. He had returned from an overnight school camping trip covered in bruises. His leaking blood vessels caused severe bruising all over his small body. The doctor immediately separated us from our son to determine if we had nearly beaten him to death. Once we were cleared of child abuse charges, the doctor suspected ITP—a blood platelet disorder. He withheld his worst fear of cancer until the treatment for ITP had a chance to work. The doctor ordered a medevac for Everett to the Ketchikan Hospital where he was admitted to ICU. At the same time, Principal Doug Rhodes had planned to take Elgin on his fishing boat to Suemez Island to hunt for one of the trophy black bears dotting the islands of Southeast Alaska.

"There is nothing you can do for Everett. He will be okay. The doctor said ICU is solely a precaution, and I can update you on any changes by satellite phone from the hospital to the boat. The Westfalls offered to watch Sutton and Ethan." I encouraged Elgin to go on his trip, which reluctantly he did. In the end, Elgin brought home a bear, and Everett went on to fully recover over the summer.

On our last day in Craig, we made one final dump run. A friendly man at the gate informed us, "You'll be back within a year. People always say they're not coming back, but they inevitably return." Elgin assured him we were not coming back, but he was wrong.

The next day, we boarded the ferry heading south to Prince Rupert, British Columbia, and then on to Ohio after only one school year in Craig. It didn't take long to realize leaving Alaska had been a mistake. As predicted, we were packing up and heading north again in a year. Alaska's teacher retirement was too generous to ignore. Educators in Ohio in their mid-sixties counted the years until retirement as opposed to their Alaska counterparts in their early forties. With my potential health issues, we had no choice.

FORTY-EIGHT

Growing Roots to the Bedrock

A year later, we rushed home from work in Ohio where we had been working as technologists in the ARCTIC program, training Alaska teachers in Ohio classrooms. Two Alaska school districts requested phone interviews before the annual job fair, which we had planned to attend in a couple of days. The first interview with Southeast Island School District (SISD), we considered a practice run for the second interview with Nome City Schools.

At the close of the second interview, Superintendent Stan Lujan offered us full-time positions, then said, "You have until six tonight to decide because we are leaving for the job fair in the morning."

Elgin thanked him as we looked at each other in disbelief. We planned to leave in the morning too. The request for interviews had been unexpected. *Ring. Ring.* Elgin answered.

"This is the superintendent of Southeast Island School District. We want to offer you the technology director position and hire Melissa as the high school technology, social studies, and language arts teacher." Elgin shot a surprised look in my direction. A second job offer, and we hadn't even left for the airport yet. Fortunately for us, we would not be taking part in a third meat market escapade at the 1999 job fair. I wonder how many copies of our 1999 CD circulated the conference room that year? We were no-shows, which probably didn't surprise many of the administrators.

We promptly put paper to pencil with little time to consider this impactful decision. Nome offered $10,000 more in salary than SISD. The cost of moving to and living in Nome was steep. We enjoyed working with the lighthearted ARCTIC intern, Robin Johnson, whom we suspected had a hand in our impromptu interview. My path had crossed Stan Lujan's a few times. He seemed friendly and competent. However, Prince of Wales Island's familiarity and the cheaper cost of living made SISD more attractive. Traveling by ferry was easier and less expensive, though not cheap by any means. What a tough decision. In the end, Nome was not to be. Though we had to grow fins to survive the continuous rainfall, the southeast's temperate weather outweighed the north's tundra despite their higher salary.

Disembarking on the *Aurora* ferry, we passed Maybeso Creek on Prince of Wales Island in August 1999. The view of steep, foggy mountains covered with endless trees filled the Bronco windows as we drove the familiar rough road. The pouring rain intensified as the windshield wipers frantically attempted to clear the downpour coming from the low-lying clouds. Condensation covered the windows inside, reminding us of our return to the humid, wet climate.

The drive across the familiar island to Thorne Bay took ninety minutes. A shipping container was waiting in our front yard. The six-year-old teacherage turned out to be a low-end eight hundred square foot modular home, barely furnished with a tiny backyard. The superintendent had kept her word, assigning us the school district's best housing. However, it was still a far cry from our beautiful suburban home in Ohio. We had been clear during our interview that we would leave if our family landed in dumpy housing—an actual possibility in bush Alaska. On the eleventh straight day of rainfall, we couldn't wait to unload the container any longer. What a mess it was—and wet, boy, was it ever wet! The rain drenched everyone and everything during the unloading.

We were here to stay. Our growing technological knowledge led to tempting, career-boosting job opportunities that knocked on our door each spring, but as our children grew older, we valued planting roots over career advancement. For the next seventeen years, those roots grew deep like an anchor, right down to the bedrock. Three out of four of our grandchildren would be born in the Ketchikan Hospital.

Thorne Bay, Alaska, a logging community nestled at the end of a bay, had mountains that rose from the ocean floor, shielding it from the worst of Clarence Strait's weather. Countless waterfalls streamed down the mountainsides. The Tongass National Forest covered the land with mammoth evergreen trees and a scarce sprinkling of red alder groves. Moss and black mold grew all over. Eagles, seagulls, and ravens squawked overhead. Boom boats pulled log rafts with fresh-cut timber through the water. Logs were brought to the sort yard at the end of the bay where loggers sorted and shipped out the lumber. The sound of boat motors and bush planes buzzed in the distance long before we saw them. Floatplane passengers watched for tiny, tree-covered islands and tattered float houses dotting the protected coastline. Logging roads zigged and zagged through the clear-cuts and forest regrowth. Wet and muddy streets with no sidewalks meant no courteous guest stepped past the front door without first removing their boots.

The lively dock hosted fishing vessels, houseboats, local floatplanes, mail planes, tiny cruise ships, and fishermen in rubber pants processing the day's catch. Float house residents docked their skiffs before climbing the ramp to their vehicles stored at the nearby parking lot. Sportsmen loaded coolers, waxed fish boxes, fancy rods, and gun cases into the courtesy four-wheeler cart at the top of the dock. Then, they descended to the water's edge to board the departing aircraft. Residents stopped to bail out their neighbor's skiffs to prevent the boats from sinking from the overflow of rainwater. The Forest Service housed seasonal workers in a floating apartment building anchored to a berth. Once a year the veterinarian arrived in a sailboat converted into a vet clinic to provide a three-day animal care clinic. There was always something happening on the dock.

Thorne Bay was once the largest logging camp in the world, with a standing record of fifteen hundred residents. When the logging industry closed in the early 2000s, the population dropped to 550. Over three years, the families who could move, did. The mass exodus affected the school, dropping the student count by half. At one point, the school district hired only two high school teachers for the town.

We would witness Thorne Bay change from an old logging camp to a poverty-stricken town over the years. Businesses closed, including the only restaurant. The community and island grew cluttered with abandoned, rusty vehicles. Trash of various types piled up everywhere. The city generator caused daily electrical brown and blackouts putting electrical appliances and computers at risk of damage. Dogs had the run of the town, and at night they competed with black bears over trash cans. Bears hauled trash bags down the street, whereas the dogs made a colossal mess in your yard. The furious wind took off with the trash cans, too, though the neighbors usually returned them after the storms.

In time, Thorne Bay somewhat rebounded. The town paved its roads, doing away with the mud and potholes. A few sidewalks went in on a couple of main streets too. The state spent years rebuilding and paving the rough shot-rock road from Klawock to Thorne Bay, cutting the drive from seventy-five to forty minutes. A new grocery store attracted people from around Prince of Wales Island. The community planted deciduous trees, tore down old buildings, hauled off the trash, and built new housing. Nick Higson accepted the principal position in Thorne Bay where he left his fingerprint on the community by leading students in multiple beautification projects just as he had done in multiple other communities within the school district over the years. In the summer, tourists arrived by modest cruise ships to stroll the streets and witness how the *real Alaskans* lived.

The Thorne Bay I will always remember had a cargo trailer, four-wheeler, or boat parked in most driveways. At least one dog peeked through each vehicle window. We had two. Four-wheelers roared down the roads with older students heading to and from school or to the dock. Young hunters trekked through the streets with rifles slung over their shoulders, and there was a different stranger in town daily, many afoot.

The people of the Last Frontier were fascinating. The land or maybe the laid-back culture seemed to call the dreamers, fortune and adventure seekers, people hiding with skeletons in their closets, and those hoping for a second chance. Tent dwellers, Russian brides, pot smokers, criminals, and children with no homes and sometimes no parents mixed in among those with teaching certificates, fishing permits, Forest Service workers, family lumber mill owners, and others. We were all in it together. It didn't matter where you came from or who you were; when you needed a neighbor, they were often there for you.

FORTY-NINE

Crashes of Every Kind

"Do you plan to fly into Port Alexander today?" I asked Elgin one morning. Residents of this unique community flew in on a floatplane or arrived by boat. Boardwalks linked the town buildings and dock. Four-wheelers rumbled by transporting loads of supplies and mail from floatplanes.

"I'm flying into Port Alexander and Port Protection if we can land at both," Elgin replied, looking out his window at the weather. As the technology director, he spent time at each school, including the other fly-in sites of Hyder, Edna Bay, and J.R. Gildersleeve. Flying was better than the alternative of spending half the day driving, which he did when he went to the schools on the road system—Coffman Cove, Naukati, Hollis, Kasaan, and Whale Pass. Technology repairs began with a phone call to the lead teacher. Teachers raved about Elgin's ability to troubleshoot by phone.

"I hate it when you fly in terrible weather. Last time you had to land in a mountain lake to wait out a storm. What if that lake hadn't been there?" I complained. On a typical day, we could expect low clouds, rain, and wind.

"JJ is always careful," he attempted to reassure me as we pulled out of the driveway, rain pitter-pattering on the roof of our Bronco. School pilot Jim Jakubek flew staff to school sites and kids and teachers in for events in his de Havilland Beaver floatplane. Not all pilots flew safely, but JJ was excellent.

Like it or not, flying was a way of life. Tell the special education teacher that, because she was not too happy one day after school.

"I was told to travel to the remote sites this week, but the fog made it impossible for the pilot to land in Thorne Bay. So, the principal told me to put on a survival suit and then the maintenance guy drove me out to Sandy Beach. I had to wade out to the floatplane in the cold water!"

I was not there and didn't see it, but I did believe it. Her story made me wonder what the heck was wrong with our administrators. The teacher was close to retirement, and that water was cold. SISD administrators had a sorry reputation for running off teachers, but this pathetic maneuver was over the top. They required no one else to wade out into the ocean to board a seaplane during our tenure.

Speaking of flying, one day I spotted the annual plane ticket ad in the newspaper. "Promech Air has a dividend special of ten tickets for $750!" I read the *Island News* aloud. Each year, the State of Alaska gave residents a dividend based on invested money from the oil heydays of the 1980s. Businesses offered sale prices in early October when the dividends arrived in our bank accounts. The Promech sale was a godsend. The cost of thirteen-year-old Sutton's braces in bush Alaska included purchasing plane tickets to Ketchikan monthly for his appointments.

"How can you send Sutton on a bush plane into the city alone?" my mother scolded me on the phone. As a teenager in the mid-1980s, I rode two buses by myself to orthodontist appointments in Tucson, a city of four hundred thousand. Ketchikan had eight thousand residents in the early 2000s. Sutton counted down the days each month. Going to town meant flying in a floatplane, eating at McDonald's, shopping at the mall, and spending the weekend with friends when he scheduled a Monday or Friday appointment.

"What if his plane crashes?" my mother worried. She had a point; pilots quit more often than teachers. And it wasn't just planes that crashed, helicopters wrecked too.

One unbelievable but true story of three helicopters crashing took place in September 1999. Flying tourists to the Juneau Ice Field, a pilot lost the ability to see in flat light conditions. Snow flurries prevented the pilot from seeing the ground, causing him to crash into the ice field. This overdue flight resulted in a second helicopter heading out to the fifteen hundred square mile ice field on a search and rescue mission. The emergency locator transmitter (or ELT) signal from the first aircraft did not transmit. The pilot used a mountain as a reference, but a brief whiteout caused him to crash into the glacier too. Juneau's control tower sent a third helicopter to search for the two missing flights. Recognizing the flat light danger, the pilot waited and refueled at the airport. Improved conditions allowed him to find the second wreckage site where he retrieved two accident victims. Together they flew on to search for the first wreckage. Suddenly, flat light and snowfall engulfed the area, resulting in the third helicopter crash of the day—a second wreck for two of the passengers. Search and rescue headed out on foot, spending the night with the victims until their rescue the next morning. Incredibly, no one died.

Around the same time, the school maintenance man died after leaving a local lodge in his floatplane. He crashed into the mountainside outside of Thorne Bay. Another daredevil coworker wrecked his plane when attempting an emergency landing on a riverbed. It was his second wreck. He survived both crashes, retired his flight logbook, and grounded himself in the name of self-preservation.

During our time in Alaska, the state averaged 112 plane crashes per year. Each year, the Prince of Wales Island and Ketchikan area averaged three wrecks resulting in at least one fatality. Some years were worse than others. In 1978, a dozen people perished in one wreck at Labouchere Bay on Prince of Wales Island. The plane crashed in deep water, preventing investigators from determining the cause. Islanders honored the victims by naming nearby Memorial Beach in their memory.

Concerns about our bush flying extended beyond our family and friends. "We can add life insurance to your house loan for a small price," Betty Webber, our Wyoming banker, offered. I shot her a confused look. "Your chances of dying in Alaska are significantly higher than here, especially with all the bush flying you do." She wasn't lying either.

Bush pilots landed on rough seas, glaciers, dry riverbeds, isolated gravel strips, and frozen lakes. To accomplish these landings, they equipped the planes with beach tires or pontoons.

Planes ran out of fuel or suffered mechanical failure. Improper modifications to aircraft and weight distribution issues also brought down planes. Pilots became disoriented or made poor decisions and outright errors. The weather closed in or changed on a dime and was a significant factor in most crashes. Aircraft collided mid-air in the crowded summer skies. The hard fact was some pilots and passengers were lost to the sea or terrain forever when their planes could not be found.

You can bet I thought about these things when it came time for me to travel because I had flown with my share of idiot pilots. Although sometimes I was the dim-witted one. I once told a new staff member, "Just because they're flying doesn't mean you have to get on the plane." A month later, I stood on the Ketchikan airport dock during an impressive storm. I heard my own words ringing in my ears as I managed to climb into a fiercely rocking seaplane. I desperately wanted to get home and sleep in my own bed. So much for my own advice!

Alaska Tennis Shoe

Someone snapped a photo of Elgin and me at the job fair in 1995 when we first arrived in Alaska. It revealed the younger version of ourselves—pre-Alaskans. Elgin wore a suit and tie and I a Sunday dress. We looked nothing like the typical rural Alaskans we became. It was just as well since there was no dry cleaning available where we were headed. Minutes following the photograph, Bob Robertson instructed us to leave the suit and dress behind.

Coworker Deanna Claus helped us change our attire in 1997. "You'll never get warm until you buy fleece. It dries quickly and keeps you warm." The dwellers of the rainforest used fleece as the main staple of their wardrobe. Fleece undercoats and jackets, fleece sweatshirts, pants with fleece lining, even fleece pajamas. It filled our drawers and closet space because it took the bite out of the cold, but I was seldom warm, no matter what time of year.

We adopted rain gear after becoming sick of being soaked to the bone in our Wyoming winter coats. A water-resistant jacket wasn't enough, and rain gear seemed to be the only proper waterproof material. Each year, I purchased an insulated rain jacket for twenty-five dollars. It required a second layer of fleece inside during the winter months but was ideal for fall and spring. Freezing temperatures caused the coat to crack first along the seams closest to my hands. The sides and front split from one too many winter layers beneath. By spring, duct tape kept the rain out. It wasn't fashionable, but it was practical, and I was dry. I will admit, wearing the tattered jacket anywhere outside of rural Alaska embarrassed me.

We purchased Xtratuf boots, referred to by Alaskans as the *Alaska tennis shoe*. The chocolate brown waterproof boot with tan rimmed sole was the typical Alaskan footwear. Many students wore these Alaska tennis shoes year-round. My grandchildren's first shoes would be Xtratufs.

Becoming an Alaskan did not happen the minute we drove across the state line. It was a process. The change began with our arrival, then the clothing on our backs, and, ultimately our mindset. I realized my transformation in the Seattle airport.

Passing eastbound SeaTac gates, I noticed the leather coats and quality clothing of my youth worn by the people awaiting their flights. Years earlier I had arrived in Alaska wearing the same clothing. I walked a little slower to savor the memory of such fine clothes.

When I arrived at the gates for flights north to Alaska, I felt relief—almost as if I was already home. Passengers at these gates were laden with the maximum luggage allowed and dressed in fleece and rain gear. Some toted backpacks filled with a supply of favorite foods unavailable in Alaska's isolated towns and villages. Here, I was not ashamed of my Alaska tennis shoes or the less than stellar raincoat I sported. These travelers understood and looked just like me.

I flew into Seattle no less than twice a year to manage neurological symptoms brought on by MS. In 1996, a Montana neurologist informed me there was nothing he could do and said to schedule an appointment if I had more symptoms. It took four years for that day to arrive.

The alarm rudely awoke us one cold October morning. I rolled back over and snuggled the warm covers where Elgin had recently been sleeping. "You'd better wake up, or we will be late," he warned.

Stretching, I opened my eyes to greet the day. Rubbing them, I sat up. Something wasn't right. Focusing on the mirror in front of me, I knew I was in trouble; I was almost blind.

"Elgin! I can't see!" I hollered over the shower from the bedroom.

"What?" He wasn't sure he had heard me correctly. Drying off with a towel, he entered the bedroom to confirm, "What do you mean you can't see?"

Alarmed, I stood there in my pajamas. "My vision is blurry, especially in my left eye, and when I move it, there's sharp pain." I had noticed flashing lights in the days before, though I thought a migraine was coming on.

"I need to fly into Ketchikan," I controlled my panic.

"You had better hurry. The first flight leaves in fifteen minutes." Elgin called Taquan Air to schedule a last-minute reservation on the morning mail plane. Next, he dialed the optometrist and handed me the phone. I left a message saying I woke up blind and was catching the seven o'clock flight to Ketchikan, hoping they had time to squeeze me in.

Fifteen minutes later, I heard the buzz of a landing floatplane and then the idling as it taxied in the bay toward the dock. Elgin helped me down the ramp to the plane, where he told the pilot about the vision issues I was having. He and the pilot helped me climb the steep, wet plane steps. Not much to see on the flight—not that I cared. I think I must have been in shock.

"Please have a cab at the dock when we land," the pilot requested over the radio. "I'll help you climb the ramp to the cab outside the office," he sympathized with me.

The cab driver guided me into the eye clinic. Standing at the counter, I apologized for the wordy phone message. "No problem. Dr. Swearingen has cleared his morning schedule for you. He'll be right out."

It took half a day of tests before the doctor concluded, "Optic neuritis, probably multiple sclerosis. You should see a neurologist." I struggled with vision issues from October until June, when I traveled south for the summer. In the meantime, I altered my instruction to include as many learning activities as possible. The blurry vision made it difficult to grade stacks of papers.

My final diagnosis of multiple sclerosis came in June 2001. Five years had now passed since my last neurologist appointment; it was time to learn what options the doctors had available to help. It floored me to discover that one round of oral steroids put me back on track, somewhat.

I learned a valuable lesson. Do not suffer from MS when medications can ease the symptoms. My vision took years to fully recover; however, to this day, blurry vision flares at the slightest hint of fatigue, heat, or stress.

Humorous moments arose when teaching with MS, though. The next fall, a new fifth-grade student arrived at the door of my fourth-seventh-grade classroom. Periodically, stress and fatigue caused language and vertigo symptoms affecting my interaction with students. They knew of my issues, what to expect, and how to help when necessary. I pulled up a chair to share this information with the new boy.

"I could tell you are sick," he responded when I finished.

"You could?" I inquired in wonder. I was okay that morning; he shouldn't have noticed. "How did you know?"

"I can see it in your hands!" I looked at my colorful stained hands. The class had tie-dyed T-shirts the previous day. I smiled with a giggle inside.

FIFTY-ONE

Loonies and Toonies

By the summer of 2001, we had formed a routine. When school let out in early June, we headed to Prince Rupert by ferry in a packed Bronco, pulling an empty cargo trailer. *Wow, it's shocking how long it takes to get to the highway—two days by water!* I documented. From there, we drove three long days through Canada and Montana to Wyoming.

Our first fast food meal in ten months meant driving through Taco Bell for Ethan and me, Wendy's for Everett and Sutton, and KFC for Elgin. Once in Wyoming, we rented a two-bedroom apartment from Northwest College for two months. Then we feasted on all the activities, stores, restaurants, appointments, and people we had missed. We knew the famine was returning in mid-August. We left each summer in debt and worked the entire next school year to pay it off. Then we did it all over again the next summer.

Tom Ryan, our first superintendent, warned us, "We spent so much money leaving for breaks! I could have bought a house with it. Stay in Alaska during the holidays and summer to retire with a fortune in the bank." His advice fell on deaf ears. Breaks kept our sanity. We had to leave in order to stay.

"Where do you live?" the Canadian border patrol asked when we reached the Alberta border on our way back to Alaska. He accepted our driver's licenses and birth certificates while glancing at the Bronco and white cargo trailer. Every border agent questioned us but never searched the trailer filled with a year's supply of non-perishable food and items we had stockpiled during our summer shopping sprees.

"Thorne Bay, Alaska. We are teachers and spend our summers in Wyoming." Another glance through the paperwork, and the border agent handed it back.

I searched the glove box for the Canadian money bag with one-dollar loonies, two-dollar toonies, and a handful of colorful bills. We would not be using the American money bag for a few days, so I stuffed it into the glovebox. Two weeks before each trip, I contacted the bank to order Canadian cash. The exchange rate was in our favor at first. One Canadian dollar cost sixty-eight cents in American money. We felt like we had hit the jackpot driving through Canada back then. By 2016, the exchange rate was $1.08 American for one Canadian dollar and we couldn't get through Canada fast enough!

"Remember, 110 kilometers is sixty-eight mph," I reminded Elgin as we gained speed on the highway. We adjusted to Canadian money, kilometers for speed and distance, and gas dispensed by liters, not gallons. It made for some fancy figuring to determine the best price per gallon in American money.

The boys played their Game Boys while Elgin drove most of the way, first through the fields of southern Alberta, then skirting Calgary. Onward we went through Banff and Jasper National Parks. The road turned lonely in British Columbia. Every town and wide spot in the road had a golf course, while bathrooms became outhouses of varying conditions along the roadside. We quickly learned which ones to bypass.

On day three, thick cloud cover overtook the blue skies near Terrace, and the rain began. To pass the time, I read a book aloud to Elgin, or we planned for retirement. Okay, so we were not retiring for a long time, but we kept our eye on the goal.

Arriving in Prince Rupert, British Columbia, three hours early for the Alaska Marine Highway ferry to Ketchikan meant sitting in a crowded car while going nowhere at the end of a lengthy drive. Mostly, we slept, read books, and watched people walk their dogs while struggling to find a comfortable position in the car seat.

Many teachers returned home during the summers and arrived at the same time to catch the last available ferry before teacher in-service in August. To kill time, the Prince of Wales Island teachers stood outside chatting beside our vehicles filled with supplies. In August, teachers discussed the new school year and inevitable changes in staff or policies while waiting in line at the ferry. In June, we often found ourselves saying goodbye to those moving on, listening to their stories of adventure and, at times, defeat.

On August 19, 2001, we drove off the ferry into Ketchikan. "Happy birthday, Everett! You're officially a teenager." Everett never celebrated his birthday on the nineteenth because we were always, and I do mean always, on the road to Alaska. So, we celebrated his birthday with Sutton's on the third with family in Wyoming.

"Thanks, Mom." Sandwiched between his brothers in the backseat of the Bronco, Everett opened the envelope. Ethan and Sutton fought for window seats, while Everett always agreed to sit in the middle to stop their bickering. After that trip up the highway, we decided to upgrade the Bronco to an Expedition giving each of the boys their own window. They were growing up and needed more space on the lengthy drives going home to Wyoming.

We had three hours in Ketchikan before arriving at the terminal to catch a second ferry to the island. Vehicles of all sorts sat bumper-to-bumper in four lanes. During the long wait, I became bored. Seagulls hopped on the ground, searching for a snack left behind by travelers. They were everywhere searching for a free meal. I reached into a Cheerio box and withdrew a handful of cereal. Elgin noticed but not quick enough.

"Don't do it!" he warned. My hand darted out the window, releasing the Cheerios. I giggled when the nearby birds flew toward us. My smile turned to horror when seagulls from the surrounding area spotted their friends on the move. Birds swarmed us, and the rest of the vehicles waiting in line. They landed, covering the Bronco's hood and roof. They even glanced in the front window while more flew in from a distance. *Click, click, click.* The sound of their claws upset Elgin.

"They will scratch the paint!" What could we do? *Nothing!* Absolutely nothing. Other vehicles blocked us in and those occupants were none too happy with me, given seagulls searched for the elusive Cheerios by clicking around on their paint jobs too. "I can't believe you did that!" Elgin scolded me. Holy cow! I never did that again. I wanted to, but I couldn't get away with it twice.

Once on the ferry, each of us wrote a letter, rolled it up, and stuck it in a glass bottle. We mixed the bottles up and pocketed one for a keepsake. Then our family stood on the deck in the rolling waves and tossed the rest overboard.

It was late in the evening when we rolled off the *Aurora* ferry onto the island, commonly referred to as "The Rock" by its residents. Drizzling rain accompanied fog that settled in patches around the mountains. The smell of evergreen trees by the millions mingled with the odor of mold and ocean water. A long line of cars from the ferry drove the curvy road home at forty to fifty mph. Few passing zones existed on the highway, meaning the first vehicle off the ship set the pace to Klawock. The shot-rock island roads beyond Klawock required heavy-duty 10-ply tires to prevent flats, but they were loud, especially when wet.

We pulled into our driveway at midnight. The chilly house felt empty and humid when we arrived. We dragged ourselves in the door and dropped into bed. Teacher in-service began at eight in the morning, so we waited to fully unload the Bronco and cargo trailer until the next afternoon.

The following evening, we stacked boxes beside kitchen cabinets, in the utility room, under beds, in the closets, and hallway. Anywhere a box fit, we stashed it. Stacked boxes of canned food in August dwindled as the year progressed, giving us some breathing space by spring in the eight hundred square foot home.

Five days of teacher in-service exhausted us. Each evening we unpacked, made a trip to the beach, or drove seventy-five minutes on rough, unpaved, rocky roads into Klawock or Craig for groceries. We passed tea-colored creeks and streams, rock cliffs with waterfalls streaming down, and an occasional meadow on the drive. Being the first to spot the downed WWII plane by the water's edge provided our entertainment until trees grew up blocking the view. We even hiked to the plane once and signed our names along with other past visitors.

We seldom had a cracked windshield from a rock flipped by a passing car. The first bug to hit the windshield surprised us somewhere in Canada on our way to Wyoming each summer. Much like Nelson Lagoon, from mid-August to June, Southeast Alaska had few flying insects aside from the gnat-like no-see-ums. The creepy, big spiders in their enormous webs spanning between trees and our house or vehicle, more than made up for the lack of other bugs though.

Heading back to school in 2001, the school district had a surprise in store for us. They hired a couple of recent college graduates as the only teachers for the high school. These new hires held provisional licenses, having not taken classes in a teaching program before entering the classroom. As a high school teacher, they reassigned me to the elementary fourth-seventh-grade classroom. To make matters worse, the district threw out the traditional instructional model and adopted an extreme form of standards-based education that was difficult and time-consuming to implement. The twenty-six teachers from ten schools in the district developed the curriculum in their spare time. Also, the instructional model discouraged the daily use of textbooks. Lesson planning and record-keeping for this system in a multi-graded classroom became insane.

At the same time, the neurologist prescribed an injectable medication to control my MS. The 18-gauge *horse* needle caused severe anxiety for this needle-phobic patient. I opted for the thinner 25-gauge needle, but that meant the shot took longer to give, and the medication was extremely painful. It took the entire weekend and forty to fifty ibuprofen pills to recover from the debilitating side effects. Sutton helped out by taking over the laundry duties every weekend. I pulled myself out of bed each morning, regardless of what MS said about it. In a couple of years, my prescription changed to a daily shot with fewer side effects, and I'm proud to say I learned to give it to myself.

One day on our way into the school, a high school teacher stepped out of his classroom as we passed by in the hall. "Terrorists have killed fifty thousand people in the World Trade Center in New York! They flew planes with passengers into the buildings, and those have collapsed!" He wrung his hands and fought back tears. The date was September 11, 2001, known now as 9/11.

Elgin and I darted shocked looks at one another. We consoled the young teacher for a moment as he filled us in on the current reports. When I reached my desk, I searched the news on the internet and to my horror saw images of planes flying into buildings as my students walked into the classroom. The high school student body of twenty or so students gathered at the lead teacher's house to watch the news for the remainder of the school day. The rest of us waited until after school to see the coverage. It was a relief to learn the missing and dead numbered in the low thousands instead of tens of thousands, though the tragedy was still immense.

My bulletin boards transformed with the rest of our country into red, white, and blue with multiple flags hanging around the room. As a nation, we stood together and mourned our dead.

FIFTY-TWO

Bear Fear

After the folks in Nelson Lagoon shared their bear stories, I developed a bear fear, though I refused to allow it to control my life. It was thrilling to see a bear, but not everyone shared my opinion. One teacher did not even stay to begin the school year before he packed up his family and left. "Bear prints are everywhere, even on our porch in the morning. I quit! This job is not worth losing one of my children." He wasn't the first, nor would he be the last teacher to leave in the middle of the night.

Wild imaginations, stories of horrific attacks from other places in the state, and large prints in the sand kept bear spray flying off Alaska store shelves. Bears avoid humans. While I lived on Prince of Wales Island, there were no bear attacks. That said, gruesome attacks happened in the state, killing one person every other year on average, with half the deaths being hunters.

During the August 2000 teacher in-service, fellow teacher, Kathy Shirley, told us about a grizzly bear attack near her community on the mainland. Hyder was in our school district, but not on Prince of Wales Island.

"The awful mauling happened at our campground outside of town. A grizzly bear tore a guy apart and ate his remains. Fish and Game shot the bear and found pieces of the guy in its stomach. I guess they had tried to trap the bear a few times, but he got away," Kathy reported. The dreadful story fueled nightmares for me hiking alone in the forest for years to come.

Adopting a dog in 2003 meant more time spent in the forest. Sampson, a gorgeous tricolor King Charles Cavalier Spaniel, greeted us at the door each afternoon. He stole our hearts so much that a second Cavalier, Josie, came along in 2004 sporting her ruby red coat. Together, the four of us hiked the logging roads of Prince of Wales Island daily after work. Rain or shine, dark and scary. It didn't matter. The dogs had to walk, so we explored the Tongass National Forest, home of the trophy black bear.

We enjoyed hiking to Elgin's favorite fishing spot on Angel Lake. Each cast of the fly pole produced a bite or appeared as though it did. The dogs played and watched the trout swim upstream in the nearby shallow creek. Sampson tried incessantly to catch one without success. Despite the thrill of Angel Lake for Elgin and Sampson, the risk was not worth the benefit. Death by a bear attack wasn't the only treacherous possibility in bear country.

"We probably shouldn't bring the dogs out here anymore," Elgin stated as we hiked the thirty minutes back to the road through the tall, thick grass one day. "I'm afraid a conibear trap might kill a dog."

Trekking through the grass, watching for bears, and then hearing about *conibear* traps, I thought he was referring to bear traps hidden in the grass. For fifteen years, I stepped gingerly through the grass and kept my eyes peeled for those baited bear traps. It turned out hunters hid conibear traps in or near the water to catch beaver and otters. They did not stash bear traps in the grass. Who knew?

Frightening situations snuck up without warning, though. One late fall afternoon, Elgin and I took the dogs for a walk at Eagle's Nest Campground on Balls Lake. The murky path included occasional boardwalks over the worst of the mud. Admiring the scenery, I fell behind Elgin and the dogs. Tall bushes lined the edge of the raised walkway, while a spectacular view across the lake made it easy to lollygag. A branch snapped behind me. Not a little snap mind you, but a *snap*! The top of a bush rustled wildly above my head while the other bushes stood still. The windless day afforded no explanation other than a bear. I hurried to catch up to Elgin, careful not to run or look back to avoid eye contact with the potential bear.

"Elgin!" I half-whispered a desperate cry for help after I put some distance between the bush and myself. "Elgin! There is a bear behind me."

"Don't be ridiculous!" He never believed me when I thought a bear was close. I don't know why; there was plenty of evidence of bears. It wasn't unusual to see fresh wet bear prints on the road where we parked the Expedition either and sometimes those prints showed up while we were hiking. Prince of Wales Island had one bear per square mile. It was not my imagination!

Elgin kept walking. I heard footsteps on the boardwalk behind me. My pace quickened without running. I heard *Thump, thump. Thump, thump* as the bear followed me down the planks. My heart shifted into my throat, and

I prepared myself for an inevitable attack by turning to face the charging bear.

I lost control of myself as a scream of terror and alarm escaped me when I turned and saw a black creature closing in on me. The size didn't matter. I continued my terrifying shriek as I watched Sampson charge past me, yowling in horror and total fear! *Sampson?* So, it wasn't a bear after all. At least the *thump, thump* wasn't a bear. There *was* a bear behind that bush a quarter of a mile back, I assure you.

"What are you doing? You are scaring the dogs. Cut it out!" a startled Elgin yelled at me, with Sampson still whimpering at his feet. There was no sympathy for my terror, nor was Elgin willing to listen to my side of the story as we climbed the stairs to our vehicle.

"Somehow, Sampson must have looped back behind us, but I can tell you a bear shook that bush, and I heard the *snap,*" my words fell on deaf ears. Elgin was mad.

Two days later, we walked the dogs on the Thorne Bay dock, a genuine treat for me because Elgin preferred to trek through the woods. We strolled alongside boats and enjoyed close-up inspections of our neighbors' planes stored in slips on the dock. A flooded skiff called Elgin's name, so he grabbed a bucket to bale the water out for an unknown neighbor. A fisherman busied himself inside the cab of a large fishing vessel.

"Look, there's a snake in the water." A snake swimming in the bay was news to me. "Hey, Elgin, this is cool," I yelled without taking my eyes off the tea-colored bay. Sampson trotted over to greet me as Elgin and Josie reached the end of the dock.

A loud *thump* followed by a heavy *thump, thump. Thump, thump* pounded the wooden planks. The familiar thumping returned my mind to the bear incident at Eagle's Nest two days prior. I whirled around to see a giant black animal trotting toward me. I shrieked in horror. My terror echoed across the bay.

Elgin did an about-face as Sampson screeched, then whimpered and dashed, like the coward that he was, to Elgin's feet. The hardy fisherman threw himself off his boat onto the dock, screaming at his huge, black beast of a dog, "Come here!"

I cried as Elgin yelled, "I am never taking you to the dock again. *Never!*" He marched by, humiliated by me. Our terrified dogs even hung their heads as they passed me. And Elgin *didn't* walk the dock with me again for several years.

"Are you okay? My dog came over to say hi, that's all. He really is a sweet dog," the fisherman kindly explained before ordering his dog onto the boat. I felt shame, total humiliation. Tears soaked my face, and my body still trembled. Friendly dog or not, I thought it was a bear.

Elgin had rounded the corner, marching in anger toward the dock's ramp. I knew there was no use explaining. Okay. So, we were in the middle of town, in the middle of the day, and it was only a dog. Yeah! *A big black dog!* And that, my friend, is *my* side of the story. I'll let Elgin tell you his side.

Bear fear crept up in even stranger places. Once I thought I saw a bear in downtown Washington, DC. My sister-in-law Merlaine and I strolled through Union Station after a late-night movie. Without a care in the world, I gazed at the magnificent buildings in the night light. Then, out of the corner of my eye, I spotted it. Large, furry, and black. I yelped in fear and grabbed Merlaine's arm, "Bear!" A lady turned the corner holding the leash of the mammoth, black dog. I giggled in embarrassment. "What can I say? I'm an Alaskan. If it's a black four-legged animal, it's a bear."

Sometimes I didn't have to *think* there was a bear. I *knew* there was a bear, like the time Elgin and I hiked on Balls Lake while it was still frozen in the spring. Momma and baby bear, fresh out of hibernation, left prints in the snow on the frozen lake, which put me on high alert. I kept a close watch along the shoreline. Those two bears were definitely out there somewhere, even if we hadn't spotted more than their prints. The island had bear prints and scat everywhere.

Not everything about bears was scary though. We loved to *bear hunt* which to us meant going for a drive in hopes of seeing a bear on one of the countless old logging roads. At times, the subject of bears struck my funny bone, for example when the State Farm agent in Ketchikan answered my question about comprehensive insurance coverage. "It covers the vehicle for anything not related to a collision. So, if a bear breaks into it, it catches on fire . . . " Before she could go on, I was laughing. Her first example was a bear breaking into a vehicle. Alaskans knew how to talk to other Alaskans!

FIFTY-THREE

Painful In-House Training

Terrified, I squirmed, lying on the clinic table. *Relax*. I coached myself. *You can do this. You need this. Pinch yourself on the leg when Michael sticks you with the IV. It will be over in a minute.* Yeah, right!

Michael, a tall local Native man, sat next to me but said nothing as he prepared to give me an IV. MS was wreaking havoc on my life, so the neurologist prescribed intravenous steroids over the phone from Seattle. With a history of fainting and hating needles, it was torture waiting for the stick. Michael sitting beside me, dashed my high hopes of the physician's assistant giving the IV, as Bob Trotter was nowhere in sight. In fact, I saw no one else. As far as I could tell, the staff left Michael and me alone in the ER of the Alicia Roberts Clinic of Klawock, Alaska.

Isn't he the receptionist? I thought incredibly to myself. He took a deep breath and wrapped the heavy-duty rubber band around my arm. Man, do those hurt! *Smack, smack.* His fingers tapped my vein, and then he sterilized the skin.

I grimaced as the needle penetrated my flesh. *Ouch!* I held my breath. Timidly, he dug to catch the vein under the skin. My muscles tightened as he pulled the needle out and plunged it in again. *The vein must have collapsed,* I guessed. He dug, and dug, and dug some more. No IV was in place. Then he wiped my arm. *It must be blood,* I thought but refused to look. Watching was not an option for me.

My right hand squeezed as I readied myself for his next attempt. It was beyond painful. I resisted the urge to pull back, scream, or cry. He dug deeper and deeper as if chasing the vein to the bone. I stiffened, ceased breathing, and prayed that Michael would find the vein, fast. I had lost track of time. It seemed like forty-five minutes, but it may have only been ten. It didn't matter because I had reached a breaking point and could no longer take it.

Half yelling, I stated with conviction, "I'm done! I'm not doing this anymore." The jerking of my arm startled Michael, who instantly rose to his feet and retreated to the back of the makeshift ER.

"I'm sorry," he whispered from his corner of the room. "I'm so sorry." Upset by the situation, Michael received consoling from a nurse while the physician's assistant stepped into the room. He had been there the whole time.

"Let me try," the physician's assistant offered. I resisted the urge to flee the room and allowed one more poke of the vein. One shot of Lidocaine, one prick of the needle, and it was over.

"The first time is tough. The next one will be easier," I heard the nurse say. I was the guinea pig for Michael's first IV. That explained a lot.

After the three-hour IV, Trotter gave me a choice, "We can take it out or leave it in for three days. Which do you prefer?" What a dumb question, as if I wanted to go through *that* again!

With limited access to medical professionals, the clinic trained in-house for some positions. In the future, Michael Brown became a friend of mine. We never discussed the IV incident. He changed to another profession, though whether our shared experience had caused that, I'm not sure.

Qualified medical staff were scarce in bush Alaska, but I will say those doctors were the best. They didn't shy away from treating their patients and seldom referred me to a specialist without first attempting to help. To see a specialist meant waiting until one visited the island or traveling into Ketchikan or Sitka, though I typically flew into Anchorage or Seattle to see a neurologist. As a result, the general doctors wore many hats and tried their best to resolve the issue before racking up travel bills for the patients.

Having excellent doctors was one thing, buying prescription medication on the island if you were non-Native, was a completely different story. Until Whale Tail Pharmacy opened in the early 2000s, we had to wait for the mail plane to bring over medication from a Ketchikan pharmacy. We also had a mail-order pharmacy for our regular prescriptions.

One day, I received a phone call from the mail-order company, "I'm contacting you to verify receipt of your prescription."

"No. It hasn't arrived yet. It should be here in a few days," I replied. I suspected he lived in a city and was wondering why the medication had not arrived as expected.

"I don't know if you realize this, but you live in a *rural* area," he emphasized.

"Yes. It is remote here," I replied. That was an understatement. I described where I lived and the potential delay issues of flights and weather for the arriving prescription.

With each drug order, I explained my location. The mail-order company always assured me it would arrive at my door within forty-eight hours. I didn't argue. I knew it was unlikely to arrive in less than a week. MS medication was expensive, often worth upwards of $10,000 per month; thus, they tracked it closely. When the shipment arrived, the local air service called me to retrieve the package at the dock.

Choosing to live in bush Alaska required planning, improvising, enduring prolonged wait times, and learning to do without, even if you needed something. There were no exceptions, not even for medical necessities. Nothing out there was quick or easy. It was a hard life. One fought with grit and determination, though having a positive attitude made a world of difference when faced with chronic medical issues.

Now that the world has changed with the COVID-19 pandemic of 2020, maybe patients in bush Alaska will have greater access to online medical appointments that were not accessible to me when I lived there.

FIFTY-FOUR

Checking One Off the Bucket List

I wheeled my luggage into the hall and let the hotel door close behind me. Turning to leave, I bumped into the same Kodiak administrator who refused to discuss the interview schedule with us at the job fair in 1995.

"Your comment to the panel today impressed me. You didn't appear to be nervous in front of all those people," the administrator complimented me. My speech before the packed Captain Cook Hotel conference room in Anchorage was a passionate one, making it easy to forget the number of people in the audience. I reported the failures of the extreme outcome-based education system in my school district and the harm I believed it was causing to our students' education.

"Thank you. Don't you work for the Kodiak School District?" I inquired, recognizing him.

"Yes. How did you know?"

"My husband and I asked to interview with you in 1995, but you said the schedule was full," I reminded him.

"Who's your husband?" he asked.

"Elgin Cook. We work for SISD on Prince of Wales Island. Kodiak was once at the top of our wish list," I informed him as I prepared to leave.

"*Elgin,* the technology director?" He could not conceal his shock and seemed somewhat troubled. "I could have hired *Elgin,* the man who only needs one name?" His exaggerated slumped shoulders and gaping mouth revealed his disappointment.

"You could have," I smiled, turned, and walked away, leaving him with his jaw on the floor—poor guy. Elgin met the growing demand for educational technology by training staff for schools and universities. He helped districts across the state with their technology issues and built complex databases to track student and state records. The Alaska Society for Technology in Education (ASTE) noted his efforts by choosing him as the Administrator of the Year. Then they elected him to their board and two years later voted him in as president, which he declined.

Elgin called while I waited for my plane at the Anchorage airport, "What time will you be flying in today? Deidre and Joel invited us to go for a boat ride and have a fish fry."

"I'm all for a boat ride, but a fish fry? I will not be eating any fish." He laughed, expecting that to be my response.

Several hours later, we were bumping along the rough water of the Thorne Bay in the Jenson's fishing boat. The Jenson family always had something fun on their schedule. They built nighttime bonfires on Sandy Beach, boated in the bay, and even threw a fish fry to convince this non-fish eater to step out of my comfort zone.

"What do you say we go home and fry some fish?" Joel suggested. I could tell something was up. "Tell you what, Melissa. I understand you don't eat fish, but you have not tried my cooking. I'll fix a little of everything; then at least you can say you tried it." And that is what he did. Joel and Deidre cooked several types of seafood, and then they watched me for entertainment as I forced myself to taste each one. I don't remember how the fish tasted because the thought of eating it overpowered the flavor. So much for turning me into a seafood fan, Joel, but now I can officially say I've tried it.

"When are your parents coming?" Deidre chatted between fish samplings.

"The end of May. They'll be here for two weeks," Elgin replied.

Before we knew it, the last week of May arrived with Kenny and Connie flying in from Wyoming. They spent the night in Ketchikan and caught the morning seaplane to the island. Two smiling faces stepped onto the dock.

"What a fantastic view from the plane!" Kenny dreamed of fishing in Alaska, and now he was checking one off his bucket list. We wasted no time loading their luggage and squeezing the boys and the rest of us into the Expedition for a tight ride out to Sandy Beach. There Kenny and the boys collected seashells and dead sand dollars at low tide. I log-hopped while Elgin strolled along the beach with Connie.

It rained throughout the night, thrilling Elgin's parents. They lived in the Wyoming desert where it seldom rained, and when it did, it fell in squalls, not all-night downpours.

"I can breathe so much better on the coast," Connie, who suffered from heart issues, realized at breakfast.

"Today, we'll go king salmon fishing with a former coworker, Kevin Castle," Elgin announced. Kenny was beside himself with excitement. They traveled twenty miles by skiff to Siketi Sound on the edge of the Pacific Ocean to find the kings. On cue, whales breached close by as Elgin and Kenny fished from the boat. Elgin's line caught the first fish. He passed the rod to Everett, who gripped the bending rod and reeled in one medium size king salmon. Then the drag buzzed on Kenny's reel as a monster king hit the bait and took off. Kenny kept the line tight while he slowly reeled in the king salmon. It was a hefty one; the battle between man and fish was on. At last, he surfaced, and Kevin swooped the fishing net under the squirming monster fish to help Kenny hoist it into the boat.

We froze the king salmon and sent it home with them to Wyoming in a waxed fish box. It was the main course at the July family reunion in the Big Horn Mountains. As a joke, we left the carcass by a stream known for its six-inch brook trout for an unsuspecting fisherman to discover. I wish we could have seen their reaction.

During Kenny and Connie's visit, we attended summer teacher in-service. As the technology director, Elgin kept busy. One afternoon, he had to work late.

"Let's go bear hunting," I suggested to his parents when I arrived home from work.

"Bear hunting?" They looked surprised, but the boys knew exactly what I meant.

"She means taking a drive, hoping to see a bear on the road," Everett informed them. We piled into the Expedition and headed down the Southside road, but we saw no bears, not one. We drove all the way to Kasaan and cruised the village streets, stopped to stroll their boardwalk along the coastline in the drizzling rain, and then headed back to Thorne Bay.

"I'm shocked we haven't seen a bear. Last week, Elgin and I spotted a mother with two cubs. The cubs climbed a tree and bawled while we watched from the window. We tried not to stay too long because we didn't want to separate the family," I told Kenny and Connie.

Suddenly, a small black bear darted out into the road from the old dump outside of town. I slammed on the brakes, throwing my passengers forward as the bear disappeared under the bumper. We all took a deep breath and then watched him emerge unscathed. He scampered the rest of the way across the road and into the forest, where we lost sight of him instantly in the thick ground cover.

"Wow! That was close!" Connie exclaimed when we started driving again. I won't lie. The near miss rattled me, but Elgin's parents did get to see a bear up close.

Two weeks flew by between work and sightseeing. We intended to expose Elgin's parents to the best of the island, so we hauled a canoe and boat motor to Sarkar Lake. We considered it the gem of The Rock. Tiny islands with trees dotted the lake. We made our way to a Forest Service cabin on the far side of the lake to eat lunch. On our way back, pouring rain forced us to seek shelter under the canopy of evergreen tree branches hanging over the water.

The next day, Connie and I walked around the Thorne Bay dock and sat on the bench to enjoy passing boats and bush planes while the guys fished for cutthroat trout from our canoe on the Thorne River. "That was the best trout fishing I have ever done!" Kenny claimed, coming through the door, having caught his limit.

We moseyed along the boardwalk in the pouring rain at Eagle's Nest Campground though being soaked didn't dampen anyone's spirits. Alaska dished out the experience we had described to them over the years. Breaking out the boys' 22-rifles, we drove an hour away to a cutaway in the mountains overlooking Clarence Strait to a shooting spot. We strolled the Craig docks admiring fishing vessels. On the last day of Kenny and Connie's visit, we all boarded the *Prince of Wales* ferry in Hollis to Ketchikan. Throughout the ferry ride, Elgin's parents eagerly roamed the decks and watched the view as we sailed by the tree-covered islands of Southeast Alaska.

The Inter-Island Ferry began daily service with the *Prince of Wales* ferry in 2002, which allowed the Alaska Marine Highway to reassign the *Aurora* to Prince William Sound. When the *Prince of Wales* first came into service, a reporter put our family's photo in the newspaper—Elgin, me, and our boys all sat in computer cubicles with our laptops open for the picture. The ship departed from Hollis to Ketchikan at 7:00 a.m. and returned at 6:30 p.m. daily—no more 2:00 a.m. ferries. The service added a second vessel, the *Stikine,* to the route in 2006.

Massive cruise ships huddled in Ketchikan's port, releasing scores of tourists into the city of fewer than ten thousand residents. From a nearby shoreline, we watched the ships come and go and walked along the water's edge before delivering Kenny and Connie to the airport ferry for their flight back to Wyoming. We drove our Bronco and empty cargo trailer to the Alaska Marine Highway ferry terminal and checked in for the six-hour ride on the *Taku* ferry to Prince Rupert. From there, we had a thirty-three-hour drive back to Wyoming for summer break.

"We should be in Prince Rupert in time to rent a hotel room," I noted as we drove onto the ferry heading to Canada. We spent the beautiful afternoon and evening sightseeing and exploring the ship before settling in the forward viewing room. The ship arrived at the Prince Rupert port by midnight. We gathered our sleepy boys from the viewing room. Driving the Expedition with a cargo trailer onto the ferry earlier in the evening placed us at the front of the loading line onto the ferry, but that did not guarantee we would be first to leave when we exited.

One vehicle after another received instruction to start their engine and exit the vessel. Finally, it was our turn. Coming off the ship, a worker waved us to the side. Vehicles cut in front of us and filed into the long lines at the border. Two open custom lines inched along at a snail's pace; we were in for a long night.

"Darn it!" We ended up last in line. It took two hours to clear customs. "It's not worth the money renting a hotel room now. Let's keep driving." And we did. Too late for a room and too early for breakfast, we hit the highway. Nine hours of driving landed us in Prince George, starving and exhausted. McBride, British Columbia, was another typical stopover. Still, it was too early to stop so we continued on to Calgary. It turned into the most exhausting trip we ever drove down the highway.

I wrote in my journal that night: *Long stretches of road offer few quality food options between Prince Rupert, British Columbia, and Wyoming. And when our timing is off, we arrive at our destination starving.*

After our long drive home to Wyoming, Connie always greeted us with a big smile and a countertop filled with freshly baked hot bread and cinnamon rolls. A cinnamon roll never tasted so good!

FIFTY-FIVE

Death Knocks Too Soon

I remember those who left us too soon with sadness at their shortened lives and with gratefulness to have once known them.

— Melissa L. Cook, January 2010

Untimely death knocked at the door too soon for a disproportionate number of people we knew in Alaska's bush communities. A landslide buried three men alive. A four-year-old girl died in a house fire, and a two-year-old boy drowned after falling off the dock. A hunter, presumed lost in the forest, was never seen again. A fisherman was crushed pulling in a crab pot from the sea. Alaska was first in the nation for drowning deaths and suicide, a sad reality for Alaskans. Living there, even for a brief time, guaranteed you knew someone who had met the Grim Reaper long before their time.

A siren blared throughout the night. I cracked the front door and saw people hurrying down the road. Fear struck me as the alarm continued to fill the sleepy town. I dialed my classroom aide, Becky Welton, to ask about the emergency. Visions of a tidal wave coming into the bay filled my imagination. It turned out to be a father of five taking his last breath in a smoke-filled trailer attempting to save himself in a shallow tub of water. After an unsuccessful attempt to pull the visiting construction worker through a tiny window, the townspeople stood feet away, helpless. The man's only exit from the trailer, the front door, had collapsed in flames.

The students arrived at school the next morning emotional and hyper after witnessing the horrific scene. Students recounted the man's cries for help, screaming when the fire took over his trailer and his ultimate death. They drew vivid images for those of us not there.

The firemen retrieved the man's body from the wreckage after fighting the fire. The man had been in the shower when his wood stove, housed in the adjacent wanigan, caught the trailer on fire. The only escape route was the front door where the fire started. There was no hope. I thought of this stranger when I walked past the site over the next fourteen years.

Down the street, I bought a sandwich plate from an estate sale in Thorne Bay several years later. It reminds me of my friend, Jim Beard. I prefer to remember Jim as the fisheries expert from the Forest Service mapping out a web of streams running into the ocean using colorful duct tape on the gym floor. At the intersections of the streams, he positioned paper cups with scented cotton balls. He gave the students a list of scents to follow from the ocean to their destination. Familiar smells gave clues as to which way to go. Jim's enthusiasm for sharing his passion for fish was contagious at the annual science fair. His death came too soon and likely by his own hand, according to his family.

Suicide was a common occurrence in Alaska. Former coworkers, parents, students, neighbors, and even friends took their lives during our tenure in the state. Each in their unique way, but the devastating result was the same—a shortened life and lost friend or neighbor. The sad fact was, I stopped counting.

Not every death by one's hand was deliberate. Accidental injury or trauma was the number one cause of death for people aged one to forty-four. Trauma was the fourth leading cause of death for all other age groups. Alcohol-related accidents were at the root of multiple former student deaths. One fun-loving student died when a drunken boater struck his vessel. More than one student died as a passenger of a drunk driver.

When I walked our dogs, I thought of the deceased residents. Car accidents, fire, suicide, suicide by cop, murder, mysteriously missing, crushed between containers on the dock, crushed by heavy equipment in the sort yard, medical aliments not treated in time, widow makers, drowning, drug overdoses, lost at sea, hunting and fishing accidents, airplane and boat accidents. Need I go on? Aside from village burials, most bush people returned to their original home for their funeral, or relatives and friends threw their cremated remains to the wind over the ocean.

One city of Craig resident's death rocked not only our world but the nation's. I learned my friend, Lauri Waterman, had been murdered when a counselor contacted SISD's administration office to offer his services. "Why do we need your services?" I inquired with confusion.

"You haven't heard? They found Lauri dead in her burning van." I had not heard about it until then. I dropped to the chair behind me in shock, immediately remembering my visit with Lauri a few days before in the grocery store. She had been the high school secretary when we lived in Craig.

It was a horrific murder. A Thorne Bay man and his friend broke into Lauri's home one stormy night in November 2004. They planned to have the murder appear as if she had driven drunk off a cliff. First, they pulled her out of bed, made her put on clothes, and then forced alcohol down her throat. Then they bound and threw her onto the backseat floor of the family van and drove over an hour down a rough road near the tiny town of Naukati. There, they beat her with rocks and tried to choke her to death as the wind howled, and rain swirled through the pitch-black night.

The plan ran amuck when it wasn't so easy to kill her. Recognizing her injuries did not match a car accident, they stuffed her back into the van and drove more than an hour to the outskirts of Thorne Bay. The murderers traveled a winding mountain road until they neared the top. The men doused the van in fuel and set it on fire with Lauri inside. Then they pushed the flaming vehicle off the road, hoping it would roll down the mountain. A tree stump in the clear-cut below caught the van a short distance from the road. It smoked like a beacon for the morning hunters to spot. Lauri's death became famous due to the allegation of her sixteen-year-old daughter's involvement.

Reporters swarmed Craig and the island for years. Trial after trial eventually landed the murderers in jail. Lauri's only daughter received three years for negligent homicide for her role in the murder after two trials. Community members still do not agree on the depth of her involvement. Some thought she had nothing to do with it, while others believed she was the mastermind behind her mother's murder. An open window gave the men access to the home. Did the daughter leave it open? Did she mislead the men into believing Lauri abused her? Only those involved will ever know the entire truth.

One of the most tragic stories ever told to me happened to a coworker five years before our arrival on the island. A boating trip turned critical when a storm blew in and capsized a fishing vessel occupied by three adults and four children. After escaping through the cabin window, the boaters found themselves drenched and freezing on the exposed, overturned hull. In the darkness, panic struck. They lost the three young children to freezing temperatures and cold water, and then the adults and teenage girl swam for shore. Only two adults and the teen crawled onto the beach. They buried themselves in vegetation for warmth while awaiting rescue. My coworker, overcome with grief, swam back to the boat in search of his lost children.

Concerned by the weather and overdue arrival, the man's brother searched the dark stormy waters until he found the capsized boat and rescued the survivors. I've left out many specific details of this story, which my coworker's sister shared. I prefer to leave it at this and express my sincere condolences to the family. Even after all these years, we have not forgotten their pain.

Two months before leaving Alaska, another coworker's husband lost several of his employees in a plane crash outside Sitka. Death continued to knock at the door until our retirement date.

Given the gravity of this chapter, I shall end on a lighter note. Being avid hikers of the forest because our dogs needed a daily walk, we wandered along many isolated logging roads in the Tongass. One afternoon, we stumbled upon bones in the grass—conceivably those of a human hand. Alarmed, I hollered for Elgin.

"Does that look like a hand to you?" I asked with anticipation as he inspected the remains from a distance.

"It does, but it may be something else," he guessed.

"Several people are missing from the island. It could be one of them. You would want someone to identify your bones. We'd better not disturb the scene, just in case," I suggested.

"I'll take a picture to show the troopers," Elgin snapped a photo with his phone, and we drove into Craig.

"We found these bones in the forest outside of Klawock. They could belong to one of the missing people from the island," I said and showed the phone photo to the trooper.

"Can you send that to me? Where did you say that is?" I pointed out the bones' location on the map and wrote my contact information on a sticky note. My phone rang a few hours later.

"I found the bones," the trooper informed me. "They were from a bear. It's not unusual for people to report bear bones as human remains, especially their paw bones. Please let us know if you run across anything suspicious again."

"I told you so," Elgin said.

"Sure looked human to me."

FIFTY-SIX

Children of the Tongass Rainforest

By the fall semester of 2004, the inadequate curriculum adopted in the spring of 2000 was failing. Several juniors and seniors had dropped out upon transferring to new schools because they had few or even no credits toward graduation. Test scores across the district plummeted. The district no longer had grade levels and had vague report cards. Students worked at their own pace and level with severely limited resources. It was a nightmare. Teachers didn't teach, they facilitated. Students struggled without daily group instruction and fell behind their counterparts in other areas of Alaska and the country.

The administrators who implemented this model quit in the spring of 2004. Not a supporter of the drastic changes, I wasted no time in writing a list of issues and proposed necessary changes to improve the curriculum and emailed them to all the staff.

"Is that how you want to start your relationship with our new superintendent?" My bold email concerned Elgin. Superintendent Jim Nygaard soon offered me the curriculum and professional development director position, beginning my school administration career. I left the classroom in October on a mission to fix the failing system. It was tough. Some teachers initially poured their hearts into the new curriculum, grew tired, and didn't finish it. Problems lingered. It was time for this change. Leading the charge won me no popularity contests amongst the die hards who had pushed this model onto the rest of us over the years.

Until our boys graduated in 2005, 2006, and 2007, I always had them in at least one class, even after transferring to administration. My boys sat in on the technology classes Elgin and I taught as adjunct instructors for the University of Alaska. One late afternoon, I shook my head in disbelief as I entered the common area.

"Hi, Mom!" sixteen-year-old Everett announced his presence with an enormous smile. A junior now, he was the class clown, always quick with a witty comment or unexpected act. There my son hung, suspended several feet in the air, strapped to a pillar with packing tape. He swung his feet and shook his head while giggling to himself.

"What are you doing up there?" I gave him the evil-eye and then smiled.

"Hanging around."

For years, we met Bob and Neva Robertson after work for pizza in Craig on Friday nights. Their boys Erik and Stuart sat with our kids at one table while the adults visited at another. As educators, we all worked in the schools and needed a break from kids. Though we never specifically planned our "weekends off" we took turns taking all the boys for the weekend.

No longer little guys, our boys regularly had friends at our house after school. Teenage boys slept over Friday and sometimes Saturday nights to play epic video games all day and night. Sutton played guitar and served as president of the student council and as the student member of the school board, which involved traveling to Juneau and Anchorage. Everett started a band, starred in multiple school plays and wooed Abbey Douglas, his future wife, during his last couple of years of high school. Ethan organized video game tournaments at the school as student council president and represented Alaska at the January 2005 Presidential Inauguration in Washington, DC. Life was busy at the Cook house.

Bush life for a teenager had many unique challenges. Take dating, for instance. Going to a movie meant watching one via satellite or DVD at the school during activity night. The internet allowed for cyber dating as kids developed friendships across the island and state. Technology was quickly changing the way of life for people in bush Alaska.

Hazardous roads made learning to drive a challenge. Our car insurance dropped us for too many accidents once the boys attended college in Wyoming. I was a nervous wreck when they drove through a major city. Prince of Wales Island only had a few stop signs and mostly rough dirt roads, which put them at a disadvantage as new drivers in the Lower-48. One son wrote, "Don't worry, Mom. I won't be driving in the city until everyone else is home for the night."

Transportation didn't always mean cars and trucks, either. Our children's friends drove four-wheelers and skiffs. The school brought students in from the south side of the bay by bus boat. Kids flew to district-wide events or traveled out of the district by ferry or plane. They canoed, kayaked, and boated on school outings.

The children came from various home styles, though none lived in igloos. Most people in the rain forest lived in mobile or manufactured homes ranging in condition. Some lived in beautiful log homes while others made do in canvas tents or camper trailers covered in tarps to keep out the rain and wind. A handful of people lived on boats and float houses. Unfortunately, some students had no beds to sleep in and lacked any private space. We even had homeless children sleeping in tents or on a friend's couch.

"Coming to school is the only time I'm warm," one seventh-grade boy who lived in a tent told me. I couldn't imagine being homeless out there in the rainforest, but I knew of many children without homes over the years. The diversity in housing was incredible.

The school district made travel a priority when my children attended Thorne Bay School. The kids in our communities traveled regularly, primarily to other bush communities. Sports teams traveled by ferry and bush plane on lengthy trips several times each year. Teachers and students slept on school and ferry floors to save money. In eighth grade, students explored Ketchikan. In high school, my boys went to Anchorage, Seattle, back east to the cities of Washington, DC, and Boston, and they even went to Canada.

When the students weren't traveling, the school kept them active with archery, kayaking, rock climbing, camping, fishing, and swimming. Special trainers taught martial arts, cold water survival, and hunter safety courses. The EMS offered high school students first responder and EMT classes. In fact, Everett and Abbey became EMTs when they were eighteen years old. The school and community provided plenty of opportunities to keep kids busy if they wanted to take part.

Several boys went fishing or checked their traps for beaver and wolf at the crack of dawn before the rest of us climbed out of bed. They hunted after school. Often these kids shared fish and deer meat with community members. Students worked in the fishing and hunting industries as guides, maids, servers, deckhands, and clerks in the summer. My children had limited work opportunities because we traveled, though they worked at the local grocery store the year it opened.

The most striking difference between bush children and city kids was the age span of their friendships. Children in the bush had friends of all ages from elementary through high school and a few of these friendships have lasted a lifetime for my boys.

FIFTY-SEVEN

A Price to Pay

"Sutton?" I opened his bedroom door as the other boys hustled past me. Everett offered Ethan a ride to school. "Do you want to walk the dogs with Dad and me this afternoon?" I asked.

"Sure," he replied. "Hopefully Sampson doesn't roll all over another stinky salmon!" He laughed at the memory of our last outing that landed Sampson and Josie in the back of our truck.

"I'd prefer not to relive that slimy, rotten ordeal!" I responded with a grin. Running off lead, the dogs could not resist rolling in dead fish that had washed ashore after spawning at the end of their life cycle. Seeing the dogs with their legs in the air was always a bad sign, *always*!

"Be ready at four. I have class tonight at five," I reminded Sutton. In 2002, I graduated with the first class to earn a master's degree in educational technology from the University of Alaska. Now I wanted a PhD in school administration to become a superintendent specializing in schools with dire budget constraints and curriculum failures.

"I have class in an hour. I'd better get up," Sutton said. He was attending college online for his first semester in the fall of 2005.

Elgin dropped me off at work with the reminder, "See you at four sharp." He knew all too well that I had to drag myself away. My administrative responsibilities had grown to include curriculum and professional development director, grants, state reports, teacher in-service, and other tasks as issues and projects arose. In 2007, my job expanded to include the special education coordinator and the evaluation of a part of the teaching staff. By then, I had settled on a second master's degree in school administration instead of a PhD due to the severity of the MS attacks I was experiencing.

When SISD hired us in 1999, they had almost no technology and were seriously behind all the other schools in the state. By 2002, Elgin had installed networks and computer labs in all the schools. Then, he and I taught college classes to train the staff. By 2004, we were on the cutting edge of technology with video teleconferencing (also known as VTC). In 2005, a laptop program loaned computers to students in grades five through twelve. To help with the workload, Becky Welton hired on as our assistant. Without her help, there would have been no sleep at the Cook house for years.

Though Elgin enjoyed his job as the technology director during these changing times, he debated the fiscal irresponsibility of the VCT project. The district spent more than half a million dollars per year of taxpayers' money to pay for the bandwidth necessary to broadcast over VTC when the alternative was less than $10,000. Thorne Bay teachers taught the core subject areas of math, language arts, science, Spanish, and social studies to twenty to twenty-five remote high school students.

Additionally, SISD applied for a three-year waiver to allow special education (or SPED) services over VTC, rather than the required in-person delivery. In exchange, we were to provide our research data and suggested protocols for other Alaska school districts to use in the future. Before VTC became available, the SPED teachers working for SISD flew into eight to ten remote sites and stayed several days at each school every month to provide student services. SPED teachers turned over each year partly because they slept on floors and couches away from home for more than half the time.

In 2005, we began the first year of fully implementing VTC. Many of the duties stemming from both the VTC high school classes and the special education waiver landed on my desk. Teaching on VTC was challenging. The teachers could see only one remote classroom on the screen when broadcasting to as many as eight to ten other rooms around the district. The teachers and students endured plenty of technical issues that affected instructional flow, such as lousy satellite connections, microphone issues, and a delayed satellite response time.

So why did SISD implement the costly VTC program? Congress passed the No Child Left Behind Act in 2001 creating a standards-based education system that required teachers to be certified in the subjects they taught. By using VTC to deliver high school courses and hiring an elementary teacher for the lower grades, school districts could meet the mandate.

In the end, SISD teachers learned how to instruct over VTC, and I presented the SPED research and protocols to the state board of education in 2007 as promised. I wouldn't say the students' education was ideal, given they sat in front of a screen all day. However, the kids were able to expand their friends from one or two kids in their town to many across the region.

These years were the busiest of my entire life. Elgin and the boys fought with me over my work hours and worried about my health. An increasing number of brain lesions dotted my MRIs each year. I didn't comprehend that multiple sclerosis would have its say and that dealing with a symptom here or there wasn't the true ugliness that MS could rain down upon me. The overachiever in me could not see another path or the fast-approaching cliff at the end of the road.

I also failed to see that these were the last years I had with my boys at home. In January 2006, we drove Sutton to college in Powell, Wyoming. I remember watching him cross the threshold of our front door for the last time, wondering if he would walk through it again. He didn't. It was expensive to travel to Alaska when he could see us during our summer vacations in Wyoming. Everett finished school in the spring of the same year. He married Abbey Douglas, and they moved to Powell too. The next year, Ethan graduated a year early and followed his brothers to school in Wyoming. Consumed by work and graduate school, I didn't see the empty nest coming. Before we knew it, they were all gone. I sat in their rooms shocked that they had already grown up and moved away. Where had the time gone?

FIFTY-EIGHT

Humor Under the Cover of Darkness

One beautiful afternoon in 2005, Superintendent Jim Nygaard convinced me to watch him bring in the district office crab pot. Not being a seafood fan, I always gave my turn for the catch-of-the-day away. The two-story district office floated in the bay. A dock bordered two sides of the facility for arriving floatplanes and boats. More often than not, sea otters used the area for family gatherings, eating dinner, and basking in the occasional sunlight.

Jim put three crabs into a five-gallon bucket. He dropped one onto the dock's wooden planks and flipped him over to show me the head, mouth, claws, and legs. The remaining crabs took turns clawing their way back up to the bucket's rim.

"Notice the crabs pull each other down when one reaches the top to escape. It reminds me of teachers who attempt to hold others back if they don't have the same opportunities." He was referring to my situation of a few teachers giving me heartburn over the curriculum changes.

One by one, the district office staff left for the evening until I was the last one in the building. It had grown dark while the tide slipped out to sea. Rain drizzled over the bay.

I exited the office loaded down with a backpack and two heavy bags filled with textbooks. An outside light had burned out, leaving me in the dark on the slimy wooden dock in heels and a dress. The low tide produced a long, steep, and slippery ramp, only partially lit at the top by a dim street-light—the rest cast in shadow.

Rushing along the eerie dock, I realized how alone and vulnerable I was out there. In the dark, I could barely see the water. The spookiness of it gave me the heebie-jeebies. A tinge of fear ran through me but I brushed it off. If I had on tennis shoes or Xtratufs, I might have dashed lickety-split down the dock and scrambled up the ramp.

Below the ramp, the rocky shoreline was not visible in the darkness.

Weighted down with excess baggage, I climbed the metal ramp, its teeth providing a grip for my heels. Raindrops fell on my face as I peered up.

A sudden movement caught my eye. Then a terrifying, earsplitting screech from under the ramp curdled my blood. The piercing cry was unlike any I'd ever heard. Panic and adrenaline caused me to lose my footing with a heel stuck in the grate. A three-foot sandhill crane rose beside the ramp, spreading its six-foot wingspan. It shrieked again right beside me. My screams of terror matched his as we faced off in the darkness.

Instinctively, I flung myself across the ramp, away from the creature. My underarm caught sharply on the guardrail, keeping me from falling into the water below. My books dropped to my feet, scattering with thuds onto the ramp and slid to the wet dock below, landing in a heap.

The crane flew above me into the night sky. Its rattling calls mimicked the sound of laughter on its flight over the bay.

I have fond memories of that ramp, despite the frightening mishap with the sandhill crane. Each day when I arrived at the top on my way into work, I paused to enjoy the gorgeous view. Mountains blanketed with trees surrounded the bay. The various cloud cover, mist, rain, snow, fog, planes flying overhead, boats cruising by, and wildlife created a majestic scene with a unique presentation each day. It stole my breath away.

The floating district office was formerly a school building built on a vessel specifically designed for the J.R. Gildersleeve logging camp sometime in the early 1980s. Gildersleeve School typically had twelve to twenty students. The children used the thirty-six hundred square feet downstairs for classrooms, a library, science lab, and kitchen. The principal's office was by the front door with the secretary located in the center of the building. Upstairs, a nine hundred square foot three-bedroom apartment provided housing for teachers.

The Gildersleeve camp moved to various Southeast Alaska locations for eighty years, with a population close to a hundred. As the world's largest float camp, it even had streetlights. The community floated in coves and bays. They tied together buildings with boardwalks. The close-knit group of people was proud of their community. On average, a worker stayed at least ten years. Once the Gildersleeve logging camp closed in 2000, the floating school relocated to Thorne Bay. The second floor remained an apartment for visiting specialists. The first floor became the administration office for SISD. My office was in the former science lab, which had plenty of counter space.

Intense storms gently rocked the building with the wave action even in the bay. Focused on work, I rarely noticed until I was seasick. At one point, the facility broke loose from the pilings and drifted away from shore. We required immediate help despite the anchor dropped below the facility.

Staff easily found themselves distracted by the waterfront views and wildlife. Killer whales swam into the bay in late spring and generated a commotion in the office. Storms, boat and plane traffic, and winter sunsets in the afternoon made it hard not to stare out the window.

Eventually, the school district moved its offices into the old Thorne Bay School library. This time, the floating school transformed into a home for a family with five children. Teachers lived in the second apartment upstairs. Can you imagine growing up there?

FIFTY-NINE

No Ship is Unsinkable

Sampson swatted my bed in the middle of the night. I opened my eyes and saw him standing there, wanting me to let him out. I swung my legs over the bedside and followed him into the dark hallway toward the front door. His black coat made him difficult to see, so I listened for the click of his toenails on the wooden floor. The clicking paused as I turned the doorknob of the front door. *Click, click, click.* He had returned to the hall and then our room. *Thump!* Sampson stole my spot on the bed. That sneaky dog!

Five in the morning sure comes early, I thought as I dragged myself out of bed and tiptoed around the house, careful not to wake Elgin as I prepared to leave. SISD was sending a group of staff members to the No Child Left Behind 2007 conference in Anchorage. I rushed to gather my bags at the door.

"Ready?" Superintendent Jim Nygaard carried my luggage to the Tahoe with a couple of other employees waiting inside. The stiff wind bit hard when I descended the steps. Rain splattered my face despite attempts to protect myself from it. The storm howled as the vehicle headlights lit up the blowing trees along the roadside.

We arrived at the ferry terminal in ninety minutes. Jim helped unload the luggage into the building while I made the case for canceling our trip. It just didn't seem wise for us to be boarding a ship in this weather.

"It'll be alright," the district principal offered, and I succumbed to the peer pressure. Jim said goodbye and headed back to the Tahoe.

"Wait. You're not coming with us?" I asked. It turned out he was flying out of Thorne Bay the next day. I wanted to jump in the vehicle with him and go home, but I stood there watching him drive away.

Our group of three settled in the restaurant at the rear of the *Stikine* ferry, the best spot on the ship in foul weather. We wasted no time ordering breakfast. On stormy days, I ate early before entering Clarence Strait, where the waters were undoubtedly rough in this storm.

In the protected waters of Kasaan Bay, the ferry encountered fierce wind and accompanying wave action. Alarm rose within the passengers; this wasn't the area we expected to be so nasty. The longer we sailed, the worse it became. The waves were endless and wicked. I had never seen them so immense. It was not long before the vessel began rolling in the high seas with driving rain. The ship plowed into each wave head-on. The bow rose above the stern as the boat rode the wave to the top. It hung there, suspended at the edge, and then crashed over the crest into the turbulent waters below. Up and down, up and down. The rocking and rolling back and forth made many people seasick. It wasn't unusual for the ferry rides to be rough, but this was taking it to a whole new level.

"I hate rides like this! And it's too late to turn back. They should have canceled this ferry! What were they thinking?" The district principal forgot he had encouraged us to board the boat in the storm. He spent his summers commercial fishing so he understood the danger of our current situation and should have known not to get on the boat in the first place. He sat across the table from me with his arms spread out along the top of the bench, his hands intensely gripped into the cushions.

Someone exited the restaurant, the door slamming behind them, startling people nearby. A lady puked a few tables away.

"Oh, man! I hate this!" The principal controlled his urge to panic as a look of terror grew in his eyes. Struggling to keep my balance, I moved to the window to watch the waves crash onto the outside corridor. Ocean water sprayed the dining room windows as I stared out at the storm.

When I returned to my seat, all hell broke loose. The ship pivoted to the side in one swoop. Loud creaks radiated from the hull beneath us. We rode the wave port side first, exposing the starboard to the bottom of the swell. The entire windowpane on the starboard side looked straight down into a sea of water. On the port side, the stormy, dark sky filled the window. We hung suspended on the wave as the *Stikine* struggled to keep us upright. Not one person uttered a word.

Silverware, trays, cups, dishes, food, book bags, and trash rained down on top of me. A loud crash came from inside the galley while pots and pans clanked. The builders wisely secured the dining room swivel chairs to the ferry floor. My chair spun me toward the window, facing the raging water. I gripped the table and planted my feet on the floor to stay put.

The ferry dropped over the wave's crest, crashing into the trough below. Spraying water covered the windows. We rocked like babies in a violent cradle as the next swell grew underneath us. Uncontrolled, the ship rode up and dropped over a few more wave crests before the captain straightened the ship.

A ten-year-old girl stood up crying and vomiting right in front of us.

"Oh, gees!" the principal responded. He gagged back the urge to vomit with her. I suspected if he didn't have two coworkers sitting with him, the grunts and whimpers of fear coming from across the table would have been sobbing tears, and full-blown swear words.

"Please do not flush the toilets. The ferry has limited tank capacity. The freshwater has run out, and the sewer holding tanks are completely full," the captain announced overhead.

Passengers puked into trash cans in the room. Others darted through the dining room doors. Good luck running in the hall in this storm, only to land in a bathroom with overflowing toilets of vomit. The air reeked of puke, which only caused more heaving. I overheard reports of sick passengers lying all over the floor in the forward viewing room and bathroom. Sick passengers were not unusual, but the sheer number and overflowing toilets were unique.

Hugging the shoreline, the captain inched his way into Ketchikan, adding ninety minutes to the already miserable three-hour trip. The typically calm waters of the Tongass Narrows leading into Ketchikan pitched a fierce fight in the wind. The ferry dock and terminals lay ahead.

Docking the ferry in this storm bordered on impossible. Passengers lined the windows to watch workers struggle to tie down the vessel. Waves splashed against the hull. Rain smacked workers in the face while the slick deck rocked and rolled beneath their feet. We wondered if the harbormaster would force us back out to sea, but the workers successfully secured the boat. With the ordeal finally over, passengers filled the hallway, ready to set foot onto steady ground.

We hailed a cab for a quick ride from the dock to the airport ferry. What a sight we must have been, arriving late, seasick, soaked, and not thrilled to be on the milk run flight up the coast to Anchorage. They nicknamed the flight the *milk run* because it originated with supplies in Seattle with stops in Ketchikan, Wrangell, Sitka or Petersburg, and Juneau. It guaranteed passengers one long, grueling afternoon flying into Anchorage.

TSA hurried us through to the waiting plane. I removed my shoes and took my computer out of its bag. With my totes on the conveyor belt, I waited in line. Something set off the alarm when I stepped through the metal detector.

"Please step over here for inspection," the TSA woman instructed. Her wand hovered over my vest, where a butter knife protruded from the pocket. "What's this?" It surprised me as much as it did her.

"It must have fallen into my pocket when the ferry almost capsized," I claimed. Only in Alaska would a TSA agent accept an excuse like that!

I sat down to wait for my flight and sent Elgin an email saying: *The ferry ride to Ketchikan was really rough and hair-raising. We were rolling, bumping, crashing, and splashing on the ferry today! It gave a whole new meaning to the phrase rock-and-roll.*

Have you heard of the *SS Princess Sophia,* referred to by some as *The Unknown Titanic of the West Coast*? If you haven't, you are not alone.

The sinking of the *SS Princess Sophia* was the worst human disaster in Alaska's history. It still holds the record as the worst shipwreck on America's west coast. I read a book about it in 1995 and thought of it when I ferried in rough seas. Given the wreck of the *Titanic* and *SS Princess Sophia,* I knew no ship was unsinkable.

The year was 1918 and the cease-fire for WWI was two weeks away. Local workers and their families from Alaska and Canada's Yukon and British Columbia Territories headed home for the winter break. On the twenty-fourth of October, at 2:00 a.m., the *Sophia* became engulfed in a winter storm with blinding snow and high winds. The ship ran onto the Vanderbilt Reef right outside of Juneau, Alaska.

"Mayday, Mayday, Mayday," sent rescuers scrambling to save the passengers.

The captain hoped for a break in the weather. He avoided risking passengers' lives by not putting them into lifeboats in strong winds on high seas near the reef. He waited a day. The storm grew worse. Though rescuers stood by, no boats approached the *Sophia* in the dark winter night. Waves violently crashed against the dangerous reef. Rescuers sought shelter in a nearby cove. Almost forty hours later, at 5:20 p.m., rescuers in the area heard the final mayday call.

Bill Morrison detailed the ship's sinking in his book, *The Sinking of the Princess Sophia: Taking the North Down with Her* (1991). "It's blowing like crazy, the tide is rising—suddenly the stern end of the ship lifts off as it turns around facing north. It blows off the reef, it rips a huge gash in the hull, and it slips stern first into the ninety feet of water."

By morning the storm had cleared, but it was too late. More than 350 souls on board perished in the dreadful night. Yukon Territory alone lost 8 percent of its Caucasian population in the tragedy.

The oil-covered bodies proved challenging to identify for the Juneau volunteers. A hundred bodies remained in the submerged cabins and hallways before being recovered by divers. Bodies washed ashore along the coast for months. The city of Juneau buried or sent the dead home by boat to Vancouver and the Lower-48.

Celebrations filled the city streets at the news of the end of World War I, which completely overshadowed the horrific sinking of the *SS Princess Sophia*. Any other time, the world surely would have mourned such a tragic loss. Instead, few even knew it happened. No famous people were aboard that day, only ordinary workers, and one Walter Harper, the first person to set foot on Mount McKinley's (Denali) summit. Not one survivor lived to tell their story.

Lost or Stuck

Which would be worse, becoming lost or being stuck on Prince of Wales Island? Scores of people disappeared in Alaska, some from the island. A few of the missing people have never been found. Hunters failed to return home. Pilots were lost at sea. Even two children ran away into the woods and stayed missing for nine months.

The school superintendent Jim Nygaard became lost in the Tongass National Forest. It was a chilly, wet November night when his wife Louella phoned to say he hadn't returned home from a hunting trip he had taken with a local. Given the late hour, no search party left until morning. No one slept as we watched the temperature drop into the thirties and listened to the rainfall. The next morning, a search plane flew over and spotted the two men, half-frozen, but waving frantically. They had walked circles in the woods. The local man hid in a hollowed-out log to protect himself from the elements. Jim leaned against a tree, exposed to the pouring rain, dressed only for a day trip. It is a wonder they escaped with their lives.

Some people became lost in the woods driving the roads on Prince of Wales Island with fifteen hundred miles of old logging roads headed out to nowhere. The miles upon miles of logging roads can become a maze to the unsuspecting driver. The mountains blocked the horizon. Rough roads made the drive a slow go, and at each fork in the road, we held our breath, hoping our choice of direction wasn't taking us further out into no-man's-land. We never ran out of gas, but I worried about it on countless trips.

Animal trails going every which way made it easy to take off in the wrong direction on foot. "Elgin, didn't we come through here an hour ago? I think those could be our tracks." We wandered in the forest with our boys, lost right before dark. I wondered if we should keep searching for the road or build a shelter while we could still see. The forest had wild animals and rain, lots of rain. We had become lost in the woods searching for Salt Chuck

Mine.

If being lost on an old road wasn't in the cards, becoming stuck was a real possibility. People found themselves stuck in snow and mud or broken down. Foul weather caught people out boating or flying. Sick patients in need of medical attention in Ketchikan could spend days waiting for a medevac.

Being stuck in Alaska didn't always mean physically. Finances could easily trap people. Fortune seekers sacrificed being near extended family, friends, and their old way of life. Young educators earning the coveted state retirement, such as ourselves, found themselves planted in the state for a minimum of twenty to twenty-five years. We felt stuck when we wanted to return to Wyoming to be closer to our aging parents. A handful of teachers arrived penniless only to discover the harsh realities of bush life overwhelmed them, but they had no way to leave. Repeatedly, coworkers banded together to help stuck teachers buy tickets home.

And then some people were temporarily stuck. A specialist flying in for a few hours to test a student for special education could wind up sleeping on the couch, floor, or a staff member's spare bed for a week. Sports teams visiting for games slept on my classroom floors for many unscheduled nights while waiting out the weather.

Occasionally, major airliners made forced landings, spilling hundreds of people into tiny towns. Cold Bay's former WWII airport has a 10,400-foot runway, which serves as a haven for planes in crisis. The school and community members open their doors and pantries to the stranded. And if it is you stranded, you had better enjoy fish because that's what they are having for dinner.

When on a tight ferry schedule, we rushed through events to avoid becoming stuck, especially in Ketchikan—the last city before reaching the island. For example, we sped from the *Columbia* ferry to the Ketchikan Hospital for a short visit after the birth of our first grandchild, Meliah Mae Cook, in late August 2009.

Everett and Abbey packed while we held the baby. Expectant mothers stayed in larger towns for weeks, waiting to go into labor near a hospital. Abbey was no exception. Now that Meliah had arrived, they had a plane to catch. Everett was already late for his third year in college back in Wyoming.

We barely had time to hold our beautiful dark-haired Meliah. Darn! As a mother of all sons, I had counted the years until I had a chance to have a granddaughter. Now I had to leave to catch a ferry after only a few minutes of bonding time.

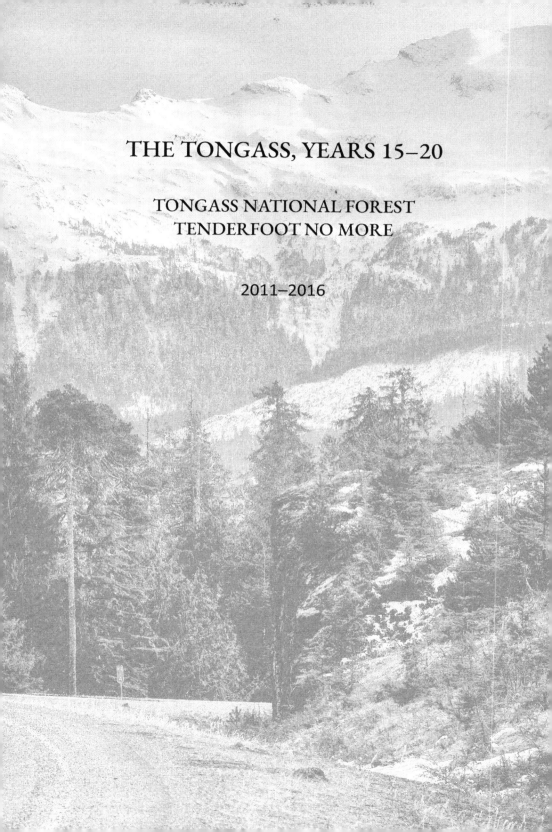

THE TONGASS, YEARS 15–20

TONGASS NATIONAL FOREST
TENDERFOOT NO MORE

2011–2016

SIXTY-ONE

Disability is Not a Bundle of Sick Days

My reflection in the bathroom mirror turned fuzzy, gray, and suddenly black. I collapsed in a heap on the cold floor. It was the beginning of the end of my career.

I had transferred to an administrative position in the fall of 2004, expecting a reduction in stress. Are you laughing? My new schedule permitted flextime, which protected my sick leave.

After four years of administrative work, stress on the job caused MS to become downright ugly by June 2008. A brain stem lesion wreaked havoc with the automation of my heart, lungs, and body temperature. Fatigue made it a struggle to keep my eyes open. All those mornings I dragged myself out of bed for work were about to pay off. *Tomorrow could be worse,* I told myself for years. Well, tomorrow had arrived. Despite pushback from the new superintendent, I took medical leave for the entire next school year.

In August 2009, I returned to the high school classroom, hoping the shorter hours and less stress would keep me in the workforce long enough to see my boys through college.

In the first week of February 2011, Elgin flew south to spend time with his ailing father. The doctors had diagnosed Kenny with ALS in late December. His condition deteriorated rapidly until he passed away that July. My stepfather, Robert Simmons, shocked us when he died suddenly in October. It was a devastating year.

Too weak to attempt another task, I plopped myself on the couch staring at the blank TV for half an hour—too dog-tired to turn the darn thing on, I wrote. My MS had spiraled out of control. Teaching was an exhausting job, and February was typically a difficult month for students and staff alike.

MS dictates my day and there's no arguing; it just is. I make the best of even the toughest days because we only get one shot at each day and then it is gone forever. There is no rewind in life, I posted on social media. Having a positive attitude about multiple sclerosis helped me stay working as long as I did, but my time was up.

For months, I wrote notes on the board between class periods to keep myself on track. Without them, I chased the white rabbit down its hole and could not find my way back to the lesson's objective. Students enjoyed that because we'd spiral into delightful academic discussions, albeit off-topic.

Vertigo forced me to use a cane and to instruct from a barstool. Vision issues meant I required additional light over my desk. Language issues tongue-tied me.

When the MS medication suppressed my immune system, sick students sat in the back of the room to prevent exposing me to their colds. Many opted to take a flu shot rather than a nasal spray to reduce my risk of contracting the illness as they shed the virus. Principal Nick Higson scheduled additional janitorial hours to disinfect my classroom daily, reduced my class size, and was there whenever I requested help. He and the students did what they could to keep me teaching, but we were fighting a losing battle.

Memory issues complicated my ability to answer student questions. It was a challenge to remember the tasks I needed to accomplish. For months, I diligently stuck reminder notes to my clothing. I realized my teaching days were over when I scolded a child for not asking to use the bathroom before leaving the room. He defended himself adamantly saying he *had* requested permission to leave. The other students agreed with him. I had no memory of it.

"Moo!" The same eighth-grader stood at the door staring at me in all seriousness the next week. "I figured I would help you remember I have permission to leave the room." With that, he opened the door and left. He amused me.

A month earlier, I had mooed at the class while they quietly studied. The students immediately glanced up in astonishment at their nutty teacher, mooing like a cow. I smiled, "To get the immediate attention of a person or group, make an unexpected animal noise." Giggling, we returned to work. One of my main teaching goals had been to develop an engaging, fun, yet disciplined learning environment, and I often used the elements of humor and surprise to do it.

Humor aside, the end of my career in education fell upon me. Despite the classroom support given to me by students and Principal Higson, it was time for me to quit. I told the students when I returned to teaching in 2009, if a first-year teacher could manage the classroom better than me, I would apply for medical disability. I left on May 1, 2011, replaced by a first-year teacher just as I had predicted.

In May 2012, I attended the annual awards night. Nick Higson surprised me with a service award for my twelve years with SISD. Students of all ages and from multiple schools filled the bleachers. Following a brief speech, I stepped away from the podium, cane and award in hand.

"Moo!" The stands came alive as the students mooed in unison. I stared at the crowd, bewildered. *Are they booing me?* A high school boy saw my confusion and leapt from his seat, yelling, "We're mooing for you, Mrs. Cook. We're Mooing!" Tears filled my eyes as I stood before a stand of mooing children. I missed them all so much. Students brought laughter into my life hourly for years. How quiet my world had now become. I returned to the podium to explain to the parents why their children were mooing.

Two more years passed. I seldom left the house except to walk Sampson and Josie. After all, I was sick. Right? Then I had an epiphany; disability isn't a bundle of sick days—it's life. It was then I put on my coat, picked up my camera, and started living again. A short time later, I wrote: *I can always find something to do but it's almost always alone. I'm not complaining, just noticing.*

In the fall of 2014, I wrote an article describing the change in my perception of medical disability for Carnival of MS Bloggers, #161:

Creating a World of My Own
By Melissa L. Cook

Papers stacked high, email flags a mile long, a budget to reconstruct on my desk, a teacher in for an evaluation, and it was already 2:30 p.m.—I would be home late again tonight. Double-timing as I navigated the halls of the school, touching base with teachers to see if they needed anything—support, supplies, a travel request. On to instruct an after-school teacher in-service, and then I would hightail it to a conference call on a new state report. I loved my job. My career as a school district administrator was, simply put, awesome. Little did I know my driven world would abruptly skid to a crawl, robbing me of my oomph and leaving me alone with no more tasks to complete than to peel myself out of bed, slip on clothes, and cook dinner. Multiple sclerosis had taken an ugly turn for me.

Initially, I was too ill to perceive my devastating launch into isolation. Loneliness was a few months off. Fearing the worst was about to befall me, I planned my final arrangements and put my affairs in order. The shock of being alone hit me like a ton of bricks. Overload at the office made it difficult to sustain meaningful relationships in the after-hours. I was alone now during the day; my life would never be the same.

A few years later, I composed a blog post called "Disability is Not a Bundle of Sick Days" with the conclusion, "It's as if I have spent the past thirty-one months out on sick leave. Disability isn't a sick day; it's life. It's about time I realized it and started living again." I hid in my home for two-and-a-half years because I thought I was sick. What would people think if I wasn't working but could mosey into the post office or store? I ventured out with a camera in hand to photograph fall colors and discovered my neighbors and friends had wondered whatever happened to me.

Creating a world of my own came from the freedom gained in throwing out the sick day mentality. Multiple sclerosis is a day-by-day illness, meaning there are times I feel normal and can do what I used to do. The first order of business was making new friends. Second, I reintroduced purpose into my life when I began blogging about my MS story and the latest research on www.MSsymptoms.me. Third, my desire to help others led me to become a first responder. People with disabilities can be an asset to EMS. I became a board member for the local domestic violence and rape crisis center, putting my administrative training and education to use. Now I am polishing up a children's story and am revising short stories on Alaska bush life.

Multiple sclerosis still hangs around my doorstep. However, I balance my new world in a way I never could with the demands of work. Resting as I need and remembering all things in moderation permits me to live an awe-inspiring life without the career I once loved.

The old saying, when one door closes, another one opens, has been true for me. My career goal of becoming a superintendent of schools with a PhD was not to be. However, my dream of writing is taking shape. In addition, I find time to play with my grandchildren, quilt, bead, take photographs, and I want to learn how to paint with watercolors. I am creating my own world. Yes, I still spend most of my days alone, but I am not lonely; I'm happy again. My best friend is home in the evenings and on weekends with me. I love you, Elgin!–11/6/2014.

In December 2014, the only poem I have ever written spilled out of me.

Sometimes

By Melissa L. Cook

Sometimes, I need a little help now and then, so I have learned to ask.
Sometimes, I have pain, so I have learned to manage.
Sometimes, I am lonely now that I am on disability, so new friends I have made.
Sometimes, I miss my career, so I have learned to write.
Sometimes, I feel sadness, so happiness I choose.
Sometimes, I must figure out how to do things differently, but I still do.

SIXTY-TWO

Reckless Insanity

The air was brisk, filling my nose with the smell of fresh snow and ice. *Crunch, crunch* sounded below my feet as I hiked through the ice-covered snow. The sun had set as the full moon rose over the tree-covered mountains. My headband flashlight lit the way for the dogs and they breezed through the snow, tails wagging behind them. They ran ahead and rounded the next corner in the dark. Jogging along the path, the evergreen branches laden with snow awed me. By far, the best hikes took place in the forest at night.

For seventeen years, I hiked in the Tongass National Forest. It didn't matter if it rained or snowed. It didn't matter if it was dark outside or blowing like a hurricane. I hiked with Elgin, the dogs, and occasionally the boys. And at times, the dogs and I walked alone.

From 2011 to 2016, I ventured out by myself on most days since I was home on medical disability. Logging roads made for easy access, as did recreational areas void of visitors most of the year. On my way home from Craig, I considered stopping to walk the dogs at Eagle's Nest Campground, one of Sampson's all-time favorite places. He begged me to stop with slight whines and his big eyes in between sniffing the air vents.

Walking around Balls Lake alone was less appealing in the spring. Just because I hiked daily didn't mean I always enjoyed it. Bears out of hibernation made me more cautious and even afraid at times.

Bears are out now. Besides, you forgot the gun. As I drummed up excuses in my head, Sampson eyed me with anticipation. His nose pressed against the truck's air vent; he detected his choice spot fast approaching.

How can you deny him a run on the boardwalk when you are driving right by the lake? The guilt trip worked, and I pulled into the parking lot at the last second. Energy burst through Sampson, and out escaped a bark. He leapt to the center console at the prospect of the outing.

Attempting to forget the hungry bears fresh out of hibernation, I stopped at the trail's entrance. Sampson tried to control his whine and hopped into my seat while I exited the vehicle. "Okay!" He and Josie flew out of the truck and sped down the path, stopping to sniff the closest tree before hightailing it into the woods.

Pretending to have more courage than I possessed, I strolled swiftly to the path leading into the forest. *I've hiked this trail hundreds of times. Why am I so spooked today?*

"Let's get this over with," I conceded aloud. Alone, surrounded by trees and thick underbrush, I knew the possibility of running into a bear was real but, honestly, remote. The dogs scurried down the gravel path to the boardwalk along the lake's edge. They sniffed for invaders to what they perceived as their personal dog run.

Walking dogs without leashes is a big no-no in bear country! I reminded myself. My brain refused to shut up. *Dogs who encounter bears will run back to their owners for protection, with the bear in tow!* I took a deep breath to calm my nerves. *Why do you do this to yourself? Quit it!*

"Frosty the snowman," I sang. The dogs tolerated my unflattering voice as I hummed and sang on our solo trips into the woods. I figured it was best to announce my presence.

You shouldn't be out here alone, my mind nagged.

Bears prefer to avoid humans, I argued with myself.

The Forest Service covered the boardwalk with black netting and roof shingles to combat the slickness. My insulated boots crunched through half-melted snow and ice. My heart pounded as I looked through the trees for bears.

"There must have been some magic in that old silk hat they found," I sang, quickening my pace. A narrow wooden staircase leading to a campsite at the top of the steep hill appeared up ahead. I knew every inch of this area and was aware the campsite trail led past a picnic table and tent clearing. If I cut through the campsite to the main road, I would not be far from where I had left my truck.

Don't run! A bear won't be able to deny himself the thrill of the chase. Don't you do it! I began speed-walking without running, closing in on the dogs who expected a full hike around the lake and back to the main road. Surprising them, I suddenly hollered, "Let's go!" The dogs stopped on the boardwalk and stared at me, unsure of what I meant.

Don't you run. Don't do it! I told myself until I broke into a clumsy sprint down the boardwalk and screamed, "Come on!" The dogs took off running toward me.

You idiot! If a bear is out there, he will be on your tail now! I was out of control and didn't care. I scrambled up the icy, snow-covered steps as quickly as my heavy insulated boots allowed. Sampson and Josie scampered between my feet in a race to beat me to the top. Reaching the path, we broke out into a wild sprint through the woods; the sudden, unexpected turn of events confused the dogs, but the change of pace excited them. Breaking through the trees and onto the gravel path, I gained solid footing and a better ability to see around me. The campground road lay ahead. I spotted the truck when we rounded the next corner.

"Jump in!" I ordered on the run and flung open the truck door for the dogs to jump into the backseat. My eyes darted from tree to tree, imagining a bear behind each one. Sampson darted by me and returned to the path, undoubtedly feeling shortchanged by the abrupt ending to his cherished time.

"Come back here!" I closed in on him; my odd behavior scared him into submission. Josie, already in the truck, panted on the floor. When the door shut behind me, my nerves calmed after our paranoid run through the forest. I'll admit, I lost my mind and freaked out over a bear that never showed himself. That doesn't mean it wasn't there!

Prince of Wales Island had one black bear per square mile. We stepped over bear prints and scat on the logging roads daily. That said, I knew not one bear attack ever happened on the island while we lived there, though I kept my eye out for them anyway. And despite routinely scaring myself on the trail, this was my one and only bout of reckless insanity.

SIXTY-THREE

Friends in Rainy Places

Elgin struggled living so far away from our Wyoming desert home, and the rain in the Tongass National Forest made things worse for him. Once, he told me he didn't *hate* Alaska, he just couldn't take the continual rain, and he wasn't alone. I wrote in 2011: *It has rained and rained and rained for days and days and days. I'm soaked to the bone and ready for a break, and we have only been back in Alaska for nine days!* Thorne Bay receives almost three times the precipitation as the rainy city of Seattle.

My love for Alaska didn't start until I left my career for medical disability. With the freedom to do whatever I wanted for the first time in my adult life, I took advantage of the opportunity to hike in the forest, wander the beach, stroll the docks, and strengthen friendships that, until now, had been challenging to nurture with my busy work schedule.

As it turned out, all of my friends were coworkers who worked during the day, and most had moved on to other school districts or states far away. So, one evening, I looked around the quilt guild meeting in Klawock to make a new friend. The group consisted of people with day jobs or ladies traveling fair distances from around the island to get to town. No one was driving the hour from my neck of the woods, though. Then, I spotted Joy Weber, an eighty-five-year-old artist from Klawock.

"Hey, Joy?" I started. "Do you teach beginners how to embroider?" I asked, looking at her show-and-tell project.

"I can. Be at my apartment on Tuesday morning at eleven o'clock," she replied. Dina Merchant, the co-leader of the guild, sat down next to her with a big hello, and they began to visit. After the meeting, Dina pulled me aside.

"Don't be late! Joy expects visitors to be on time." I heeded Dina's advice and arrived at 11:00 a.m. sharp.

"Hello! Come in!" Within seconds of my knock, Joy appeared with a bright smile and a wide-open door. It was the beginning of our dear friendship. That day Joy gave me the grand tour of her two-bedroom apartment, including her craft room. For several years, Joy and I spent two days a week together. We went to lunch, ran errands, attended quilt guild meetings, and spent Saturday afternoons with a handful of other ladies in Dina's quilt shop located in her converted garage. I especially enjoyed listening to Joy talk about her experience working in the laundry office serving the soldiers during WWII and hearing her laugh, which she did often.

Joy and I spent much of our time at the quilt shop in Craig. Dina provided a place for friendship to anyone who wanted to get out of the house, work on a craft, sew, quilt, or just hang out snacking on her platter of cheese and crackers. When a quilter showed up with a carload of project supplies, the ladies often dashed out into the rain and were blown back into the shop by the wind, bags and boxes in hand.

Several of the ladies were teachers who had or were teaching in the small schools on the island, including me, Dina, and Neva. Nonie Dixon owned and operated a restaurant in Klawock. She was the resident sewing expert and co-leader of the guild who patiently taught sewing skills to anyone who asked. Neva was always quick to help carry in supplies. During a weekend sewing retreat, when fatigue slowed me to a crawl, she put her project aside to help me catch up on mine. On my good days, I helped the others carry in their boxes. We were there for each other.

On Saturday, sewing machines hummed while we chatted about the latest events in town, reminisced about where we had come from and the lives we had once lived in those places. Fishing stories, recent whale sightings, the latest house fire (the island averaged one a month), upcoming school events, and Neva's latest find in the local bargain shop were regular topics. Neva always seemed to know what people were looking for and showed up with something in hand weekly. Dina was always in the know and shared the latest appropriate news, but she wasn't a gossip. Nonie outsewed everyone while sharing some of the most exciting stories about Alaska fishing and her childhood in Washington. At ten years old, Nonie was charged by an injured bear and saved by her father, who spent a week in the hospital recovering from the injuries he sustained protecting her.

Despite all the story sharing, snacks, and friendship, by four o'clock, Joy was typically ready to go home, and to be honest, MS fatigue made the drive back to Thorne Bay about all I had left in me.

It was dark by four in the winter months, which meant I had to keep a sharp eye out for deer who hung out on the winding road between Klawock and Thorne Bay. In the spring and fall, the beauty of the drive entertained me all the way home. The rain kept roadside puddles full, and on calm days they reflected gorgeous views, which were distracting at times. Wildlife posed a risk all year long. Once, I hit an eagle with the truck grill coming out of Klawock. *Thump.* An expanding cloud of feathers flew up over the hood, and my heart sank.

Heading into the sleepy town of Thorne Bay, I called Elgin to let him know I was coming around the bay. He knew I would be tired by now and stood at the doorway waiting to haul in my sewing machine and bags of fabric. Though I drove to town chasing friendships, I returned home to my best friend, who spent his day off alone so that I could spend Saturdays with the ladies.

SIXTY-FOUR

The Kamikaze Raven

Bundled in a winter coat, I headed out to photograph the city dock at night. Misty air hung over the deserted streets of Thorne Bay. I passed Old Man Russell's house. He sat day and night by his kitchen window, visiting with friends or watching movies on his computer. Disabled, this hardy fisherman and logger still limped along to chop and store firewood in his tiny yard. At least once a week I stopped by for a short visit and delivered my latest baked goods to him. I felt a connection with Russell because we were both alone most of the time sitting by our windows across the street from each other.

The damp streets gave me an eerie feeling as I rounded the corner and carefully made my way down the hill to the waterfront. The tide was out, meaning an ocean level drop of twelve to fifteen feet or more. Grated metal teeth on the ramp gripped my boots, helping me safely descend to the dock below. Fog rolled in waves around the bay. Lights on the three-foot-tall utility meters dimly lit the fork-shaped dock. Skiffs floated in slips near the ramp while fishing vessels of various sizes, sailboats, and powerboats mixed with the fog. A yellow Piper Super Cub rested in a slip on the far-right side.

Stepping onto the dock, I took a deep breath of cold air. Low tide exposed the dock's pilings, which appeared to be tall black figures hovering fifteen feet overhead. A large piece of seaweed fell from the top of a piling and dropped right past my head landing at my feet, scaring me half to death. Fog drifted over the bay, floating in between the boats and at the far end of the walkway.

Kneeling, I composed an image of the meters lining the dock. They grew smaller and closer together as they stretched the length of the walkway. The fog mingled around the boats. Not a soul was out.

The wet wooden planks glistened before my lens. A visitor's bench faced the peaceful bay at the end of the dock. I sat in the quiet night remembering the days I brought the dogs here to play. Sampson had recently stopped eating and lost his energy. I flew him into Ketchikan to see the vet expecting him to return on the afternoon flight, but the news was grim, so they kept him in town. The next day, I caught an early morning flight only to find my beloved friend who loved every minute in life too sick to hold up his head. I held him for hours after they put him to sleep, unable or unwilling to release him to the nurse. He had been *my* dog. He stole my heart and took a piece of it with him when he died. Pushing back the tears, determined to hold onto the fun memories of him sniffing every nook and cranny, I stood and gazed across the foggy dock.

Wandering alone, I climbed the steep ramp. The windless night meant still water ideal for photography. The dock meters turned out to be my favorite image of the area.

That night, I discovered a new love. Insomnia ruled my life, so on restless nights, I threw caution to the wind, strolling by myself while the rest of the town slept. It would have displeased my mother and possibly Elgin, but it was my secret. Rare clear skies with a full moon drew me out. Blizzards drew me out. Pouring rain even coaxed me out of the house to gallivant on the dock and watch the boats rock in the waves. I slipped out to marvel at the bay in heavy fog or admired the moonlit planks covered in rain, frost, ice, or freshly fallen snow. The dock and beach are what I miss most from my Alaska days.

I began each day sitting in the dining room admiring the view, something I had never done when I worked. One day, I posted on social media:

I glanced out the window this morning at the tree-covered mountains. Bears fish in the creek below us, though we can't see them through the trees. Eagles soar overhead constantly. Bluebirds sit in the trees peeking in through the leaves while ravens watch from above for any opportunity to steal something from our trash can. How marvelous it is to wake up in Alaska!

One morning, I heard a ruckus outside the living window. It wasn't unusual for ravens to rustle around in the trash cans. The previous night, I had locked the lid to prevent the trash pickers from stopping at my house. One must have been dancing on top, plotting to remove the lid but peeking out now, I could see nothing. I returned to the dining room to watch the blue birds.

Boom!

"What the heck?" Alarmed, I darted to the front door, swung it open in time for another *boom*. A kamikaze raven torpedoed my trash can to take the lid off. I laughed. He dislodged it, slipped inside, and came out the victor. He flew over the treetops with the bones of an entire chicken carcass! Amused, I watched him until he flew out of sight.

This crafty thief's behavior explained why the local Natives told stories about the trickster who created our world—a place he transformed through magic and thievery. The Haida culture taught that the Raven found human beings in a clamshell and fed them salmon and berries. He taught proper behavior to children, despite his poor example. In reality, the ravens stole fascinating items from our yard. A good example would be when my grandchildren were hunting for Easter eggs at my house one spring.

"Are you ready to hunt for Easter eggs?" I asked my grandchildren. Meliah, now four years old, stood in the yard with her two-year-old brother, Auron. They waited patiently with their baskets in hand.

"There's one!" Meliah spotted a blue egg hidden in the grass.

"Eleven," I counted when Auron found an egg under the stairs. "I put out eighteen eggs. Where could the other seven be?" We searched high and low. Then I saw them, ravens in the trees above us—waiting.

"I have an idea," I took Auron by the hand. "Leave an egg in this planter and one over here. Quick, let's go inside and see if the birds steal the eggs."

"Ah-ha!" By the time we reached the window, a raven had already stolen an egg. We watched him fly off with the colorful treat. We kept an eye out for a few more minutes before the kids grew bored. "Now we know where the eggs went!"

I glanced out the window after the kids settled into a game and discovered the second egg was now missing. I decided to see what else the ravens would loot from the yard, so I put out spoiled chicken breasts. They were there and then they were gone! Funny birds. From then on, I stuck old eggs in the planter pot outside. It didn't take them long to vanish.

After Everett and Abbey picked up the kids, Elgin and I headed out to hit a few golf balls. Okay, so hitting golf balls in Thorne Bay wasn't quite the same as, let's say, Tucson. We drove a mile outside of town, made our way through a fast-growing red alder grove, and climbed a long hill to the former dump. The sourdoughs of the island called it Kmart, back when residents went to the dump to find items they needed. Anything with potential worth was not merely tossed into the pile but set aside in case someone else could use it. The area made for fabulous bear viewing opportunities too. As you probably realize by now, I had a constant radar for bears.

Years ago, the city had thrown wood chips over the dump. Trees and vegetation now grew on top of the chips. The constantly wet climate encouraged peat moss growth, which made for slippery conditions when plodding through there.

Evergreen trees lined the perimeter of the wide-open space surrounded by mountain peaks. The Thorne River skirted the edge of the mounds, and on some days, a heavy fog hung over it.

At the top of the hefty climb, we set out the golf mat, dropped a few balls, and began swinging. Each round, we hit thirty to forty-five balls, depending on how many we had left in our stash. Retrieving them included hiking down the hill and up the next mound of covered trash. It was futile to search for balls that landed in the woods. Did I mention the goose poop? The geese used one area of the hillside as their personal toilet! I avoided hitting a ball toward that spot to escape searching for it later. We lost one in three balls to the rotting debris or forest every time we went out.

We putted on fake grass strips in the hallway at home throughout the winters and practiced swings and chips on the covered trash heaps in the spring and fall. We also watched plenty of golf on TV. What can I say? We were hard up for a game of golf!

SIXTY-FIVE

It's Winter Again

It was winter again! Snow and ice covered the landscape. Daylight dwindled to seven hours on the shortest days of winter, all of which took place during the workday. And the long days of loneliness and cabin fever were once again upon us.

Humor lurked around the corner, though. One morning I slipped outside in my pajamas to drive Elgin to school. Thin ice coated the truck, and the door refused to open. I repeatedly tugged and pulled on the handle. Nope, it was not going to open.

"The door is frozen shut again," I hollered.

"Unlock it," Elgin replied.

The daylight decreased by minutes each day in the fall. With the end of daylight-saving time, we plunged into the darkest period of the year with a shocking loss of an additional hour overnight. I wrote: *It's that time of year when it's dark before Elgin leaves the school in the afternoon. The television provides a vivid reminder of cities and people during these long winter months. I yearn for the world outside.* Keeping a positive attitude was paramount to overcoming the negative aspects that accompanied the darkness and isolation.

But life continued when the sun set mid-afternoon in Southeast Alaska. "We'd better walk the dogs," I reminded Elgin one afternoon at 1:30. "The sun will set in an hour and a half." We drove out to Sandy Beach or Eagle's Nest on the weekends until the snow blocked us out. The dogs couldn't wait to hike a trail or log hop on the beach. On the weekdays during the winter, headlamps lit our way.

The Alaska Permanent Fund dividend arrived in our bank accounts each October. We bought either plane or ferry tickets on the same day, then we counted the weeks until winter break. We spent the three full weeks of vacation time in either Arizona or Wyoming.

When we left for Wyoming, we drove the highway through British Columbia, plowing snow and crawling over mountain passes in blizzards with near whiteout conditions. We white-knuckled it over snow-packed and icy roads and saw many cars, trucks, and semi-trucks in the ditch along the way. On one winter trip, a plow drove us off the road and into a snowdrift in the wee hours of the morning. Then the grumpy man had to pull us out.

If we flew to Tucson, the change from sunny warm weather to Alaska's winter temperatures shocked our systems. Sometimes, we lucked out and arrived in Ketchikan to rain and wind. Other times, it was snow and ice.

"You claim the dogs and luggage. I'll bring the truck to the front door to meet you," Elgin instructed. Bundled up, he exited the airport into a blizzard.

Loaded down with baggage, two crates with anxious dogs inside, and layered in coats prepared to greet the winter storm, I waited. And waited. And waited. I am not talking twenty minutes, but possibly over an hour. It was a three-minute walk, at the most, to our truck. I peeked outside to determine if Elgin was coming, but I could see nothing through the blizzard and darkness. Finally, Elgin drove up in the ice-covered truck with snow accumulating on the newly scraped-off hood. Frozen. That's the best way to describe the vehicle and outside conditions, frozen.

"What took you so long?" I shouldn't have asked. Obviously, there was a problem with the truck.

"*What do you mean?*" Elgin looked at me incredibly. "Do you see the truck?" I looked at my feet, immediately regretting my question. "Not to mention, I didn't have a shovel! The snowplow piled four feet of snow behind our truck. It melted, froze into ice, and then they piled more snow on top of it! Idiots! How do they expect people to get their vehicles out? Simply finding it in the dark was a trick! The blizzard blocked what little light was out there. Deep snow covered the vehicles, so I dug out feet of snow in the dark only to find the truck covered in ice and frozen shut! I chipped as much ice away with the tire iron as I could. Then I drove in four-wheel-drive to back over the ice wall, which is when the air dam broke off the front bumper. What took me so long? *That's* what took me so long!"

His skin was wet from melting snow on his beet-red face. Snow covered his hat and coat. The biting wind passed right through our clothes. I handed him the first bag, and he put it in the back. We loaded the rest of the luggage, crates, and dogs, then drove to the airport ferry to cross the channel over to Ketchikan. At the hotel, I walked the dogs along the coastline in the dark. The storm chilled me right down to the bone.

It snowed, and snowed, and snowed that winter. Our favorite hiking spots remained snow-covered most of the spring. I'm grateful not all winters were so long and rough.

Diminished daylight limited the already few options available for outdoor activities in the dead of winter. Satellite television brought the outside world into our living room. Puzzles sat on the kitchen table. Elgin played chess over the internet with his brother, Myron. Both brothers mastered photography and image editing and spent evenings critiquing each other's work. Elgin chatted with his mother and Myron nightly while I spent hours on the phone with my mother during the day. It was lonelier when it was quiet.

After the boys left for college, I began quilting as a pastime. Elgin put together a quilting studio for me in our living room, turning the spare room into the TV room. I spent the lion's share of my days in the studio at my desk, sewing table, or in front of the twelve-foot-long quilting table.

Being home alone day after day during the winter was especially difficult. I wrote home: *I'm bored and lonely in the Last Frontier in the middle of the winter. I can't wait until I live in society again. The days are long, dark, and silent here. Sometimes I get all dressed up with no place to go, which makes it hard to find a reason not to stay in my pajamas on some days.*

An email from early spring revealed life under cover of darkness:

The brilliant stars come out when the cloud cover dissipates in the Tongass National Forest. One of my favorite memories is jogging with my dogs in complete darkness with only the moon and the truck headlights far behind me to light the way. Running along the snow and ice-covered truck tracks on the road, I gazed up at the enormous snow-covered trees. Above me was the unusual sighting of the moon and stars twinkling in the black night sky. It was as if I was running through a painting, a cold one at that!

Winter ended when rain melted the last of the snow—and rain it did. I described one afternoon dog walk in an email:

I took the dogs for a walk in a hurricane! Well, maybe not a hurricane, but the wind was raging, the freezing rain was blowing sideways, and it sounded like the ocean was coming ashore. I expected the dogs to hurry about their business in such weather, but no, they sniffed every bush, stick, rock, and log! We were all soaked by the time we got in.

It was almost never dry in the rainforest. Even when the rain stopped, everything was wet. Water dripped off the trees, the truck, the house, the trash can. Drip, drip, drip, and drip some more. It was this time of year I became desperate to dry out. And then, the yellow flowers of the skunk cabbage plant popped out of the marshy mess surrounding us each spring. Every year we competed to see who could spot the first stinky skunk cabbage and then rejoiced. It meant summer break lay straight ahead.

SIXTY-SIX

Evey's Mountain

"Mom, I want to live off the land. I'm a survivalist and love the woods. I hate being in the city." Ethan attended college in Spearfish, South Dakota, a town with less than ten thousand people. It resembled a big city to him after growing up in bush Alaska. Eager to finish school, he dreamed of a subsistence lifestyle in the Tongass National Forest.

Ethan returned with his family to Prince of Wales Island in the fall of 2014. He completed his student teaching with Native children at the two-teacher school in Kasaan. After graduating in December, he accepted a job working with Craig's disadvantaged children until a caretaker position opened at a remote lodge on the north end of the island.

The heydays for Bear Valley Lodge had long since passed. The buildings stood on their last legs. Even in its state of disrepair, it was magical looking out at El Capitan Passage and the surrounding forested mountains. And they didn't name it Bear Valley Lodge for nothing. I saw more bears within one mile of that lodge than all the bear sightings I ever had on the island, combined.

Eight musty cabins had a boardwalk connecting them to the lodge. Showcase windows with a spectacular view once entertained diners in the main building. A single wood stove heated the entire upstairs, including a living room, galley kitchen with a food storage area, and a game room. The downstairs housed a damp and smelly laundry, office, and two more guest rooms. An employee bunkhouse next door rested precariously on the steep side of a ledge above the bay. A boathouse with an attached workshop stored the lodge's fishing boat, fuel barrels, and tools. The nearby spring supplied the lodge with water, but it wasn't potable unless it was boiled.

A generator ran ten hours every other day using diesel from the 5,000-gallon tank outside. It recharged the backup batteries lined in rows on the shed floor. While it ran, Ethan and his family used the microwave, TV, and turned on all the lights they wanted. When it shut off, they kept power usage to a minimum to preserve the batteries for the fridge and freezer.

Driving to the lodge from Thorne Bay took two hours and up to five in the wintertime. Breaking up the drive, we stopped at favorite spots such as Sarkar Lake. We admired the sinkholes while strolling on the path at Beaver Falls and avoided the massive spider webs strung between tree limbs. Potholes made the road from the Whale Pass turn off a slow go. It narrowed into one lane for the final thirteen miles, meandering through a maze of trees with a rare logging truck startling us on blind corners.

"Do you feel like a trapped rat in this maze of trees?" Elgin asked.

"No. I see the creeks, rivers, old man's beard moss hanging from the tree limbs, rock cliffs, waterfalls, and so many trees with character," I replied.

"They do have character, I'll give you that," he agreed. We entertained ourselves by counting fourteen piles of bear scat on the road from the Whale Pass turn off to the lodge.

Ethan unlocked the gate and we pulled up next to the lodge looking over the passageway. Coming into the lodge, I noticed something odd in the water. I grabbed the binoculars and spotted a sea otter and a dolphin. The dolphin was nodding his head as if they were having a conversation.

Elgin got right to work checking out the utilities to ensure safety and helping with necessary repairs. I put the binoculars away and busied myself deep cleaning old, gross leftovers from past owners and visitors. The tedious tasks distracted me from the recent passing of my dad, Robert Tyler, who had died a month earlier.

For years, we worried about not being able to get home in time if one of our parents became seriously ill. I received the dreaded call for my dad the day before we were scheduled to drive back to Alaska in August 2015. I left Elgin to make the trip alone while I flew to Florida to be with my dad and my sister Debbie. I regretted the missed opportunities to spend time with him over the years, though I know he took pride in my endeavors. He loved the Alaska shows and enthusiastically listened to my stories as I drafted notes for this book.

On my next trip to the lodge, I arrived with a truckload of bottled water and canned food, then spent several days helping Ethan fill the empty woodshed. A winter road closure could last months, meaning Ethan had to prepare for weeks or months without town access.

A change in MS medication was giving me new freedom to be outside living my life. Good thing too; we were in for two hard days.

"Where are we headed?" I asked as Ethan hopped into the truck after locking the road gate.

"Everett and Abbey came over last weekend, and we cut down several dead trees a couple of miles from here. Since I didn't plan to cut the trees into rounds right away, we went deeper into the forest so no one would spot the easy firewood." That hidden firewood was by no means easy to get.

We hiked back into the woods, where Ethan started up his chainsaw to cut the fallen trees into rounds—a large but manageable segment of a tree. I threw every single round twenty-three times from where they fell in the woods to the truck. Twenty-three times I lifted and heaved logs as far as physically possible. Between the trees, over a creek, through more forest, down a hillside, and then up to the road, I chucked them one-by-one while standing on slick, wet vegetation.

Catching my breath, I stood by the pile of rounds at the edge of the forest, looking down the hill where I planned to throw the logs next. The smell of fresh-cut wood filled the air. A misty rain forced me to keep my insulated raincoat on, even though the heavy work caused me to sweat. The sound of the chainsaw echoed through the trees. I bent over, lifted a round, tossing it with all my might over the rocky hillside into the ditch. Then, I chucked it one last time up the hill to the roadside behind the truck. I rested the heavy rounds on my legs to hoist them into the truck, bruising my thighs.

Two truckloads later, we finished unloading the logs into the woodshed. We made a quick meal, and I headed into the game room to sleep. We would be at it again in the morning.

"Grandma, can you sleep with me tonight?" Five-year-old Evey grinned as she patted her bed. I limped over and plopped down next to her, beat from an intense day of cutting firewood with Ethan, who had been her age when we came to Alaska. A crib divided Ethan and Erika's bed from Evey's. A play area lay beside her bed with a couch across the room, where I intended to sleep tonight.

"I must rest, but I will lie with you for a minute, and then I'm sleeping on the couch," she moaned but snuggled into me. I peered through the window at the mountain beyond El Capitan Passage. The sun had set, but the mountain was still visible.

"See the mountain over there?" I asked Evey. She leaned up to look, her long blond hair covering her back.

"Uh-huh," she replied.

"That is Evey's Mountain," I told her. Not another soul lived out there during the offseason, so it seemed fitting that the mountain she saw out her window be named Evey's Mountain.

"It can't be Evey's Mountain. It wouldn't be fair to Ezio," she looked at me with concern. Her baby brother had been born a few months ago, in May 2015. I looked around.

"See the tree outside the window by his crib?" She nodded. "We can name it Ezio's Tree." She smiled.

The next morning, Evey and I hiked the steep hill down to the dock before breakfast. Fog on the still water traveled down the passageway, veiling Evey's Mountain. We heard the sea otters cracking shells on their bellies as they floated nearby on the water. A boat buzzed by while a black bear investigated the water's edge further down the beach.

"I have an idea for hauling the trees to the road," I told Ethan on our way out to cut firewood.

"You cut down the next tree and tie a rope around it. I'll pull it out of the woods with the truck. Then you cut it into rounds on the road, and I'll load them into the truck bed." And we did exactly that.

By 5:00 p.m., we were driving under the colorful canopy of fall leaves on the one-lane road to the lodge with the third load of the day. At the gate, Ethan hopped out and unlocked the chain.

"Last load today," Ethan announced as we passed the lodge to the woodshed.

"If we hurry, we can still haul in one more load," the overachiever in me argued. Exhausted, Ethan gave me the *not-a-chance look,* so we unloaded the logs out of the truck and stacked them in the woodshed. This was no easy feat. Each log weighed a ton. It turned out to be a good idea to quit.

We both groaned in pain, climbing out of the truck at the lodge. Our muscles hurt.

"Do you have to go home today?" Evey asked as we enjoyed the last bit of evening light standing on the dock.

"Yes, but I'm taking you with me. We will visit the library, see Meliah and Auron, play at the park, and Grandpa has his guitar ready to sing a few songs with you." She turned and ran up the steep hill back to the lodge to pack her bag. She spent at least seven to ten days out of each month with us. We turned our spare room into her bedroom. Erika used the time to rest with Ezio while Ethan collected more firewood, organized the shop, and cleaned the lodge.

"The firewood trips took more gas than I expected," I told Ethan. He busied himself securing a freezer in the back of the truck to drop off at Bear Trail Store in Whale Pass. Don and Patty Alsup, the owners, had befriended Ethan and helped him learn how to hunt, fish, and cut down trees for firewood. He assured me their store had gasoline.

The thick clouds blocked the moonlight; it was pitch-black outside when I left the lodge. Whale Pass had few residents spread out far and wide in the mountainous forest. I drove up one road and down another, searching for the store. The gas gauge pointed to the line above empty. In desperation and fear of running out of gas in unfamiliar territory, I stopped the only car I saw on the road to ask for directions. After a few more wrong turns, I finally spotted the sign pointing to the store.

"We have plenty of gas," Patty Alsup pointed to the five-gallon jugs lining the side of her house-slash-store. I poured a few into my tank, collected all her empty tanks, and promised to fill them up before returning next week when I brought Evey home.

That winter, Ethan achieved his dream of living alone with his young family in bush Alaska. He hung a deer on the porch only to have a bear steal part of it. A storm ripped the dock apart, leaving him to brave the weather and water to secure the remaining pieces for repair. A medical emergency caused Elgin and me to bust through the snow to open the road and drive Erika to the plane. Wolves howled. Bears visited. The sea otters floated on their backs in the bay, snacking on shells. And Ethan kept the fire burning to keep the lodge warm for his family.

SIXTY-SEVEN

Lights and Sirens

Take an EMT class, a voice kept saying when I lay awake at night. I ignored the prompting. At the sight of blood, I became faint, and for that reason alone, I had no business becoming an EMT. It hadn't been too long ago that I sat in a diner figuring out how to hold a spoon because MS had played muscle memory tricks on me. *Disabled people don't run on ambulances. How could I consider becoming an EMT?* I didn't even *want* to be an EMT.

Take an EMT class, the intrusive voice nagged. For a year, I stood behind my excuses, but the voice kept nagging. So, I became an EMT.

Though I had envisioned most ambulance calls as bloody accidents, I was wrong. The majority of patient calls came in for chest pain, vomiting, falls, stroke symptoms, and other non-blood-related issues. And my other concern about being disabled with MS wasn't a problem either. EMTs work as a team. My medical issues did not stop me from showing up for a call or performing my duties. My disability allowed me to serve the community by manning the day shift when most people worked. I discovered a new calling in emergency medicine.

In the winter of 2016, the overworked EMS director Chaundell Piburn in Craig advertised for a temporary, part-time assistant to help with a few projects. Despite our plans to move back to Wyoming in four months, I returned to work and saved my wages to cover the ferry tickets and barge fee. Chaundell taught me how to put on an active shooter scenario we planned and implemented for the first responders on the island. Working with her gave me a fun-loving person to share part of my day doing something worthwhile for our community. I felt useful again working for her and the Craig EMS.

With a low call volume and a constant turnover in population, an EMT in bush Alaska had limited opportunities to practice their skills in real time. Each call was potentially a new situation for them. Alaskans found all sorts of ways to injure themselves, meaning any call could be a doozy. Trainers warned EMTs of calls lasting hours or days because of weather. Instructors told us, "In the Lower-48, we would not teach you this skill, but here you can dart a chest for tension pneumothorax." When the medical director or sponsoring doctor for the ambulance agreed, instructors trained basic level EMTs to perform higher-level skills in cases of severe emergencies.

Prince of Wales Island residents faced other unique issues in EMS. Critical patients flew out to Ketchikan, Sitka, or Seattle by helicopter or plane. Coast Guard helicopters flew in as backup when regular service providers were unavailable or unable to transport sick or injured patients. However, there were times even the Coast Guard could not fly in due to storms.

In populated areas, the coroner responds to calls involving death, and they transfer the deceased to a cooler at the funeral home or morgue. Prince of Wales Island had no coroner, no cooler, no funeral home, and no morgue. We wrapped one deceased patient in a sheet, descended a narrow staircase, and seat-belted them into the passenger seat of their truck. A relative drove the body to Hollis to catch the ferry into Ketchikan the next morning. The alternative was to transport the deceased by ambulance to the Klawock clinic for the night and then to the morning ferry bound for Ketchikan at the family's expense.

If your emergency wasn't in town, you could wait hours. An ambulance rushing down the rough logging roads at speeds greater than thirty mph was not feasible. When the ambulance returned to pavement, the winding road to Klawock kept our speed under fifty. Many Alaskans had first responder training when they lived far from medical services.

EMTs work under a medical director, a doctor. Securing and keeping one on record was no easy feat. Would you put your malpractice insurance on the line for a transient population of new EMTs?

The EMS communication system was archaic in bush Alaska, with 25 percent of residents not having access to 911. If you had an emergency in Thorne Bay, for instance, you had to call the city hall. Hopefully, you knew the number. The person manning the phones at night then paged out the ambulance.

Thorne Bay EMS was voluntary, meaning if the responders were not available or did not care to respond to a call, they didn't have to. You definitely wanted to stay on good terms with the local EMTs. Transporting a patient required a minimum of two volunteers from the limited group of

EMTs. That is a sobering thought for a newbie to the state, now isn't it? When necessary, the ambulance from Craig or Klawock drove forty-five to sixty minutes across the island to provide care.

I never regretted serving as an EMT despite my initial hesitation and am proud to have saved several lives. Could that be why the little voice nagged me until I gave in? Maybe.

SIXTY-EIGHT

It's Worth It

Standing on the porch in my pajamas, I shivered in the wind while waving goodbye to Elgin. My hand pressed the front door closed as I thought about how some days I didn't miss preparing for school and leaving so early. This was one such day. Old Man Winter laid a thick blanket of snow over the trees, homes, and narrow streets of Thorne Bay, Alaska.

Elgin's ringtone rang on my phone. "Hey! Grab your camera and hurry down to the dock. The fog on the bay is fantastic. I'd go myself, but I have to work. I promise it's worth it."

"I'm tired this morning, and now it's snowing," I dragged my feet at the idea as I gazed out the snowy windowpane. A cold walk to the dock did not appeal to me, though it wasn't too far. "Maybe," I replied without enthusiasm. MS fatigue held me back.

"Whatever you want to do. It's worth it! Love you," he hung up as he entered the school.

Enormous fluffy snowflakes drifted down from the thick layer of snow-filled clouds. The beauty enticed me to come out to play.

"What the heck!" I sprang into action with a sudden burst of oomph and grabbed my blue jeans from the bedroom. Living in Alaska for nineteen years taught me to dress in layers with a sweatshirt, fleece, and an insulated rain jacket. A scarf wrapped around my neck, hat, gloves, and waterproof, insulated boots, which slipped on easily and completed my ensemble. I was ready to go.

Once outside, the cool air invigorated me. *Why had I been so reluctant to go?* The snow accumulation grew by the minute while oodles of fat flakes partially obstructed the view. My boots left deep prints on our narrow street as I made my way to the dock.

Oh, wow! Fog and snow on the south side of the bay engulfed the mountains right to the trees on the water's edge. Gray clouds blended into the water in several places.

Gorgeous! I thought, snapping a photograph. I continued down the slick hill to the dock. Gravel under the snow caught my boots with each step, making it easier to inch my way to Shoreline Drive. I took another picture.

High tide lifted the dock, leveling the ramp; it required no extra care to descend it today. During low tide, the ramp turned steep, though its rooftop kept it from becoming treacherous. It also provided protection from the buckets of rain and snow accumulation. I passed by the carts used to haul cargo, and a water hose curled neatly on the platform at the bottom of the ramp.

Moseying alongside the fishing vessels with my camera, I shot one image after another. I snapped photos of snow-covered buoys, fishing rods, reels, coiled thick rope, and booms. Dinghies in their slips overflowed with snow.

"Oh! Oh! Oh!" I cried in delight as a perfect picture appeared through the fog. Sunlight beamed through the heavy snow to reflect on the bay with a tugboat pulling a barge in the distance.

I cannot believe this! I thought to myself in awe. I broke out into a run despite the slick conditions. *Thud. Thud. Thud.* My boots pounded the dock.

The sunbeam faded as I sprinted on the snowy planks. I abruptly stopped. Too late. The clouds closed in, eliminating the spectacular view and leaving me without a single photograph of the scene.

"Darn it!" I yelled to myself. I was alone out there, staring off into the snowfall, engrossed in my disappointment. Breathtaking. That's what it had been.

A plane flew in through the storm, buzzed by, and skimmed the water fading into the blizzard as it flew across the bay toward The Port—the local post office, mini-store, and airport. And when I say the airport, I mean a tiny dock for waiting passengers and a radio in the store for the pilot to report arrival times. It surprised me that a floatplane flew in at all. Low visibility made it a dangerous endeavor for those onboard.

I wandered to the far end of the dock to watch the heavy snowfall over the darkened bay. The gigantic snowflakes created low visibility almost as blinding as thick fog. I tilted my head back, sticking out my tongue to catch one.

Standing next to the bench at the end of the dock, I watched the tugboat and barge approach Thorne Bay. *It must be Tuesday and high tide,* I thought, knowing the barge schedule. A motorboat hummed in the distance, though the abundance of snow made it impossible to spot.

Without warning, delight and terror struck me simultaneously. In the limited visibility, a third boat crossed the bay in the congested area. And now, I could hear the plane taxiing for takeoff nearby!

Planes rarely flew in such conditions. It should have stayed in Thorne Bay to wait out the storm. Yet, I heard the plane coming.

Oh, no! A collision seemed inevitable. I could not see the plane! *Where is it?* I could hear it.

I flipped on the camera and snapped photos of the tugboat pulling a barge and another approaching boat. The plane closed in on my position, yet I still couldn't see it. *They are going to crash!* The aircraft sounded like it was right next to me.

Out of the snowstorm taxied the plane. It passed between the dock and the boats in front of me. *Snap. Snap. Snap.* I captured the scene—one picture with the plane in front of the boats, one beside them, and another with it taxiing away. The pilot must have planned to taxi around the mountains to takeoff for Ketchikan in Clarence Strait.

So lucky! I rejoiced at the once-in-a-lifetime photo opportunity. The boats and plane narrowly missed one another. What a relief!

The snowstorm engulfed the bush plane while the hum of the engine faded in the distance, the crazy pilot. *I would not want to be a passenger on that flight! No way, no how!*

SIXTY-NINE

The Bush Pilot

I needed a break from The Rock today, even if it was only a quick flight into Ketchikan.

– Melissa L. Cook, March 2015

The demand for flights in Southeast Alaska ballooned from late April to October when scores of people descended upon us. Lodges were booked with outdoorsmen who arrived to fish for halibut and salmon or hunt the island's trophy black bear. Bush planes dropped sportsmen into isolated places to camp for a week or more. Tourists flew out to see the bears and Misty Fjords. With the flood of visitors came an influx of seasonal pilots. Many arrived with little or no training on the challenges found in Alaska flying. New pilots had a steep learning curve on the dangers of thick overcast skies, treacherous terrain, williwaws, and other unpredictable winds.

Bush planes filled Ketchikan's tight airspace, making collisions inevitable. Some planes escaped with near misses, clipped each other, or crashed, one on top of the other. A few wrecked into mountains while others snagged the treetops, casting the planes and their passengers to the forest floor. Glaciers were no haven either, with their deep crevices and flat light. The fog, wind, rain, low visibility, unpredictable downdrafts, and occasional snow flurries added to the dangers awaiting seasonal pilots and guests.

With 250 villages off the road system, the highways of bush Alaska were the air and sea. One-third of commuter flights in the United States occurred in Alaska. The state averaged eight dead bush pilots annually from 2003 to 2009—"approximately 36 times the mortality rate of all U.S. workers during the same time period" (NIOSH, 2014). *Alaska Air Tales* could rival hair-raising books such as *Alaska Bear Tales* by Larry Kaniut.

The state has a distinct dependency on bush planes for mail, cargo, and passengers' daily transportation. Less than fourteen thousand miles of paved roads existed for over 663,268 square miles, an area over twice the size of Texas. To put that into perspective, Texas has 250,000 miles of roads meaning Alaska's roads would total half a million miles if they were comparable.

The bush pilot was the taxi driver, UPS, and semi-truck driver of the Alaskan skies. The sheer number of flights explains why the state had six times the number of pilots per capita as the Lower-48.

Small aircraft were no match for the wicked storms, mountains engulfed in clouds or runways bogged down with heavy snow. Unique and remote airstrips were challenging enough without adding ice, mud, or snow.

Desperate for supplies, some people provided misleading weather reports on wind or snow depths, hoping the plane would fly in. Once the wheels touched down in thick snow, it committed the aircraft to the landing. It then forced the pilot and remaining passengers into a frightening departure if they wished to go on to their destination. Mind you, many bush communities do not have accommodations for the stranded.

We cannot overlook pilot error in bush wrecks. In the 1990s, the NTSB identified bush syndrome as a factor in some accidents. Pilots with bush syndrome took unwarranted risks while in flight. They misjudged, overloaded, or inaccurately distributed weight. Reckless pilots became overconfident, flew too low, or tried to beat the weather. Some carried out risky maneuvers or goofed off.

Famous people and several politicians were not immune from dying in bush flights either. Wiley Post, the renowned pilot who flew the first solo around the world and discovered the jet stream, died with actor Will Rogers in a 1935 bush crash. In 1978, Alaska's Senator Ted Stevens survived a plane wreck at Anchorage International Airport, though his wife did not. He lived on with a premonition he might die in a plane crash. On August 9, 2010, Senator Stevens flew out for a fishing trip, but his plane crashed in the mountains north of Dillingham. The single-engine floatplane encountered foul weather. His flight had several high-risk factors, making it a typical wreck as far as Alaska plane crashes go. He did not survive.

One pilot's death will forever be ingrained in my heart—Charles Thomas Madsen Sr., also known as the *Aleutian Aviator*. Tom flew out of Unalaska under the company name Aleutian Air. He shuttled students and teachers to events in the Aleutians East Borough School District's bush schools when we lived in Nelson Lagoon. I felt safe flying with the veteran Alaska bush pilot of twenty years. I stood on the gravel strip many times watching for the *Aleutian Spirit,* his 1959 Beechcraft E18S tail dragger.

Flying to False Pass in 1995, Tom told me about a plane crash in the area. "The plane took off and nosedived into the Bering Sea. They overloaded it, killing the pilot and passenger." It was sad that Tom found his untimely end, in the same manner, less than seven years later.

On April 10, 2002, Tom Madsen died flying out of Juneau to deliver a load of shingles to a friend in Southeast Alaska. He pushed his overloaded plane to its limits and may have encountered a flap problem he could not overcome with the heavy load. The *Aleutian Spirit* went down in the mudflats of the Mendenhall Wetlands outside of Juneau. The Last Frontier lost a remarkable hero when Tom crashed doing what he loved most, flying.

"What I remember about flying with Tom was his friendly personality. Plus, he let me fly his plane," Elgin, who was a private pilot, reminisced.

"I remember Tom's kindness and how he always carried my bag and told me the latest news from around the school district," I replied. Bush pilots like Tom were significant people in our lives. They were friends, carriers of news, providers of a lift into town, and deliverers of freight, packages, and mail. To describe them as a lifeline would be an understatement, and Tom Madsen was no different.

The sponsor statement below was written in support of changing the Unalaska airport name to the Tom Madsen Airport. It conveyed Tom's acts of heroism:

> *Thomas Madsen was a bush aviator for nearly twenty years throughout the Aleutians and is well known for willingly jeopardizing his own life in order to save the lives of others. He was instrumental in many medical emergencies and search and rescues. He knowingly flew in extremely hazardous weather in order to transport persons with medical crises. If he had not acted selflessly, lives most certainly would have been lost. In one particular incident, he flew in one hundred mph winds with heavy snow and sleet in order to save the life of a toddler who had ingested a fatal amount of iron pills. Thomas Madsen epitomized the term "bush pilot" in selflessly putting others' needs above his own to meet the needs of humanity.[2]*

---

2 State of Alaska. 22nd Alaska State Legislature. http://www.akrepublicans.org/pastlegs/22ndleg/spst/spsth-b523.shtml. April 25, 2002.

In December 2020, Tom's wife, Stephanie, wrote to me, "I find comfort in knowing Tom died doing what he loved. Old pilots often lose their commercial licenses. That would not have been ok for Tom . . . it was flying the passengers he enjoyed the most."

Today, Alaska averages one hundred plane crashes each year, down from the annual 140 in the 1990s when we lived in Nelson Lagoon.

SEVENTY

Don't Squish the Bread

Before leaving for the regional EMS conference in Sitka, I sent Ethan a message saying, *It was with sheer sadness that I packed my first box yesterday and another one today. It will take us a while to empty this house. I sure hate to leave. It's scary and yet thrilling to be stepping out into the world and seeking opportunities that, until now, have been unavailable. Let the next adventure begin.* I sent the email and then headed to the dock to meet the floatplane.

The plane's engine buzzed in the sky across the bay long before I spotted it. I held my camera and waited to contrast the aircraft's white wings against the trees' dark color on the mountainside in the distance. The pontoons touched down, spewing white misty spray, contributing additional contrast to my picture. As it taxied toward me, I clicked another photo framing the dock in with the plane.

As the plane approached, the pilot turned off the engine and jumped onto the dock to grab the rope and secure the plane, holding it steady to bring it to a standstill. I handed him my bag, and he climbed the stairs to set it in the back of the five-seater de Havilland Beaver floatplane. My foot rested on the first step with hesitation. I was less than enthusiastic about the flight to Ketchikan to catch a jet to Sitka. Five days previously, three people had died in a plane crash north of our island. The only survivor had been sitting in the backseat.

Planes go down. Air travel was our mode of transportation, and accidents happened. The wreckage was often devastating and challenging to reach quickly. We accepted this risk living in a remote area accessible only by boat or plane. And yet today, I paused. A little voice inside me said, *sit in the back seat.*

I argued with myself. *In two months, we are moving to Wyoming, and I want to have a splendid view from the air before I leave.* Ignoring the little voice, I slipped into the copilot seat.

Front seat passengers seem to be the ones who die in wrecks. It's not too late. Sit in the back seat. The voice begged. I buckled up, pulling the seat belt extra tight, knowing all too well it would make no difference if we flew face-first into the mountain. The pilot hopped into his seat, turned to me, and smiled. He looked twenty years old!

Oh, shoot. I should've sat in the back seat! We taxied away from the dock. The engine blared through the cabin as we gained speed, crossing the misty bay. The plane got on step, and then the pontoons lifted off the splashing water. We bumped through air pockets, flying low over the treetops. Our flight plan included puddle jumping to retrieve Craig passengers before flying back across the island and on to Ketchikan.

I sent a text message to Elgin, *This guy is blowing the dust off the treetops as we fly over.* I had been flying in Alaska since this pilot was a toddler and knew air pockets could drop a plane fifty feet or more in one downdraft. Skimming the trees was asking for one to catch the plane, snatch it from the air, and hurl it to the forest floor. I don't know about you, but that was an adventure I could live without.

Regardless of the gorgeous view, it was a nail-biting fifteen-to-twenty-minute flight. Fish Egg Island appeared in the distance as we flew over Klawock Inlet. The pilot tightly banked one wing and swiftly dropped onto the water near Craig. That was enough for me! This daredevil pilot displayed either inexperience, cockiness, or both.

Upon landing, I asked the boarding passengers if anyone cared to "share the joy and ride in front." An eager traveler gladly took my place. Riding without the view was safer in the event of an untimely, unexpected, premature ending of our flight.

The floatplane sprayed water outside my window as we bumped along the waves during touchdown in the Tongass Narrows. Arriving at the Ketchikan airport's seaplane dock, I dashed up the steep ramp to the airport for a quick jet ride with Alaska Airlines to Sitka.

Sitka's airport had another one of those hairy, scary runways. Surrounded by water and tiny islands, the runway was short with unpredictable weather. Sea birds posed a safety hazard for flight traffic. Not too many passengers landed here without gripping their armrest; I was no exception. The plane always touched down much harder than at other airports, as if putting an exclamation mark on the ordeal.

I settled into an old dorm room of the now closed Jackson College.

Knowing the weather was forecast to turn ugly within hours, I spent the evening hiking along the beautiful coastline and docks nearby. Despite landing here countless times over the years, this was my first time visiting the two-hundred-year-old town. The Sitka dock and fishing boats dwarfed those found on Prince of Wales Island.

I made the trip to Sitka for the regional EMS Symposium, which brought together doctors, nurses, EMTs, and first responders from around Southeast Alaska. Together, we shivered through training for days in freezing buildings with little to no heat. The dorms were no warmer at night. Chilly rain and wind plagued the weeklong EMT training. To ensure I had breakfast in the morning without hiking into town, I brought peanut butter and bread for sandwiches in my bag. For lunch and dinner, I trekked through blowing, drenching rain half a mile one-way into Sitka's shopping district.

When the conference ended, I was eager to get home to Thorne Bay and warm up. I packed my bag and phoned a cab. The initial cab and second turned out to be no-shows, so I flagged down a sympathetic lady near the dorm who drove me to the airport—another example of Alaskans helping each other out in their time of need.

The jet flew low over Prince of Wales Island for the short milk run flight into Ketchikan. On the north end of the island, I scanned the mountains below to locate Bear Valley Lodge, where Ethan lived. I spotted Thorne Bay on the east side of the island before we crossed Clarence Straight. Landing in Ketchikan had its tense moments, often resulting in forceful touchdowns too.

I gathered my bags from the single carousel at the airport and stood in line at the busy Pacific Airways counter—a commuter service the locals referred to as PacAir. Waiting there gave me an excuse to sneak a peek at the travelers around me. Living remotely afforded few opportunities to see new people.

The couple in front of me lived on the island and were returning home from a medevac. The woman accidentally stabbed herself in the stomach with a knife while teaching a newbie how to skin an animal. I've forgotten which kind. The lady in front of them held a large bag from Cinnabon, which wasn't available locally. It reminded me of the trips when I had carried the same bag of sweets back home for my eagerly awaiting boys. Hunters, loaded down with travel bags of supplies and guns, slipped into line behind me.

"I'm flying over," a professional lady informed her traveling companion as she stepped into line behind the hunters.

"I plan to be on this afternoon's ferry to the island. See you in Craig," the other replied. The flying traveler landed by floatplane on the island in twenty-five minutes. The ferrying traveler had a three-hour wait, three-hour ferry ride, and a forty-five-minute drive to get to the same destination. I shook my head at the situation.

I pondered the reasons someone would do such a thing. I guessed either money, a savings of sixty-two dollars in the difference between the plane versus ferry fees, lack of open seats on the plane, or fear of flying. The man may have incurred too many close calls on bush flights or lost too many friends in wrecks. I had my list of people I once knew.

Arriving on the airport dock, I watched white mist blowing in the breeze as the floatplane pontoons set down. The pilot thanked the assistant for catching the plane's rope hanging from the wing as they both secured the aircraft to the dock. The excited hunters pushed their way toward the plane. Reaching past them, the pilot took my carry-on and backpack.

"Please put the computer bag on top. There's a loaf of bread in it and I don't want it squished," I warned the pilot as he set my bags in the cargo space. The hunters turned in unison and laughed at me. Not being from here, the rude hunters did not understand. However, the pilot recognized the request as coming from a seasoned bush traveler and gently laid my bag on top.

Only shows their ignorance, I thought to myself. I traveled with bread to be sure I didn't go hungry, a lesson I had learned twenty years ago.

The hunters piled in while one stood behind to ensure he had a window seat. The pilot offered me his hand as I climbed the first step. My mind flashed back to those who had died in the plane wreck two weeks ago. Falling back into the false sense of security took time after recent tragic deaths. The mountainous terrain, harsh weather, and low visibility made it an unforgiving place for crashes, and the locals knew it.

The hunter climbed in after me. Being squished between two overweight hunters was no picnic. The level of excitement in the floatplane was a dead giveaway; this was their first bush flight. The large bodies blocked my view of the beautiful scenery as they hovered in the windowpanes, snapping photos with their phones. Arms reached over me to share their pictures.

As we approached Thorne Bay, I leaned forward to peek out the window and saw Elgin waiting for me on the dock. He was a sight for sore eyes. I was home at last. We circled the bay on approach and flared to a touchdown on the water. The aircraft taxied through the bay to the dock.

"A full flight," Elgin noticed as we hugged. I couldn't wait to jump in a hot shower.

Funny, it was the hunter's first bush flight and my last as an Alaskan.

Elgin began earnestly packing boxes for our move to Wyoming while I attended the conference. The house already didn't feel like home when I came through the door. No fast talk on my part could convince Elgin to sign another teaching contract when he qualified for retirement. For months, I had tried. I would soon miss this adventurous life and those I was leaving behind with it.

SEVENTY-ONE

Terror on the Back Road

Our last days in Alaska slipped away like sand in the hourglass. With each day that passed, Elgin's excitement grew. His smile broadened. His step quickened. But for me, the excitement mixed with heartache. From my sewing studio window, I saw Everett's car parked at his work across the street. It symbolized what I was leaving behind. I choked back tears packing boxes and forced a smile for Elgin's benefit whenever he was nearby. Together, we had counted the two decades to retirement. It wasn't his fault I had changed my mind. And no matter how many times I asked if he would consider staying another year, his answer was always no.

Even Elgin savored our walks on the beach or through the woods in our final months on the island. Fighting off the pesky no-see-um bugs, we visited our favorite island spots one last time. We hiked on boardwalks through muskeg, around blowdowns, and along trails spotted with the skunk cabbage's yellow flowers. We discovered new places and wondered why we hadn't found them before now.

Josie and our new rescue dog, Solomon, sniffed along Gravelly Creek on an afternoon hike when I noticed a giant widow maker lying across the trail. "Yikes! Sure glad I wasn't here when this widow maker fell." Splintered wood scattered in pieces with larger segments reaching into the woods beyond—a reminder of the dangers lurking from above in the forest.

"I bet it blew down in the windstorm last night. I'm not surprised, it sounded like a volcano going off outside our bedroom window!" I said as Elgin stepped over the branch to inspect it. I contemplated the vulnerability of our sons when they harvested firewood, often alone.

I must admit, though, falling trees was an adrenaline rush when "timber" echoed through the forest. First, a tree creaked as it leaned. Cracking and splintering indicated the beginning of the fall, followed by near silence with only the wisp of air rustling through the branches. The trunk collapsed to the ground with a heavy thud, the branches snapping and wood crackling. You hoped the tree landed where you had planned and not directly across the road, which happened occasionally.

A month before we left for Wyoming in June, my ailing seventy-six-year-old mother, Patricia, flew in for her last visit to the island. The buzz of the plane in the distance hummed through my kitchen. Grabbing my rain gear, I jumped into the truck. At the dock, I watched the five-seater Beaver floatplane fly into sight. Descending the ramp beside the post office, I was relieved to see the high tide. My mother would be able to walk up the ramp without help.

They say there are bold pilots and old pilots but no old, bold pilots. I thought of that as I stood on the Thorne Bay dock, watching the pilot skim the top of the trees in an unusual flight pattern. It was the young, bold pilot I had flown with last month. Not impressed, I watched the wing bank too steeply, and the plane dropped from the edge of the treetops to the water in one swoop. I suspected he could be on the next episode of the *Alaska Aircraft Investigations*.

Mom smiled, sliding across the three-person seat to the door. The pilot held her hand and took her portable oxygen machine as she climbed down one step at a time. A break in a recent storm that had weathered my mother in Ketchikan overnight prevented a risky exit from the plane. Boarding a rocking floatplane from a dock wasn't easy to begin with; it was a recipe for disaster for the elderly or weak in foul weather.

That night the storm resumed. Rain poured down, wind blustered through the trees, and even a single crack of rare thunder shook the house, causing all sorts of fear throughout the town. Vibration in the floors and walls made it feel as though it hit the house. My heart pounded heavily in my chest. *Is that a landslide coming down the mountain?* I wondered. Landslides were common on the island; the evidence lay across the road at times.

A local EMT hopped in her car and drove around town looking for a downed airplane. My neighbor thought an explosion had occurred. Others recognized it for what it was—thunder. In twenty years, we heard thunder rumble twice. We never had a tornado warning either. Most of Alaska lacked the unstable warm air required for lightning.

Despite the stormy weather, my mother's brief visit meant we needed to get out to see the kids and grandkids without delay. We spent time at the lodge with Ethan and his family. The next day, we visited Everett's home.

My mother learned how each of the boys managed to live in the temperate rainforest. Catch systems filled water tanks with rainwater coming off the roof. Hikes to the bay allowed the kids to fetch dishwater when the water tanks ran dry. They filled jugs with drinking water from the spring off the side of the road. Subsistence fishing and hunting filled their freezers with meat. Berry picking, beachcombing, and creating whimsical art from dried vegetation provided entertainment. Everett's place had the famous indoor honey buckets and an outhouse.

On Saturday morning, Mom and I headed to Craig for an early lunch at Annie Betty's Cafe with my sewing pals Joy and Neva. I dreaded leaving our little group.

Sunday afternoon, the grandchildren stopped by to play. "This will probably be the last time I see them," my mom accurately predicted before the boys brought their kids over. She knew what I refused to accept; her clock was ticking in this visit and in life.

My mom's plane pulled away from the dock and taxied into the bay the next morning. She waved goodbye through the window as the plane bumped along the water, gaining speed. The engine blared and misty water shot out from underneath the pontoons. Then they were airborne and skimming along the bay before lifting into the sky. I stood on the dock, waving for as long as I could see the plane. The buzz of the engine lingered after the plane flew out of sight.

With a lump in my throat, I climbed the ramp and left for the EMS office in Craig. After seventeen years of living in Thorne Bay, I seldom tired of the drive across the island. Trees lined the curvy road. Seagulls, eagles, and ravens soared in the sky. An occasional bear, deer, or eagle flying too low kept me on my toes. I enjoyed the sunlight coming through the forest, the creeks flowing along the roads, and waterfalls running down the mountainsides.

I approached an inherently dangerous *S* curve lined with evergreen trees on one side and a rock wall on the other. A loaded red logging truck came into the turn too fast, forcing himself into the oncoming lane, *my lane,* to navigate the second corner. My truck approaching the same tight corner must have surprised him as he jerked back into his lane to avoid a head-on collision.

My heart stopped when his trailer, loaded with huge logs stacked high, swerved across the corner and into my lane right in front of me. A steep and narrow ditch beside the road afforded me no options. My foot slammed on the brakes as the passenger side tires hung off the pavement. I barely squeaked by.

As soon as the truck passed, I sucked in a breath of air, and tears immediately sprung from my eyes. In shock, the image of the loaded trailer filled with logs burned into my memory.

A couple of weeks before the near accident, I stood on a logging road in the forest and photographed the exact truck that darn near killed me. The trucks rumbled along the rocky roads, back and forth between the timber cut and the lumber mills. The sound of the engines announced their arrival long before they drove around the corner if you were outside to hear them. I stood; camera ready to snap photos when they appeared. The truckers waved at my camera which followed them as they passed. I shot a few more images when the trucks began to round the next corner, disappearing behind the trees.

After the incident, anger flashed over me when I passed that red log truck. The driver nearly cost me my life driving too fast. How quickly it can all be over. With its beautiful mountains, tea-colored streams, and gorgeous trees with character, Prince of Wales Island could also be dangerous for drivers. Miles upon miles of no-passing zones, blind corners, narrow tree-lined roads, and an abundance of wildlife made it an unforgiving road, especially at night or in the winter.

Even in the daylight wrecks on the road were a constant danger. In June 2015, a deadly head-on collision with a logging truck outside of Klawock took the life of Johnny Botello, a recent Thorne Bay graduate. The rumor was he might have fallen asleep at the wheel. He lingered for a month in a Seattle hospital before succumbing to his injuries, never regaining consciousness. Sadly, the small town of Thorne Bay lost two young men that same day in Seattle's hospitals; our daughter-in-law's brother, Justin Douglas, also passed away after a brief illness. They are dearly missed by all who knew them.

Days before our departure, I saw the red logging truck up ahead. Anger instantly filled my heart, and then he slowed way down and waved vigorously out of his open window as if to say, "I'm sorry." Tears filled my eyes again as I waved back. The near accident probably scared him half out of his wits, too. Until then, I had only been contemplating my own terror.

SEVENTY-TWO

Penguins, Igloos and Real Alaskans

Alaska's motto could be, "If you don't fit in anywhere else, you are welcome here!"

– Melissa L. Cook, May 2016

Alaska's early prospectors, known as sourdoughs, heard the call of the Last Frontier and began arriving in the late 1800s. The veteran survivalists carried a yeasty bread starter in a pouch worn around their necks and inside their shirts to keep it warm. Sourdough John Peterson, the epitome of a mountain man and a forty-year Alaska resident from Ennis, Montana, gave us a container of sourdough starter the first month we lived in Thorne Bay.

The bush Alaskans we knew were Native Alaskans, sourdoughs, or people like us. Many arrived from the Lower-48 and Canada to work. The sourdoughs Tom Madsen, Snake Eyes, Harvey McDonald, and the Castle brothers Brian and Kevin spent their adult lives earning a living flying, logging, fishing, and teaching in bush Alaska. Fisherman Glen Douglas and his wife Donna moved to Southeast Alaska to raise seven children on their fishing boat and then built a retirement cabin in the woods on Prince of Wales Island. Educators Joel and Deidre Jenson brought three children from Minnesota to the bush and loved it so much they stayed. Road workers Bill and Becky Welton worked for decades on the island before retiring back home in West Virginia. Ryan and Crystal Nelson taught school for five years before moving to our little town in Wyoming to raise their family. And then there were the tenderfoots, who came and went in the blink of an eye, unable or unwilling to live through the harsh realities of bush life.

People often wondered about our life in Alaska. I don't blame them for asking. Many television shows they watched tried to depict life in bush Alaska, though only a few did a decent job at it.

"Are there penguins where you live? Do you live in an igloo? Can you see Russia from your house?" The answer to these questions was no. Penguins live in the Southern Hemisphere. Modern-day Eskimos make igloos for emergency shelter in northern Alaska and Canada. Alaskans can see Russia from St. Lawrence, Little Diomede Islands, and a rare spot on the northwest coast of the mainland. Or so I am told, I haven't seen Russia from Alaska myself. I have heard of people crossing the frozen Bering Strait between Big and Little Diomede Islands. Beware, though, the Russians threw one Bering Sea crosser in jail once he stepped ashore.

"Don't they pay you to live in Alaska?" The secret is out. The State of Alaska pays out a dividend from a fund set aside during the 1980s oil boom. You have to be a resident for one full year before applying for the next year's check, which arrived in October, so it took a while to receive the first payment. In 2021, the future of the dividend is uncertain, and the amount continues to drop.

"Is it cold there? Is it dark all winter long?" Yes, to both questions. I froze practically every single day for twenty years despite wearing long johns throughout the school year. The humidity in Southeast Alaska's rain forest made the moderate temperatures feel ice cold. A dehumidifier kept our home warm, and our blankets dry. The lengthy dark winters increased the risk of depression and cabin fever. Sadly, Alaska leads the nation in suicide.

"Does the sun stay up all night? What's the weather right now? Do you know Sarah Palin?" Alaska is comparable in width and height to the Lower-48—see the Alaska Comparison Map at the front of the book. In northern areas of the state, the sun does not set during the summer or rise in the winter. In Southeast Alaska, it rained, and rained, and rained. In other areas, it snowed, snowed, snowed. Prince of Wales Island averaged one hundred inches of rain and thirty-nine inches of snow annually. Ketchikan kept a rain meter downtown for their 150 inches. And no, I have not met Sarah Palin; however, she was a competent governor in a state dealing with corruption.

"You shouldn't be cold; you are from Alaska." I heard this comment regularly in conversations. The truth is, I am always cold, perhaps because I spent so much time freezing in Alaska. A handful of crazy people in the northern part of the state wore shorts when it reached twenty degrees. Then there was me, wearing long johns at sixty. A windy sixty degrees in the humid rain forest was chilly.

"Are you calling me from Alaska?" When I phoned family, friends, or people I had business with in the Lower-48, they often acted like I had called from Mars, especially in our earlier years.

"Do you live close to the *Alaskan Bush People*?" Are you kidding me? Those people are not real Alaskans, and I believe they filmed the show in Washington. According to the news, two of the show's actors served jail time in 2016 for lying on the Alaska Permanent Fund application. You must be an Alaska resident to qualify for the dividend.

"Do you watch TV shows about Alaska?" Absolutely. Alaskans loved to watch shows on Alaska. The state is vast. I never saw the Iditarod Trail Sled Dog Race because it didn't occur anywhere near the fifty-sixth parallel where I lived. The *Alaska State Troopers* show was real to life, along with *Flying Wild Alaska* and the *Deadliest Catch*. I enjoyed watching *Gold Rush*, *Bering Sea Gold*, *Edge of Alaska*, and *Port Protection* (filmed on Prince of Wales Island). These shows amused us, but they had plenty of setup scenes and embellishment. For example, in *Port Protection*, a couple collected firewood, and the wife didn't realize they would be throwing the cut logs down the mountainside. Worse, they showed a woman fishing in a boat with a rifle on her lap to fend off the bears. That just doesn't happen on Prince of Wales Island.

"Are Alaskans similar to the old mountain men?" Most were not, however, we knew a few unique people. Swede and Shirley Ecklund come to mind as being quite distinct. You can find their pictures online taken for *National Geographic Magazine's* July 2007 article, "Tongass National Forest." Swede stood on the dock of his float house near Thorne Bay in Piggy Cove—self-named. Shirley's photos show her driving a skiff into Thorne Bay, demonstrating how to prepare crab on the dock, and dishing out food to guests with her husband Swede. Their family pet pig greeted the guests at the door.

A former military man, Swede cooked for loggers in camps and sportsmen at lodges. I met Swede when he was a board member for our school district and a foster parent to young men I taught in class. A colorful, older, balding hippy, he wore his blond-gray hair in a ponytail and always had a smile to go with his mustache. He delighted in telling jokes, though many went over my head due to his exceptional command of higher-level vocabulary and love for obscene content. Whenever our paths crossed, he placed his hand on my shoulder to inquire how I was doing. My boys cherish the time they spent with Swede at his float house.

Shirley wore her long dark hair to her waist, often in a braid or tied on top of her head. She always had on an orange and black survival suit to protect herself from the wet, inhospitable environment while taking the fifteen-minute open skiff ride into town. As rugged as the men, Shirley could outswear a sailor. When all dolled up, she was beautiful.

Together, she and Swede fostered thirty teenage boys over the years. They made it their life's calling to provide troubled teen boys with a second chance. They gave them a home, a job, and the structure required to become successful. Swede taught them to cook and serve groups while Shirley cracked the whip to keep them in line and progressing in school. They made a reliable team for these young men who truly needed them.

Swede's death at seventy-eight years old in July 2016 captured national and international headlines when Shirley took his body on what the press dubbed a "Rolling Wake" in Southeast Alaska. To preserve his body, she had his aluminum casket placed in her truck bed packed with ice. She replenished the melting ice at the fish canneries along the way. The *Juneau Empire* quoted the Ketchikan chief of police as saying, " . . . You can't make this stuff up." Swede would have loved it! Shirley passed away in June 2020 with one last young man by her side. Those two were the real sourdough Alaskans of our day.

SEVENTY-THREE

Balance Sheet of Our Alaska Life

More than two decades ago, they called my name as the grand prize winner at the Alaska Teacher Placement Job Fair in 1995. It occurred to me the grand prize I took home wasn't the Alaska shaped wooden clock, it was my first teaching job. That job set me on the path to the real grand prize—a life filled with adventure that ended with an early retirement at forty-nine years old.

Carrying boxes through the living room with wet, muddy shoes was exactly how we moved into our Thorne Bay home seventeen years ago. It's how we moved into Craig back in 1997. It poured for days in Homer while we waited for a break in the storm to fly out to Nelson Lagoon. With a brief window in the foul weather, we flew over the Alaska Peninsula to my first teaching job in 1995. I wrote home: *Rain weaved its way throughout all of our time in Alaska, so why should it be any different now as we load up to leave?*

The speaker at the 1995 job fair ordered adventurers to go home. I wasn't an adventurer, but I certainly experienced it. On our eleventh day in Nelson Lagoon, a rogue wave swept Elgin out to sea on his four-wheeler. By the third week, I had watched the village become submerged by the Bering Sea when a high tide arrived at the peak of a storm. We opened the front door each morning in the fall and spring to see Alaska brown bear prints beside the Suburban. During our second year, one of the school pilots died in a plane crash, swallowed by the sea. Pavlof Volcano, forty-eight miles away, blew its top twice and huffed and puffed for four months. And before leaving the village, Sutton survived falling into the last known underground Aleut shelter from World War II.

Alaska was a place where many pursued their fortune, and we were no different. For centuries, people made the trek to the Last Frontier to get rich quick. Explorers, gold miners, trappers, fishermen, oil workers, and loggers set their sights on rural Alaska, hoping to roll in the dough. It took us twenty years, but we brought home a little nest egg too.

We had intangible personal gains. Bush communities are small, making each member a bit more valuable than, say, in a city of a million people. Neighbors were assets in your life, and you in theirs.

As in business, we suffered through the liabilities of our Alaska bush life. Long, hard winters were not for the faint at heart. We lost out on a lengthy list of opportunities to spend time with family and friends for special events and day-to-day gatherings. And sadly, not everyone was still alive when we retired. Our grandparents, fathers, and my stepdad died during our time in Alaska. Our mothers passed soon after our return, which left us seriously pondering our decision to have spent so many years so far away from home.

Old Man Russell once told me, "When you move to Alaska, you give up everything." Transplants to the state, and there were many, understand precisely what he meant. Moving to Alaska was expensive in dollars and relationships with family and friends. We also had to adjust to a new culture.

Each of us missed different aspects of our former lives, but we missed them just the same. In Nelson Lagoon, I could not stop craving a meal I didn't cook. In the Tongass, I dreamed of a sidewalk in front of my house and a nearby best friend. I have those things now.

We understood our children's sacrifice for our retirement plans. To compensate, we spoiled them in the summer when we arrived in the Lower-48, a costly expense to our bottom line.

I thought we'd always be young, or at least that our time here wouldn't take such a toll on our youth, I wrote the year before we retired. You could say we depreciated or aged over our tenure there.

The dogs aged with us, and our beloved Sampson did not live to see our retirement day. He sure loved being an Alaskan dog though. Solomon and Josie passed away in 2017. I prefer to believe the dogs' spirits are frolicking in the forest, running down logging roads, playing along the creeks, and chasing the scents of Alaska's critters.

The boys left long before we did. Sutton played guitar in Seattle for a few years before settling close by in Billings, Montana where he grows medical marijuana for a living. He shares a love for music, rock hounding, guns, and exploring the outdoors with us. Everett and Ethan graduated from college with teaching degrees and returned to Alaska with their families. They have taught our grandchildren how to live off the land and survive on a subsistence lifestyle—a dividend we hadn't expected. Our boys did not fear becoming a little wet in the rain chopping wood for heat, building their home from scratch, or filling their freezer from Mother Nature's store.

The bottom line is, we did not leave rich by any means, but we achieved our goal of early retirement. It wasn't easy, and countless times we considered leaving. But in the end, we stuck it out and grew to cherish the opportunities the adventure provided us.

SEVENTY-FOUR

Goodbye Alaska

Insomnia again. In a week, we would be on the road to Wyoming for our final trip down the highway. *Where did the years go?* I rose, tiptoed in the hallway so as not to wake Elgin and sat at my computer to write.

> *The house is almost empty. The walls are bare except for the tick marks depicting our children and grandchildren's heights over the years. The loaded trailer and container are already on the barge to Seattle. My heart is not ready. Not yet. I never will be completely prepared to leave behind my children, grandchildren, daughters-in-law, students, friends, neighbors, and community. Darn it. It wasn't supposed to be so hard to leave. Twenty years of dreaming of retirement didn't include wanting to stay!*

In the days leading up to our departure, we visited the last of our favorite spots on the island. Elgin was particularly nostalgic, knowing he never planned to return to the rainforest. He had about as much rain as he could take for being raised in the desert.

Two days before leaving, we took six-year-old Evey home to the lodge. Stopping at Eagle's Nest Campground, she rode her bicycle along the boardwalk, stopping to hug the old-growth trees along Control Creek. It had been our beloved Sampson's favorite spot to walk. We hiked Beaver Falls looking into the depths of the sinkholes one last time. Flashbacks reminded me of our young boys running down the boardwalk. Then we counted bear scat on the one-lane road to the lodge.

We spent the day helping Ethan move into the employee bunkhouse. He and Everett had repaired the building for safety. Afterward, Ethan remodeled two of the bedrooms into a family room and installed a kitchen in the second bathroom.

Evey and I played outside on the dock. The view always took my breath away. Tall, white Alaska daisies popped up everywhere. The lodge was a little piece of heaven with its abundant wildlife and waterfront mountain views.

"Watch me ride my bike, Grandma!" Evey rode along the isolated road while I strolled admiring the flowers. A bear grunting in the trees put me on alert. We avoided playing too close to the woods for the rest of the afternoon.

I won't lie. I dreaded the moment we had to leave. We took last-minute pictures and then gave tearful hugs to say goodbye, for now.

We drove to Whale Pass and on to Coffman Cove and Luck Lake. The winding road can cause carsickness if you take the road too quickly. Between the lake and Thorne Bay, we drove along the water's edge enjoying the view of Clarence Strait.

That night before going to bed I wrote: *All those years of wishing I was somewhere else, dreaming of places with sidewalks, stores, restaurants, and most of all, people. I finally feel at home here now that we are ready to leave.*

Elgin had one final day of work to clean out his classroom. We celebrated our retirement by having lunch with Bob and Neva Robertson at the Dockside Cafe in Craig. The Robertsons planned to stay in Klawock for their retirement years, and we were moving on. Our twenty-year friendship wasn't ending, but the distance would affect it.

"If your boys need anything, call us. We'll be here for them," Bob offered. And true to his word, when we called, they helped the boys. Sadly, Bob passed away unexpectedly in August 2019.

On our way home, we stopped at Gravelly Creek, where we had regularly walked the dogs. The trail led to a set of stairs down to the Thorne River. We hiked in the rock beds, remembering the times we had taken Sampson and Josie there to play. We walked along the river on sunny days and snowy days, rainy days and windy days. Only high water kept us out of there. Today, we relished the last visit, walking through the trees covered in old man's beard moss.

We finished packing the truck and ate ramen noodles for dinner. Fitting. We ate those noodles nearly every day in Nelson Lagoon. After leaving the village, we seldom ate them again, but tonight ramen was the only food left in the house. We laughed.

"Let's take the dogs to Sandy Beach," Elgin suggested. When the beach road was open, we visited at least once a week for seventeen years taking quiet strolls, storm watching, supervising class field trips, and student kayak training. We log-hopped with our boys and dogs here, sat around bonfires with friends, had picnics with Evey, and walked on the beach under a full moon at night. It was Elgin's favorite spot, so we saved it for last.

Elgin lifted Josie out of the truck, and I helped Solomon. Our old dogs ran through the trees on their way to smell the beach. Elgin walked in peace, lost in his thoughts and memories. I fell behind and snapped photos of him with the dogs on the wet sand. He was quiet, took his time, and watched the last of the light on Clarence Strait. We drove the six miles home in silence. *Home.* The island wouldn't be our home after tonight.

Five in the morning came early. "It's time," Elgin said, standing in our bedroom doorway. I took photos of the near-empty house and then stood in the kitchen looking over the eight hundred square feet filled with memories of our family through the years. There was a story to be told from each scratch and mark I saw.

We drove the Thorne Bay Road to Klawock where we turned onto the Craig-Hollis Highway, passing Maybeso Creek before arriving at the terminal in Hollis seventy-five minutes later. The worker wasted no time waving us onto the ship.

Climbing the metal stairs to the *Stikine* ferry's main floor, we headed to the seats in the back by the window. The moment the vessel pulled away from the Hollis dock, I knew our departure was real. No longer were we preparing for retirement; we *were* retired and now departing for the last time as Alaska residents.

As we sailed, the rolling gray clouds stole my last glimpses of the mountains and trees. Prince of Wales Island became engulfed, and with it, my family and the life I had known. My heart ached. Our love-hate relationship with bush Alaska was over. Alaska was staying, but we were leaving for another place, a new life, to live a dream we held dear for so long. But nothing is free. The price again was people left behind. We would not be there to watch our grandchildren grow up or cross paths with our boys and daughters-in-law.

I pouted internally for a while, holding back tears. A red *X* had marked this day on our calendar for two decades, I didn't want to spoil it for Elgin. We had plans, lots of plans. My heartbreak was not included in those plans. Somehow, I would have to adjust, but that would happen tomorrow. I put on a smile and pushed away my pain.

To stay busy and distracted, I pulled out my laptop and worked on my book, *this* book. I composed the ending:

Goodbye, Alaska. I've given you my youth, and you've given me adventure. I'm leaving you with two of our sons and all our grandchildren. You are taking a piece of my heart and soul. I will remember you daily with amazement and intrigue. Though I have put pen to paper, you and I both know the words only go so far in describing the decades we have spent together. Some things, despite my best effort, were simply indescribable. Farewell, my friend.

"Would you do it again?" I asked Elgin a year later.

He thought for a minute, and to my surprise replied, "I believe I would."

Me (53) and Elgin (54) standing by a boiler at an old mine. A snapshot of one of our many adventures since we left Alaska in 2016.—*Absaroka Range, Shoshone National Forest, Wyoming 2020.*

EPILOGUE

In 1995, I left the job fair wearing heels, traded them in for the Alaska tennis shoe, and now I run around in hiking boots. I arrived a teacher and left an adventurer. We spent twenty Alaska winters planning for early retirement and returned to rural Wyoming with an extensive bucket list in June 2016.

When we left for Alaska, we had parents and grandparents. We returned to our mothers, but only for a short time. My mom passed away in December 2017, and Elgin's mother passed away one year later. Becoming parentless wasn't in our plans. When did our parents grow old? When did we grow old? We hadn't anticipated that! We totally missed the mark for reasonable expectations as to who would be here for our retirement days. Without them, several bucket list items no longer mattered.

We always equated golfing with retirement. As it turned out, we did most of our golfing before 2016 during Christmas breaks in Tucson, summer vacations in Wyoming, and on the Thorne Bay reclaimed trash heap. I haven't sewn a quilt since we left either. Who has the time now? We've been busy checking off other bucket list items. Turned out we had missed more than we thought, putting golf and quilting on the backburner—for a while anyway.

The first bucket list item we checked off was spending the fall of 2016 in my childhood home state of Michigan, enjoying apple cider and donuts while exploring the Upper Peninsula. Then we became snowbirds and headed to Tucson, Arizona for the only winter we would get to spend with my mother.

Next, we remodeled and added one thousand square feet to our Wyoming home, which delighted Elgin's mother who lived next door. Doing the labor ourselves, that one item took three years to check off—so much for camping trips, golfing, and catching up on the twenty years of movies we had missed.

My MS is under control with new medication and with the ability to adjust my schedule to rest when needed. I continue to maintain my EMT certification, volunteer for the local fire department, and serve on the Wyoming Writers board. We adopted another rescue dog, Ginger, who keeps me hiking daily, fortunately without so much rain and wind. Speaking of rain and wind, I had planned to return to Alaska at least once a year, but life happens, and I have only returned every other year.

All the boys are in their thirties as of 2021. Sutton lives two hours away in Montana and has not returned to Alaska after leaving in 2005. Living in rural Alaska was never his dream. We now have plenty of opportunities to grab a meal or go on a hike with him when we are in town. Everett and Abbey continue to raise Meliah and Auron in bush Alaska, living a subsistence lifestyle. They added a large indoor chicken coop to their property. Ethan and Erika returned to Wyoming in 2019 after five years in Alaska because they were tired of living without basic utilities, missed raising the kids around their grandparents, and Erika wanted to attend college. Now divorced, Ethan is raising Eveymarie and Ezio as a single parent and Erika has almost completed her associates degree in a nearby town.

It has been twenty-six years since we left for Alaska. Today, we seek out adventures weekly Jeeping and hiking with Elgin's sister Elaine and her husband, Dan Flores. Together we explore northwestern Wyoming's backroads, publishing videos of our excursions on www.WyomingJeepers.com and on our YouTube channel, at least for now. We picnic on frozen lakes in the badlands, winch the Jeeps through snowdrifts in the mountains, rockhound in riverbeds, four-wheel through grizzly bear country, and so much more. Most of Elgin's other siblings also live in the area, lessening the sting of losing our parents too early.

Our lives are full and busy and like other retirees; we are shocked we once found the time to work.

Thank you for reading my story. Reviews are critical to a book's success. Your time is greatly appreciated in writing a book review and following me online at one or more of the following:

www.Amazon.com
www.BarnesandNoble.com
www.BookBub.com
www.Goodreads.com

ACKNOWLEDGEMENTS

As educators, we claimed it took a village to raise a healthy child, and now I have learned that it takes a team to write an amazing book! My hat is off to my supportive, incredible, and dedicated team. This book would not be what it is without each of you.

A huge thank you to my husband Elgin Cook for sticking with me through the never-ending round of edits. You never quit on me. Your fingerprint adds accuracy of detail and flow of events we lived through together over two decades. Your artistic talent created an unbelievable cover and typesetting which sets this book apart. Thank you for humoring my idea of teaching in bush Alaska and staying the course to achieve our early retirement goal.

Sutton Cook, Everett Cook, and Ethan Cook, thank you for answering my questions to get your perspectives on stories that happened to you. Together, we have the most accurate account possible, which meets the primary goal of the book. I am grateful to you for your ability to adapt to a significant change in life at a young age.

Lana Gunderson, you reminded me of forgotten details from our first two years in Alaska. You responded quickly to my questions and sent me items from Nelson Lagoon to further my publishing efforts. The encouragement you gave motivated me to hone my story. During the Nelson Lagoon years, you served as our rock. Thank you!

Becky Ord Welton, you added to the accuracy and interest in the Tongass years of the book. You provided quick responses to my questions with links to research, images, and people. Your memories filled in parts of Thorne Bay history I was not there to witness, such as the earlier residents referring to the dump as Kmart and more. Thank you for being an exceptional classroom aide, administrative assistant, and friend to Elgin and me for years.

Cilla Rysewyk, my former student, thank you for sharing information and answering questions promptly. You contacted me twenty-three years after I moved away and asked if I remembered you. Cilla, I never forgot you or your final wave of goodbye that still brings tears to my eyes.

To my fourteen beta readers, I give you a heartfelt thank-you for your time and input. A special thanks to my first draft beta reader, my sister-in-law TaMara Robertson. I appreciate the hours you spent providing feedback and helping to draft the book club questions. Sister-in-law Elaine Flores, thank you for being the only beta listener of the audiobook. I genuinely value both of your input.

Aaron Linsdau, the American adventurer, polar explorer, author of *Antarctic Tears,* owner of Sastrugi Press, and fellow YouTuber, thank you for guiding me through the editing, publishing, and audiobook creation process. I am grateful for the hours you spent helping me deliver the best possible edition of my story. May our paths continue to cross in our publishing and video endeavors.

Editors, Rachel Robson, owner of 100% Proof: Proofreading and Editorial, and Kimberly Steinke of Parker Mayne Editorial, thank you for the multiple rounds of editing and proofreading. I am especially grateful for your suggestions to enhance the story and expert use of your editing scalpels. My story is more complete as a result of your guidance.

This book is my story, written by me but created by many. Without the input, long hours and commitment to my dream of publishing this book, the end product would not be what it is today. For this reason, I am truly grateful to not only those listed here but for every one of the people who have helped me along the way. I am truly grateful to all of you.

Me (53) standing by my Jeep—*Elk Fork Canyon, Shoshone National Forest, Wyoming, 2020.*

GLOSSARY

(As used in this book)

Alaska Marine Highway—the ferry system connecting the coastal communities in Alaska, Bellingham, Washington, and Prince Rupert, British Columbia

Alaska time—lackadaisical approach to life, no rush

altimeter—an instrument measuring altitude

anemometer—an instrument measuring wind speed

AVO—Alaska Volcano Observatory

Aurora Borealis—also called northern lights—colorful skies of greens, reds, and purples—the further north one goes, the better the display of color and movement

bush—or *the* bush, the parts of rural Alaska with no main road or ferry connections to the rest of the state, fly in or boat access only

bush syndrome—risks pilots take due to attitude, financial gain, fatigue, the relaxed environmental factors of Alaska's lifestyle, and pressures to reach one's destination

cabin fever—Seasonal Affective Disorder (SAD), side effects of being indoors for prolonged periods during the winter months causing irritability, loneliness, restlessness, depression, etc.

crab landing—a crosswind technique when the pilot approaches a runway skewed in relation to the center, also referred to as crabbing

crosswind landing—perpendicular winds force a plane to approach the runway with the nose off-center

fish bowl—lack of privacy, being on display for the community, being in the community but not truly part of it

float house—house on floatation devices that floats in protected bays

floatplane—plane with pontoons to land on water

honey buckets—five-gallon buckets with extra thick bag liners and a toilet seat, used in place of a typical indoors toilet

Iditarod—dog sled race from Anchorage to Nome, commemorates the serum run in 1925 when the village of Nome required diphtheria antitoxins following a serious outbreak

IFR—instrument flight rules, a rating for flying in low visibility with instruments

igloo—Eskimo dome shelters built from blocks made of pressed snow, temporary shelters used by Inuit people of the Arctic in Alaska, Canada, and Greenland

Inside Passage—a sailing route in Southeast Alaska and Canada with a course between hundreds of islands and the mainland

Last Frontier—a nickname for Alaska

Lower-48—the rest of the country excluding Hawaii and Alaska, continuous states

mail plane—a routine flight carrying mail and sometimes passengers to a village or town

milk run—the daily puddling jumping jet flight that brings supplies and passengers into several bush communities with no road access along the coast of Southeast Alaska—Seattle, Ketchikan, Wrangell, Sitka, Petersburg, Juneau, and Anchorage

muskeg—sphagnum moss, a sponge-like plant life, floating over unseen water or wetlands

old man's beard—light green moss which hangs from the trees in the Tongass National Forest

RATNet—Rural Alaska Television Network which in the 1990s, broadcast limited television programming to rural Alaskans rotating between major network programming each evening

rogue wave—an unexpected wave much larger than current waves

rookery—a breeding ground for birds or mammals, in this case for fur seals

party line—one phone line shared by two or more separate entities

PFD—permanent fund dividend, oil boom money set aside in 1976 by the Alaska State Constitution for the people, the state distributes a portion of the annual interest to qualifying residents of Alaska in October each year

socked in—weather, clouds causing low to zero visibility

sourdough—old-timer Alaskans

Southside—the southern land of Thorne Bay across the bay, a seven-minute boat ride or a thirty-minute drive down a rough road

subsistence—living off the land and local environment—people fish, hunt, chop firewood, building homes from beach logs, or by cutting down trees in the local forest

teacherage—referring to teacher housing units

tender—the drop off location for fisherman out at sea, a ship with a large haul to store fish from multiple smaller fishing vessels

tundra—vast areas of flat, barren, permanently frozen, Arctic lands

VPSO—village public safety officer with less training than a state trooper

wanigan—storage area added onto a home

weathered in or out—passengers stuck in or out of a location based on weather

widow maker—a falling tree or branch large enough to kill a person should it land on them

williwaw—a violent gust of wind blowing offshore from a mountain to the coast

Glossary

BOOK CLUB QUESTIONS

1. Melissa regretted leaving. Does this surprise you? Why?

2. At the job fair in 1995, the speaker told adventurers to go home; they wanted to hire teachers. After reading the book, do you agree with the speaker's message?

3. Does this book change your perception of Alaska? How would you feel about living in the bush?

4. Why do you think Elgin and Melissa misjudged the difference twenty years would have on their lives?

5. In chapter 73, Melissa lays out the benefits and the costs of the decision to live in Alaska and raise their family there. If you could trade places with Melissa, what would your balance sheet have?

6. Between 1995 and 2016, technology changed the world. It took years for these new gadgets and services to arrive in bush Alaska. What technologies became available during this period? What effects do you believe they had on those living in bush communities once they became available?

7. In your twenties, would you have had the forethought to consider the lack of medical access moving to Nelson Lagoon? It is a gamble at any age, but is there an age or circumstance in which you would draw the line?

8. Does this story inspire you to step out of your comfort zone and do something different? What lessons can you learn from their story?

9. Was there a point in this story where you would have decided enough was enough and returned to Wyoming?

10. The Craig dump worker told Elgin and Melissa most people return to Alaska within a year of leaving, and they did. Would you have returned for the Alaska Teacher Retirement?

11. What would you miss most if you moved to Alaska's bush for twenty years?

Made in the USA
Monee, IL
30 May 2022

be9b58df-9d72-4c64-9910-a242f1029f97R01